W9-BCD-159

The Leonard L. Milberg Collection

The Leonard L. Milberg
Collection of American Poetry

COMPILED BY
J. HOWARD WOOLMER

WITH BIOGRAPHICAL ESSAYS BY
MOLLY WEIGEL

PRINCETON UNIVERSITY LIBRARY
PRINCETON, NEW JERSEY
1994

PHOTOGRAPH CREDITS:

Miriam Berkley: EMILY GROSHOLZ

Philip A. Biscuti: WILLIAM MEREDITH

Star Black: LOUISE GLÜCK, BARBARA GUEST

John Blazejewski: JAMES RICHARDSON

Dan Carraco: WENDELL BERRY

Nancy Crampton: JAMES SCHUYLER, CHARLES WRIGHT

Bruce Davidson: C. K. WILLIAMS

Chris Felver: EDWARD DORN

John Forasté: MICHAEL HARPER

Douglas Haynes: GUY DAVENPORT

Bruce Jackson: ROBERT CREELEY

Jack Loeffler: GARY SNYDER

H. Lundeen-Whittemore: REED WHITTEMORE

Charlotte Mandell: ROBERT KELLY

Rollie McKenna: A. R. AMMONS, JOHN ASHBERY, JOHN BERRYMAN,
ELIZABETH BISHOP, LOUISE BOGAN, PHILIP BOOTH, JOSEPH BRODSKY, JAMES
DICKEY, RICHARD EBERHART, ALLEN GINSBERG, DONALD HALL, ANTHONY
HECHT, JOHN HOLLANDER, DAVID IGNATOW, RANDALL JARRELL, DONALD
JUSTICE, X. J. KENNEDY, GALWAY KINNELL, KENNETH KOCH, STANLEY
KUNITZ, DENISE LEVERTOV, J. D. McCLATCHY, JAMES MERRILL, W. S.
MERWIN, HOWARD NEMEROV, SYLVIA PLATH, ADRIENNE RICH, THEODORE
ROETHKE, ANNE SEXTON, DELMORE SCHWARTZ, KARL SHAPIRO, LOUIS
SIMPSON, W. D. SNODGRASS, MARK STRAND, MAY SWENSON, THEODORE
WEISS, RICHARD WILBUR, JAMES WRIGHT

Joel Meyerowitz: DANIEL HALPERN

Renate Ponsold: FRANK O'HARA

Sheppard Powell: DIANE DI PRIMA

Virginia Schendler: AMY CLAMPITT

Bern Schwartz: RICHMOND LATTIMORE

Robert Selden Smith: ROBERT HASS

Kit Stafford: WILLIAM STAFFORD

Robert Turney: DIANE WAKOSKI

Thomas Victor: ALFRED CORN

Copyright © 1994
by Princeton University Library

ISBN NO. 087811-038-0

Designed by Judith Martin Waterman

Printed in the United States of America
by Princeton Academic Press
at Lawrenceville, New Jersey

The Leonard L. Milberg
Collection of American Poetry
has been given to the Princeton University Library
in honor of
Richard M. Ludwig.

Preface   ❀

When Richard M. Ludwig, Associate University Librarian for Rare Books and Special Collections in the Firestone Library, retired in 1986, Leonard L. Milberg, Class of 1953, offered to fund a small collection of the works of contemporary American poets in Ludwig's honor. Ludwig, who had been teaching graduate and undergraduate courses in contemporary American poetry at Princeton for twenty-five years, knew that although the Rare Books Division already had extensive holdings of many major modern poets such as T. S. Eliot, Robert Lowell, Marianne Moore, Ezra Pound, Wallace Stevens, William Carlos Williams, and others, the Library still lacked representative collections of contemporary American poets. I met with Leonard Milberg at the Century Club in New York to discuss the collection, and we decided to concentrate on poets who had not been collected extensively by Princeton. Eleven were chosen: A. R. Ammons, John Ashbery, Elizabeth Bishop, John Hollander, Galway Kinnell, Denise Levertov, James Merrill, W. S. Merwin, Adrienne Rich, Anne Sexton, and May Swenson, an unusually well-balanced list of male and female poets, although this had not been a planned aim of the collection.

As might be expected, after the names of these poets became known, questions were raised as to why certain other poets had been omitted. We carefully considered each of these suggestions, accepting many of them, and the result was that the list continued to grow. When we reached a total of seventy poets we decided that it was time to call a halt.

Most of the poets on our list were first published commercially after the end of World War II. Others (John Berryman,

Randall Jarrell, William Meredith, and Frederick Morgan) were included because of their connection to Princeton, or because we felt them to be too important to be excluded (Louise Bogan, Richard Eberhart, Theodore Roethke, Delmore Schwartz, and a few others). These earlier poets were included when the Rare Books Division had only a few of their works, and we felt that significant additions could be made.

Because the collection is primarily intended for the use of students and scholars, we thought that it would be most useful if we gathered all printed materials in depth. We therefore included broadsides, translations made by the poets themselves (but not translations of their own works), and ephemeral items such as poetry postcards and greeting cards as well as first and significant editions of the poets' books. And every item purchased had to be in fine condition. In cases where the Rare Books Division already held a book by one of our poets, we did not duplicate it by adding another copy. Therefore the absence of an important title in this catalogue does not necessarily mean that the Library lacks a copy. Even though the catalogue had to be closed at the end of July 1993 to meet production deadlines, we had already acquired more than eighteen hundred items, a remarkable tribute to the generosity of Leonard Milberg. We are continuing to add to the collection, and Milberg has even suggested adding some of the younger American poets.

Compiling this catalogue required the cooperation and enthusiasm of many hands. Chief among these were Mark Farrell, Stephen Ferguson, John Logan, and Patricia Marks from the staff of the Library, and A. Walton Litz and Richard Ludwig from the Princeton University faculty. We are particularly indebted to Molly Weigel who wrote the biographical essays for the catalogue; to Princeton University graduate students Barton C. Beebe, Talia N. Bloch, Julie E. Burkley, Wendy Hui Kyong Chun, Sarah B. Churchwell, Suzannah E. Clark, Mike Lee Davis, Judith Jackson Fossett, McKay B.

Jenkins, Gavin R. Jones, Tamara S. Ketabgian, David M. Kasunic, Melissa McCormick, David L. Sedley, Yumi Selden, Bruce N. Simon, Cynthia L. Snyder, Edward H. Sparrow, Ellen C. Wayland–Smith, and Laura W. Yavitz, whose assistance in verifying the text was indispensable; to Frederick Tibbetts for his critical reading of the page proofs; and to Judith Martin Waterman who designed the catalogue. Special thanks also to Rollie McKenna and her assistant Judith Bachmann who were so generous in the arrangements for using the McKenna photographs.

J. HOWARD WOOLMER
Revere, Pennsylvania
October 1993

The Leonard L. Milberg Collection

A. R. Ammons

The poetry of A. R. Ammons (b. 1926) explores the dialectic of the random, peripheral events of nature and the process by which the mind creates wholeness from them. Reminiscent of Walt Whitman in his inclusiveness and of William Carlos Williams in his concern for the particular and the local, Ammons is a quintessentially American poet. He often writes about walks along the beaches and through the fields of North Carolina, where he grew up, or New Jersey, where he worked as manager of a glass-making company, or upstate New York, where he has taught at Cornell University since 1964. The poems themselves are walks of a kind, in which many-sided perceptions coalesce into a vision and disperse in a continually repeated movement. In a walk on the beach in "Corsons Inlet," the poet lets himself be directed by sight:

> *I allow myself eddies of meaning:*
> *yield to a direction of significance*
> *running*
> *like a stream through the geography of my work:*

> *you can find*
> *in my sayings*
> > *swerves of action*
> > *like the inlet's cutting edge:*
> > *there are dunes of motion,*
> *organizations of grass, white sandy paths of remembrance*
> *in the overall wandering of mirroring mind:*

But "I have / drawn no lines: / as / manifold events of sand / change the dune's shape that will not be the same shape / tomorrow."[1] Ammons says an event can be like "a flock of swallows flying in so many different directions and yet seeming to assume a single shape." It therefore "has the capacity to criticize" narrow, single points of view. "The event in its power and unexpectedness is more material to be considered against the too narrow symmetry of a previous definition."[2]

Formally, Ammons tends toward long poems that allow details and shifts of perception to accumulate (much like Charles Olson's field composition), and sparse punctuation, with an emphasis on colons which propel a poem forward from one idea to the next and also suggest the possibility of motion either forward or backward. Ammons's series of long philosophical meditations on poetry and its relation to nature include *Tape for the Turn of the Year*, typed on a roll of adding-machine tape which determined the length of the lines and of the poem as a whole, and *Sphere: The Form of a Motion*, comprising 155 twelve-line stanzas that form a single sentence. More recently, Ammons has been able to apply his dialectic of random perception and unifying vision to the exploration of human relationships in poems like "Easter Morning," which poignantly treats childhood trauma and loss.[3]

He won the National Book Award in 1973 for *Collected Poems 1951–1971*, the Bollingen Prize in Poetry for 1975, and the National Book Critics Circle Award in 1982 for *A Coast of Trees*.

~ POETRY

"Breaking Out." Winston-Salem, North Carolina: Palaemon Press, 1978. Broadside, illustrated by the author. One of 100 copies in a total limitation of 126. Published at $10.00.

Changing Things. Winston-Salem, North Carolina: Palaemon Press, 1981. One of 26 lettered copies in a total limitation of 126. Signed by the author. Wrappers with gilt paper dust jacket.

A Coast of Trees: Poems. New York: W. W. Norton, 1981. Dust jacket. Published at $12.95.

Collected Poems, 1951–1971. New York: W. W. Norton, 1972. Dust jacket. Published at $12.50. Three thousand copies printed.

Corsons Inlet. A Book of Poems. Ithaca, New York: Cornell University Press, 1965. Dust jacket. Published at $3.95. Fifteen hundred copies printed.

Easter Morning. Winston Salem: North Carolina Humanities Committee, 1986. Wrappers. One of 220 signed copies printed at the Shadowy Waters Press for distribution at "The Home Country of A. R. Ammons: A Tribute."

Expressions of Sea Level. Columbus: Ohio State University Press, 1963. Dust jacket. Published at $4.00. One thousand copies printed.

Lake Effect Country: Poems. New York: W. W. Norton, 1983. Dust jacket. Published at $15.50.

Northfield Poems. Ithaca, New York: Cornell University Press, 1966. Dust jacket. Published at $3.95. Fifteen hundred copies printed.

Ommateum: With Doxology. Philadelphia: Dorrance & Company, 1955. Dust jacket. The author's first book, privately published. Ammons states that 300 copies were printed of which only 100 were bound; of these bound copies about 40 were purchased by his father-in-law and mailed to business associates.

"Pecker's Peak; or, Piker's Pique." Winston-Salem, North Carolina: Palaemon Press, n.d. Broadside. "One of a very few copies privately printed for friends of Palaemon Press." Not dated, but published after 1980.

"For Doyle Fosso." Winston-Salem, North Carolina: Press for Privacy, 1977. Single sheet folded twice to make four pages. Sixty copies were printed, of which 36 were for sale at $5.00. Enclosed in a printed envelope.

The Really Short Poems. New York: W. W. Norton, 1990. Dust jacket. Published at $15.50.

Selected Longer Poems. New York: W. W. Norton, 1980. Dust jacket. Published at $12.95.

Selected Poems. Ithaca, New York: Cornell University Press, 1968. Dust jacket. Published at $5.95. There were 1,500 copies bound in cloth and 4,000 in paper.

The Selected Poems. Expanded edition. New York: W. W. Norton, 1986. Dust jacket. Published at $15.95.

The Selected Poems 1951–1977. New York: W. W. Norton, 1977. Dust jacket. Published at $7.95. There were 2,500 clothbound and 4,000 paperbound copies.

"Shit List; or, Omnium-gatherum of Diversity into Unity." Winston-Salem, North Carolina: Stuart Wright, 1979. Broadside. One of 30 copies privately printed, Christmas 1979. Not for sale.

Six-Piece Suite. Winston-Salem, North Carolina: Palaemon Press, 1978. Wrappers. One of 200 copies signed by the author in a total limitation of 230. Published at $20.00.

The Snow Poems. New York: W. W. Norton, 1977. Dust jacket. Published at $12.50. Three thousand copies were printed.

Sphere: The Form of a Motion. New York: W. W. Norton, 1974. Dust jacket. Published at $6.95. Two thousand copies were bound in cloth; 5,000 in paper covers.

Sumerian Vistas: Poems. New York: W. W. Norton, 1987. Dust jacket. Published at $15.95.

Tape for the Turn of the Year. Ithaca, New York: Cornell University Press, 1965. Dust jacket. Published at $4.95. Fifteen hundred copies were printed.

"Thaw." London: Eric and Joan Stevens, ca. 1986. Christmas card. The poem is reprinted from *Corsons Inlet*.

Worldly Hopes: Poems. New York: W. W. Norton, 1982. Dust jacket. Published at $12.95.

John Ashbery

J John Ashbery (b. 1927) asks us to question how we read, how we construct meaning; he shows us that language creates its own shifting reality, that the ways in which we know ourselves and our world are not transparent or direct. Hence images have a life of their own, and an "I" or "creator" is no longer at the center of the poetic enterprise. Like the other members of the New York School, Ashbery incorporates techniques and discourse from the visual arts, drawing on abstract expressionism, pop art, and film. Ashbery's acclaimed *Self-Portrait in a Convex Mirror* takes its title from a painting by Parmigianino, an Italian mannerist painter whose work prefigured surrealism by emphasizing the painting's surface and the deformation of space. The first sentence of the poem is a long adverbial phrase with no subject:

> *As Parmigianino did it, the right hand*
> *Bigger than the head, thrust at the viewer*
> *And swerving easily away, as though to protect*
> *What it advertises.*[1]

The "I" is removed, making the manner in which things are done the real subject of sentence and poem.

Ashbery's disjunctive poetics has profoundly influenced

the recent Language Poetry movement. The collage tech-
niques of *The Tennis Court Oath* opened the possibility of a
free-flowing fragmentation that did not have to make sense.
Yet there are still associative threads to follow: "They Dream
Only of America" is a Whitmanesque narrative of the expan-
siveness and danger in American possibility, here played out in
a clandestine homosexual affair rife with signs that are
uninterpretable but laden with meaning. In *Three Poems* Ashbery
uses prose poetry as a medium to explore the idea of selection
in poetry, in life, and in love.

> . . . *Not choose this or that because it pleases, [but] merely to
> assume the idea of choosing, so that some things can be left
> behind. It doesn't matter which ones. I could tell you about some
> of the things I've discarded but that wouldn't help you because
> you must choose your own, or rather not choose them but let
> them be inflicted on and off you. This is the point of the
> narrowing-down process. And gradually, as the air gets thinner
> as you climb a mountain, these things will stand forth in a relief
> all their own—the look of belonging. It is a marvelous job to
> do, and it is enough just to approximate it. Things will do the
> rest.*[2]

Choosing is not controlling but remaining open to the forces
of chance that shape us and determine the direction of our
lives even as we help to create them. This sense of our
fundamental interpenetrability also informs and is informed
by Ashbery's view of homosexual love, and *Three Poems* enlarg-
es the love lyric by narrating the aftermath of the break-up of
a love relationship in a ruminative language full of double
meanings, out of which startling images briefly rise, like the
mountain in the passage above. We should look for meaning
in the contingent rather than in the absolute, Ashbery suggests
in "October at the Window":

> One must always
> Be quite conscious of the edges of things
> And then how they meet will cease
> To be an issue, all other things
> Being equal, as in fact they are.[3]

Ashbery won the Pulitzer Prize, the National Book Critics Circle Award, and the National Book Award in 1976 for *Self-Portrait in a Convex Mirror*. In 1985 he was awarded the Bollingen Prize in Poetry.

≈ POETRY

Apparitions: Poems, by John Ashbery, Galway Kinnell, W. S. Merwin, L. M. Rosenberg, Dave Smith. Northridge, California: Lord John Press, 1981. Boards. One of 300 copies signed by each poet in a total limitation of 350.

April Galleons: Poems. New York: Viking Press, Elisabeth Sifton Books, 1987. Dust jacket. Published at $15.95.

As We Know: Poems. New York, Viking Press, 1979. Dust jacket. Published at $12.50. This copy is signed by the author on the title page.

Flow Chart. New York: Alfred A. Knopf, 1991. Dust jacket. Published at $20.00.

Fragment. Illustrated by Alex Katz. Los Angeles: Black Sparrow Press, 1969. Boards; glassine dust jacket. One of 250 copies signed by the author and the artist in a total limitation of 1,020. Published at $15.00.

Haibun. Illustrated by Judith Shea. Columbes, France: Collectif Génération, 1990. Loose signatures in cloth folder and slipcase as published. One of 30 copies numbered and signed by the artist. English text, extracted from the Penguin Books 1985 edition of *A Wave*.

Hotel Lautréamont. New York: Nadja, 1991. Wrappers. One of 125 copies signed by the author in a total limitation of 151.

Hotel Lautréamont. New York: Alfred A. Knopf, 1992. First trade edition. Dust jacket collage by Joseph Cornell. Published at $23.00.

The Ice Storm. Madras, India, and New York: Hanuman Books, 1987. Wrappers, in dust jacket. A miniature book.

John Ashbery. New York: DIA Art Foundation, 1987. Wrappers. "Readings in Contemporary Poetry, Number 1." One of 500 copies.

The New Spirit. New York: Adventures in Poetry, 1970. Photocopied sheets stapled in wrappers. One of 65 copies signed by the author in a total limitation of 165.

From *The New Spirit.* State University of New York at Brockport, 1972. One sheet folded to make four pages. Advertisement for a reading by Ashbery under the overall title "The Writer's Forum."

"Offshore Breeze." New York: Viking Press, 1987. Poetry card used to advertise Ashbery's *April Galleons* published the same year.

Selected Poems. London: Cape, 1967. Dust jacket. Published at 18s. First issue with lines 7–8 of the copyright statement reading "© 1957, 1959, 1960, 1961, 1962 by John Ashbery." This was later corrected by a pasted-in errata slip and finally with the correction integral.

Selected Poems. New York: Viking Press, Elisabeth Sifton Books, 1985. Dust jacket. Published at $22.95.

Self-Portrait in a Convex Mirror: Poems. New York: Viking Press, 1975. Dust jacket. Published at $5.95.

Shadow Train: Poems. New York: Viking Press, 1981. Dust jacket. Published at $8.95. This copy is signed on the title page by the author.

Some Trees: Three Poems for Three Voices. Words by John Ashbery, music by Ned Rorem. New York: Boosey & Hawkes, 1970. Wrappers. Sheet music. Published at $3.50.

"Spring Day." Winston-Salem, North Carolina: Palaemon Press, 1984. Broadside, signed by the author. Limitation not stated.

The Vermont Notebook. Illustrated by Joe Brainard. Los Angeles: Black Sparrow Press, 1975. Boards; glassine dust jacket. One of 250 copies signed by the author and the artist. Published at $15.00.

A Wave: Poems. New York: Viking Press, 1984. Dust jacket. Published at $14.95.

☙ PROSE

Along the Dark Shore: Poems, by Edward Byrne. Foreword by John Ashbery. Brockport, New York: BOA Editions, 1977. Boards. One of 26 copies signed by Ashbery and Byrne in a total limitation of 500.

"Frank O'Hara Award for Poetry." New York: Marlborough Gallery, 1970. Invitation to the presentation ceremony, with text by Ashbery. In the original printed envelope.

Ipousteguy. London: Hanover Gallery, 1964. Wrappers. Exhibition catalogue, with text by Ashbery. Plates.

John Ashbery and Kenneth Koch (A Conversation). Tucson, Arizona: Interview Press, ca. 1965. Wrappers. Published at $1.00.

"John MacWhinnie." New York: Borgenicht Gallery, 1974. Single sheet folded to make four pages. Exhibition catalogue, with text by Ashbery.

A Nest of Ninnies, by John Ashbery and James Schuyler. New York: E. P. Dutton, 1969. Dust jacket. Published at $4.95. Six thousand copies printed.

Reported Sightings: Art Chronicles, 1957–1987. New York: Alfred A. Knopf, 1989. Dust jacket. Plates. Published at $35.00.

❧ TRANSLATIONS

Melville, by Jean-Jacques Mayoux. Translated by John Ashbery. New York: Grove Press, 1960. Paperback, not issued in cloth. Published at $1.35. Illustrated. "Evergreen Profile Book 9."

Murder in Montmartre, by Noël Vexin. Translated from the French by Jonas Berry and Lawrence G. Blochman. New York: Dell Publishing Co., 1960. A paperback original. Jonas Berry was a pseudonym for John Ashbery.

Wendell Berry

Wendell Berry (b. 1934), like his parents and grandparents before him, farms the land of his native Kentucky. An eloquent and passionate defender of traditional small farming against agribusiness, he also sees farming and poetry as interconnected, two kinds of making: "human work is all art." As Paul Merchant says, Berry aligns farming, marriage, and poetry as "three crafts requiring patience, an understanding of conditions, and an investment of time and energy in a future."[1]

In his poetry and essays, Berry explores responsible and responsive ways in which human beings can exist in a natural place. Farming, and the farming of words, are one such way. We plant, and are planted by, the natural world: as the seasons change, we die and are reborn. In "History" Berry describes how the history of the land he has come to farm lives in him. He has

> . . . made the beginning
> of a farm intended to become
> my art of being here.
> By it I would instruct

my wants: they should belong
to each other and to this place.²

Belonging to each other and to the place involves recognizing that the poem is part of the cyclical process of transfer and use of energy:

Now let me feed my song
upon the life that is here
that is the life that is gone.
This blood has turned to dust
and liquefied again in stem
and vein ten thousand times.
Let what is in the flesh,
O Muse, be brought to mind.³

For Berry, allegiance to a place also forms the basis of a community; sharing the same knowledge of place, history, and work allows a precise, shared language to develop, a kind of "community speech." Words, things, deeds, people need to be faithful to one another. Thus in "An Anniversary"

What we have been becomes
The country where we are. . . .
Darkened, we are carried
Out of need, deep
In the country we have married.⁴

❧ POETRY

The Broken Ground: Poems. New York: Harcourt, Brace & World, 1964. Dust jacket. Published at $3.95.

Clearing. New York: Harcourt Brace Jovanovich, 1977. Dust jacket. Published at $6.95.

Collected Poems, 1957–1982. San Francisco: North Point Press, 1985. Dust jacket. Published at $16.50. Signed by the author on the title page.

The Country of Marriage. New York: Harcourt Brace Jovanovich, 1973. Dust jacket. Published at $4.95.

The Discovery of Kentucky. Frankfort, Kentucky: Gnomon Press, 1991. Boards. One of 100 signed copies in a total limitation of 1,000.

"Falling Asleep." Austin, Texas: Cold Mountain Press, 1974. "Cold Mountain Press Poetry Post Card, Series 11, Number 8."

Farming: A Hand Book. New York: Harcourt Brace Jovanovich, 1970. Dust jacket. Published at $4.95.

Findings. Iowa City, Iowa: Prairie Press, 1969. Dust jacket. Published at $4.50. This copy is signed by the author.

"From the Distance." Madison, Wisconsin: Black Mesa Press, 1982. Broadside, signed by the author. Limitation not stated. Printed for a reading by Berry at Woodland Pattern Book Center, 11 December 1982.

The Gift of Gravity. Illustrated by Timothy Engelland. Deerfield, Massachusetts: Deerfield Press, 1979. Dust jacket. One of 300 signed copies.

The Hidden Wound. Boston: Houghton Mifflin, 1970. Dust jacket. Published at $4.95.

Horses. Monterey, Kentucky: Larkspur Press, 1975. Wrappers. One of 949 copies.

How Ptolemy Proudfoot Lost a Bet. New York: Dim Gray Bar Press, 1992. Boards. One of 100 signed copies. Advertising flyer for the book loosely inserted.

"I go from the woods into the cleared field: . . ." N.p., ca. 1987. Broadside, signed by the author. Designed by Eric A. Johnson. Limitation not stated.

The Kentucky River: Two Poems. Monterey, Kentucky: Larkspur Press, 1976. Wrappers. One of 1,000 copies in a total limitation of 1,026.

A Native Hill. Introduction by Raymond D. Peterson. Santa Rosa, California: Santa Rosa Junior College, 1976. Wrappers. "The 200 Series No. 6," published in celebration of the nation's bicentennial year.

Openings: Poems. New York: Harcourt, Brace & World, 1968. Dust jacket. Published at $4.50. Author's compliments slip loosely inserted.

A Part. San Francisco: North Point Press, 1980. Dust jacket. Published at $12.50.

"The Peace of Wild Things." Berkeley, California: Black Oak Books, 1991. Broadside. Publisher's New Year's gift. Limitation not stated.

"A Place Unmade." Illustrated by Max Hein. Santa Rosa, California: Calliopea Press, 1984. Broadside, signed by the author and the artist. Limitation not stated.

The Rise. Lexington: University of Kentucky Library Press, 1968. Boards; glassine jacket. One of 100 copies, total limitation. This copy is signed by the author.

Sabbaths. San Francisco: North Point Press, 1987. Dust jacket. Published at $12.95. Dedicated to Donald Hall.

Sabbaths 1987. Monterey, Kentucky: Larkspur Press, 1991. One of 26 signed hardbound copies in a total limitation of 1,000.

Sabbaths 1987–90. Ipswich, England: Golgonooza Press, 1992. Paperback; not issued in cloth. Poems selected from *Sabbaths 1987* (Larkspur Press, 1991) and adding 19 poems here first published.

The Salad. Berkeley, California: North Point Press, 1980. Wrappers. Limitation not stated.

Sayings & Doings. Lexington, Kentucky: Gnomon Press, 1975. Boards; not issued in dust jacket.

Sayings & Doings; and, An Eastward Look. Frankfort, Kentucky: Gnomon Press, 1990. Boards. One of 50 signed hardbound copies.

"VII." Lexington, Kentucky: Black Swan Books, 1987. Broadside. One of 125 copies signed by the author.

There Is Singing Around Me. Austin, Texas: Cold Mountain Press, 1976. Wrappers. One of 300 signed copies in a total limitation of 326.

Three Memorial Poems. Berkeley, California: Sand Dollar Press, 1977. Tissue dust jacket. One of 100 signed copies. Accompanied by a copy of the trade edition in wrappers, one of 1,000 copies.

Traveling at Home. Wood engravings by John DePol. Lewisburg, Pennsylvania: Bucknell University, Press of Appletree Alley, 1988. Boards; not issued in dust jacket. One of 150 copies signed by the author.

Traveling at Home. Wood engravings by John DePol. San Francisco: North Point Press, 1989. First trade edition. Boards; not issued in dust jacket.

Wendell Berry. American Authors Series, ed. by Paul Merchant. Lewiston, Idaho: Confluence Press, 1991. Dust jacket. Published at $24.95.

"What can turn us from this deserted future. . . ." N.p.: Okeanos Press, 1991. Broadside. Published to honor the legacy of North Point Press, 1980–1991.

"The Wheel." Winston-Salem, North Carolina: Palaemon Press, 1980. Broadside. One of 26 signed copies in a total limitation of 126.

The Wheel. San Francisco: North Point Press, 1982. Dust jacket. Published at $10.00.

⪼ PROSE

The City and the Farm Crisis. Great Barrington, Massachusetts: E. F. Schumacher Society, 1986. Wrappers. Sixth Annual E. F. Schumacher Lecture, October 1986, Philadelphia, Pennsylvania. One of approximately 500 copies.

Civilizing the Cumberlands: A Commentary. Lexington: King Library Press, University of Kentucky, 1972. Boards; glassine jacket. One of 100 copies, total limitation. Also contains James Lane Allen's *Mountain Passes of the Cumberland.*

A Continuous Harmony: Essays Cultural and Agricultural. New York: Harcourt Brace Jovanovich, 1972. Dust jacket. Published at $5.95.

Fidelity: Five Stories. New York: Pantheon Books, 1992. Dust jacket. Published at $20.00.

The Gift of Good Land: Further Essays, Cultural and Agricultural. San Francisco: North Point Press, 1981. Dust jacket. Published at $16.50.

Harlan Hubbard: Life and Work. Lexington: University Press of Kentucky, 1990. Dust jacket. Plates and text illustrations. The Blazer Lectures for 1989.

The Landscape of Harmony. Madley, Hereford, England: Five Seasons Press, 1987. Wrappers. Published at £5.40. "Two Essays on Wildness & Community by Wendell Berry with an Introduction to the Writings . . . by Michael Hamburger & a Checklist of Wendell Berry's Books."

Nathan Coulter. Boston: Houghton Mifflin, 1960. Dust jacket. Published at $3.50. The author's first book.

Nathan Coulter: A Novel. San Francisco: North Point Press, 1985. Boards. One of 26 lettered and signed copies. Revised edition of the author's first book with a new author's note.

A Place on Earth: A Novel. San Francisco: North Point Press, 1983. Printed tissue dust jacket. One of 100 signed copies. "Pace Trust Edition," a revision of the 1967 edition.

A Place on Earth. Revision. San Francisco: North Point Press, 1983. Paperback, in dust jacket; not issued in cloth. Published at $15.00. Extensively revised from the Harcourt, Brace & World edition of 1967. Review copy with flyer loosely inserted.

Recollected Essays, 1965–1980. San Francisco: North Point Press, 1981. Dust jacket. Published at $15.00. Signed by the author on the front endpaper.

Remembering: A Novel. San Francisco: North Point Press, 1988. Dust jacket. Published at $14.95.

Standing by Words. West Stockbridge, Massachusetts: Lindisfarne Press, 1980. Wrappers. An earlier version was given as the opening talk at the 1978 meeting of the Lindisfarne Fellows.

Standing on Earth: Selected Essays. Introduction by Brian Keeble. Foreword by Jonathon Porritt. Ipswich, England: Golgonooza Press, 1991. Dust jacket. One of 250 hardcover copies signed by the author.

The Unforeseen Wilderness: Kentucky's Red River Gorge. Photographs by Ralph Eugene Meatyard. San Francisco: North Point Press, 1991. Wrappers. Revised and expanded edition; first published by the University Press of Kentucky in 1971.

The Unsettling of America: Culture and Agriculture. San Francisco: Sierra Club Books, 1977. Dust jacket. Published at $9.95.

What Are People For? Essays. San Francisco: North Point Press, 1990. Dust jacket. Published at $19.95.

The Wild Birds: Six Stories of the Port William Membership. San Francisco: North Point Press, 1986. Dust jacket. Published at $13.95.

John Berryman

Quirky, allusive, in turn colloquial and grand, John Berryman (1914–1972) explores nuances of changing feeling and multiple selves, giving us a psychological portrait of "modern agony." His poetry "reflects his life-long effort to find or fuse a style equal to the terrible psychological pressures of his themes of self-revelation and self-discovery."[1] Often associated with the Confessional poets, Berryman's close friends included Robert Lowell and Delmore Schwartz, whom he eulogizes in the *The Dream Songs*. Berryman was an alcoholic haunted by early memories of his father's suicide, and he ended his own life by jumping from a bridge in Minneapolis.

Berryman's wit always has a painful bite, or at least a poignant edge, as in "A Professor's Song," where the boredom and didactic inanity of the classroom threaten to kill the literature under discussion, but also give rise to a barely contained ironic despair:

> *Twelve. The class can go.*
> *Until I meet you, then, in Upper Hell*
> *Convulsed, foaming immortal blood: farewell.*[2]

Among other things, *The Dream Songs* is an anatomy of ennui, showing that boredom, like anger, can be righteous and justified, a fitting, even creative, response to a rigid and alienated society:

> *Life, friends, is boring. We must not say so.*
> *After all, the sky flashes, the great sea yearns,*
> *we ourselves flash and yearn,*
> *and moreover my mother told me as a boy*
> *(repeatingly) 'Ever to confess you're bored*
> *means you have no*
>
> *Inner Resources.' I conclude now I have no*
> *inner resources, because I am heavy bored.*
> *Peoples bore me,*
> *literature bores me, especially great literature,*
> *Henry bores me, with his plights & gripes*
> *as bad as achilles,*
>
> *who loves people and valiant art, which bores me.*[3]

Berryman uses personae to explore aspects of his own psychology. *Homage to Mistress Bradstreet* attempts to work through an ambiguous attraction-repulsion relationship with Puritan guilt and judgment as personified in Puritan poet Anne Bradstreet as "loved" woman addressed in epistolary form. *The Dream Songs* features Henry, "a white American in early middle age, sometimes in blackface, who has suffered an irreversible loss and talks about himself sometimes in the first person, sometimes in the third, sometimes even in the second."[4] The dislocated Henry speaks a black minstrel dialect which is contrasted with a more weary, ironic, deliberate poet's voice. So the dream songs represent an alternative, almost voluntary alienation, a series of displacements of the self, and a creation of marginal positions from which to speak: the dream world, the unconscious, a minstrel show.

Berryman won the Pulitzer Prize in 1965 for *77 Dream Songs* and the National Book Award in 1969 for *His Toy, His*

Dream, His Rest. He shared the Bollingen Prize in Poetry with Karl Shapiro in 1969.

ᔰ POETRY

Collected Poems, 1931–1971. Edited and introduced by Charles Thornbury. New York: Farrar, Straus & Giroux, 1989. Dust jacket. Published at $25.00.

Columbia Poetry, 1935. With an introduction by William T. Brewster. New York: Columbia University Press, 1935. Cloth boards. Berryman contributed four poems, his first appearance in a book.

"A Dream Song." Derry, Pennsylvania: Rook Society, 1976. Broadside. One of 150 copies issued on the occasion of the publication of *Once in a Sycamore: A Garland for John Berryman* (Derry, Pennsylvania: Rook Press, ca. 1976).

Five Young American Poets. Norfolk, Connecticut: New Directions, 1940. Dust jacket. Published at $2.50. Precedes his first book by two years. The other poets included are George Marion O'Donnell, Randall Jarrell, Mary Barnard, and W. R. Moses.

The Harvard Advocate: John Berryman Issue, vol. 103, no. 1 (Spring 1969). Wrappers. Contains three new dream songs and an interview with Berryman as well as contributions by Adrienne Rich, William Meredith, Howard Nemerov, Robert Lowell, Elizabeth Bishop, Conrad Aiken, and others.

Homage to Mistress Bradstreet and Other Poems. London: Faber and Faber, 1959. Dust jacket. Published at 18s. Many poems have been revised from their American publication. One thousand copies printed.

One Answer to a Question. Portree, Isle of Skye, Scotland: Aquila Publishing, 1981. Wrappers. First published in *Shenandoah XVII* (Autumn 1965) and then reprinted under the title *Changes* in 1966. This is apparently a pirated edition.

"Two Dream Songs." Minneapolis: K. & J. Berryman, 1965. Single sheet folded to make four pages. "Season's Greetings, 1965. Kate and John Berryman." One hundred fifty copies printed.

❧ PROSE

Homage to John Berryman. Minneapolis, University of Minnesota Library, 1973. Wrappers. Exhibition catalogue. Text by Richard J. Kelly.

Stephen Crane: The Red Badge of Courage. Portree, Isle of Skye, Scotland: Aquila Publishing, 1981. An essay first published in *The American Novel from James Fenimore Cooper to William Faulkner*, ed. Wallace Stegner (New York: Basic Books, 1965). This is apparently a pirated edition.

We Dream of Honour: John Berryman's Letters to His Mother, ed. Richard J. Kelly. New York: W. W. Norton, 1988. Dust jacket. Published at $22.50.

Elizabeth Bishop

From her first collection of poems, *North & South*, to her
last, *Geography III*, Elizabeth Bishop (1911–1979) is con-
cerned with place and the human consciousness—
how we delineate and create what surrounds us. Travel be-
comes a metaphor for our approach to reality, which we view
as if from a distance, not fully inside or outside it. Bishop, born
in Worcester, Massachusetts, and raised in Nova Scotia, trav-
elled widely and lived in Brazil for more than sixteen years. As
she asks in "Questions of Travel,"

> *Should we have stayed at home,*
> *wherever that may be?*[1]

Focussing on details with a sharp clarity, she works somewhat
as the sandpiper does in her poem of that title:

> *His beak is focussed; he is preoccupied,*
> *looking for something, something, something.*[2]

Sometimes these details seem to point straight to a direct
knowledge: the sea in "At the Fishhouses" is

> *like what we imagine knowledge to be:*
> *dark, salt, clear, moving, utterly free,*
> *drawn from the cold hard mouth*

of the world, derived from the rocky breasts
forever, flowing and drawn, and since
our knowledge is historical, flowing, and flown.³

Often the objects she fixes take on their own logic, standing in relation to each other in ways that do not conform to conventions of seeing. A child's perspective expresses an unselfconscious freedom from convention, as in "Squatter's Children," where brother and sister play in a thunderstorm:

wet and beguiled, you stand among
the mansions you may choose
out of a bigger house than yours,
whose lawfulness endures.
Its soggy documents retain
your rights in rooms of falling rain.⁴

Other poems written from a child's point of view contain a painful awakening, such as the late "In the Waiting Room," which describes a lonely, disconcerting recognition of social and sexual identity.

Bishop's fine translations of Brazilian poets such as Carlos Drummond de Andrade and João Cabral de Melo Neto, and her *Anthology of Contemporary Brazilian Poetry⁵* constitute a vital link between the poetry of North and South America. She won the Pulitzer Prize in 1956 for her second book, *Poems: North & South—A Cold Spring*, and the National Book Award in 1970 for *The Complete Poems*. In 1977, she won the National Book Critics Circle Award for *Geography III*.

⤳   POETRY

All These Cafes Have Lots of Tourists on Week-Ends: A Letter from Elizabeth Bishop to Robie Macauley. New York: Glenn Horowitz; Detroit: Richard Levey, 1987. Wrappers. Glassine dust jacket. One of 200 copies.

The Ballad of the Burglar of Babylon. Woodcuts by Ann Grifalconi. New York: Farrar, Straus & Giroux, 1968.

Dust jacket. Published at $3.95. Ten thousand four hundred copies printed.

The Complete Poems. New York: Farrar, Straus & Giroux, 1969. Dust jacket. Published at $7.50. Fifty-five hundred copies printed.

Geography III. New York: Farrar, Straus & Giroux, 1976. Dust jacket. Published at $7.95. Seventy-five hundred copies printed.

North & South. Boston: Houghton Mifflin, 1946. Dust jacket. Published at $2.00. The author's first book. Winner of the Tenth Anniversary Houghton Mifflin Award for a volume of poetry. One thousand copies printed.

"North Haven: In Memoriam—Robert Lowell." Los Angeles: Lord John Press, 1979. Broadside, illustrated by Kit Barker. One of 150 copies signed by the poet.

Poems. London: Chatto & Windus, 1956. Dust jacket. Five hundred copies published at 8s6d. A selection from *Poems: North & South—A Cold Spring*. No comparable American edition.

Poems: North & South—A Cold Spring. Boston: Houghton Mifflin, 1955. Dust jacket. Two thousand copies printed at $3.50.

Selected Poems. London: Chatto & Windus, 1967. Dust jacket. Twelve hundred copies printed at 21s.

❧ **PROSE**

Brazil, by Elizabeth Bishop and the Editors of *Life*. New York: Time Incorporated, 1962. Boards; not issued in dust jacket. "Life World Library." Two hundred fifty thousand copies printed at $2.95.

⤞ TRANSLATION

The Diary of "Helena Morley." Translated from the
   Portuguese. New York: Farrar, Straus and Cudahy, 1957.
   Dust jacket; first issue with the uncorrected publicity
   notice on flaps. Published at $4.75. Four thousand
   copies printed.

Louise Bogan

Louise Bogan (1897–1970) draws on the metaphysical and symbolist traditions to create spare yet dense poems that explore emotional and psychological complexities. Bogan's poetry and criticism (she was poetry editor of *The New Yorker* from 1931 until 1969) show a deep ambivalence toward women and women poets:

> *Women have no wilderness in them,*
> *They are provident instead,*
> *Content in the tight hot cell of their hearts*
> *To eat dusty bread.*[1]

Her formal restraint is a creative response to what she saw as the difficulties of female experience and expression. As Bogan says in a letter to Sister Angela, "You will remember . . . in dealing with my work, that you are dealing with emotion under high pressure—so that *symbols* are its only release."[2] Marianne Moore calls Bogan's poetry "compactedness compacted. Emotion with her, as she has said of certain fiction, is 'itself form, the kernel which builds outward form from inward intensity.'"[3]

Her poetry of dreams and confrontations with unconscious processes retains a sense of their mystery as it illuminates. In the early "Medusa," the entire world freezes for Medusa as her own gaze in the mirror turns her to stone. The act of recognition creates a form, but this form is death:

> *This is a dead scene forever now.*
> *Nothing will ever stir.*
> *The end will never brighten it more than this.*
> *Nor the rain blur.*[4]

The surreal power of trapped emotion questions the poetic enterprise: Does it release emotions or turn them to stone? In later poems like "The Dream" and "The Meeting," Bogan confronts figures "which may very well be the psychic demon," seeking reconciliation or understanding, in a dreamlike language of portent and dread.

> *For years I thought I knew, at the bottom of the dream,*
> *Who spoke but to say farewell,*
> *Whose smile dissolved, after his first words*
> *Gentle and plausible. . . .*
>
> *Now I am not sure. Who are you? Who have you been?*
> *Why do our paths cross?*
> *At the deepest bottom of the dream you are let in,*
> *A symbol of loss.*[5]

In Bogan's poetry, life and death are close together; like love and loss, they contain each other. "Night" treats the theme of her own approaching death:

> *The cold remote islands*
> *And the blue estuaries*
> *Where what breathes, breathes*
> *The restless wind of the inlets,*
> *And what drinks, drinks*
> *The incoming tide; . . .*
>
> *—O remember*
> *In your narrowing dark hours*
> *That more things move*
> *Than blood in the heart.*[6]

Bogan was the co-winner with Leonie Adams of the Bollingen Prize in Poetry in 1955.

✾ POETRY

The Blue Estuaries: Poems 1923–1968. New York: Farrar, Straus & Giroux, 1968. Dust jacket. Published at $4.95.

A Final Antidote: From the Journals of Louise Bogan, ed. William Maxwell and Charles McGrath. With an etching by Priscilla Steele. Omaha, Nebraska: Cummington Press, 1991. Dust jacket. One of 220 copies. The etching is signed by the artist.

"July Dawn." San Francisco: Poems in Folio, 1957. Broadside. One of 150 signed copies in a total limitation of 1,150. Accompanied by a copy of the prospectus containing a long publicity notice by the author.

The Sleeping Fury: Poems. New York: Charles Scribner's Sons, 1937. Dust jacket. Published at $2.50.

✾ PROSE

Achievement in American Poetry 1900–1950. Chicago: Henry Regnery Company, 1951. Dust jacket. Published at $2.50.

Emily Dickinson: Three Views, by Archibald MacLeish, Louise Bogan, and Richard Wilbur. Amherst, Massachusetts: Amherst College Press, 1960. Boards, issued without dust jacket. Papers delivered at Amherst College as part of its observance of the bicentennial celebration of the Town of Amherst, 23 October 1959.

A Poet's Alphabet: Reflections on the Literary Art and Vocation, ed. Robert Phelps and Ruth Limmer. New York: McGraw-Hill, 1970. Dust jacket.

What the Woman Lived: Selected Letters of Louise Bogan, 1920–1970. Edited and with an introduction by Ruth Limmer. New York: Harcourt Brace Jovanovich, 1973. Dust jacket. Published at $14.50.

⫘ TRANSLATION

The Journal of Jules Renard. Edited and translated by Louise
    Bogan and Elizabeth Roget. New York: Braziller, 1964.
    Dust jacket. Published at $6.00. Prefaces by the editors.

Philip Booth

For Philip Booth (b. 1925), the Maine coast, where he owns a house that has been in his family for five generations, provides the essential metaphors for human existence. He is a poet of edges and margins, of tides that ebb and flow, of the uncertainty of fog, of the endurance of rock:

> *The late fog, lifting . . .*
> *The long tide, at ebb.*
>
> *And cast off finally,*
> *into that perfect hope,*
> *the fishboats: going out.*[1]

As Hayden Carruth says, Booth's poems "are laconic in manner, suggesting the speech of Maine; suggesting, too, the hard-bitten quality of mind that casts off into a 'routine hope.'"[2]

Booth is wary of human arrogance, which seems to come from a lack of connectedness to the land and weather that teach us how to live. In "The Day the Tide," an apocalyptic drying-up of the ocean implicitly suggests a human cause. The result is the end of mystery, of hidden things:

it left us looking down
at what the sea, and our
reflections on it, had
. . . saved us from.[3]

For Booth, the ocean and its weather shape us; we emerged
from them and will return to them. In their presence, we learn
that complete control is impossible, because at every moment
we are on the edge of our experience, casting off into the
unknown. In "The Way Tide Comes," the changing tide erases
old markings and makes "distances shift"; time and our
movement through it are neither linear nor retraceable, but
rather a series of ebbs and flows, pulls of desire and necessity
where we live in the margins. For Booth, it is important to live
according to the tide's laws, relinquishing the urge to measure
or know completely:

There's nothing left, nothing to add,
for which the tide will not account:

fire, our awkward toes where
we yield, the periwinkles' slow track;
no matter how we want, beyond doubt,
to stay the tide or inform it, we
come in time to inform ourselves: we have
to follow it all the way out.[4]

᧞ POETRY

Available Light. New York: Viking Press, 1976. Dust jacket.
Published at $5.95. Review copy with photograph and
related material loosely inserted.

Before Sleep: Poems. New York: Viking Press, 1980. Dust
jacket. Published at $12.95.

Margins: A Sequence of New and Selected Poems. New York:
Viking Press, 1970. Dust jacket. Published at $5.95.
With the author's presentation inscription on the front
endpaper.

Relations: Selected Poems, 1950–1985. New York: Viking Press, 1986. Dust jacket. Published at $25.00.

"Seal Cove." Winston-Salem, North Carolina: Palaemon Press, 1984. Broadside; signed by the author. Limitation not stated.

Selves: New Poems. New York: Viking Press, 1990. Dust jacket. Published at $17.95.

Weathers and Edges. New York: Viking Press, 1966. Dust jacket. Published at $4.50.

Joseph Brodsky

Joseph Brodsky (b. 1940) came to the United States from
his native Russia as a political exile in 1972. He has
described an exiled writer as one "who survives like a
fish in the sand";[1] but since his arrival he has made a place for
himself in the Anglo-American literary tradition, publishing
English translations (often by himself) of his poems, and
writing more and more of them in English.

Persecuted in the Soviet Union for his early writings
despite their lack of overt political content, Brodsky is inevi-
tably engaged with totalitarianism, with "the challenge of
writing music after Auschwitz," as he says in his 1987 Nobel
Prize acceptance speech, quoting Theodor Adorno, and add-
ing that we can substitute the name of any Russian camp.[2] His
poetry reflects the suffering caused by an oppressive regime
(according to Stephen Spender, it "has the air of being ground
out between his teeth"[3]), and the determination to oppose
that oppression. As Czeslaw Milosz said, "I find it fascinating
to read his poems as part of his larger enterprise, which is no
less than an attempt to fortify the place of man in a threatening
world."[4]

For Brodsky, language is a constitutive element of human freedom and autonomy. Art teaches the writer "the privateness of the human condition." Therefore, literature should not belong to an elite group, another form of totalitarianism, and we are responsible to language and the ways we use it. "The poet . . . is language's means for existence," and when writing, one should be guided by the language toward new territory, unexpected events.[5]

In "The Fifth Anniversary"—the anniversary of the beginning of Brodsky's exile—writing is the only possible home or refuge:

> *Scratch on, my clawlike pen, my pilgrim staff, my salvage!*
> *Don't rush our shuffling words: the age wheel-deep in*
>   *garbage*
> *Won't overtake us and won't grab you, barefoot savage. . . .*
>
> *This won't be heard up North, nor where hot sands hug*
>   *cactus.*
> *I don't know anymore what earth will nurse my carcass.*
> *Scratch on, my pen: let's mark the white the way it marks*
>   *us.*[6]

∾ POETRY

Elegy to John Donne, and Other Poems. Selected, translated, and with an introduction by Nicholas Bethell. London: Longmans, 1967. Dust jacket. Published at 25s. Brodsky's first book in English.

"The Funeral of Bobo." Translated by Richard Wilbur. Ann Arbor, Michigan: Ardis, 1974. Broadside. One of 100 copies signed by Brodsky.

A Part of Speech. New York: Farrar, Straus & Giroux, 1980. Dust jacket. Published at $12.95.

Selected Poems. Translated from the Russian by George L. Kline. Foreword by W. H. Auden. New York: Harper & Row, 1973. Dust jacket. Published at $5.95.

"To a Tyrant." West Branch, Iowa: Toothpaste Press for
Bookslinger, 1982. Broadside. One of 90 signed copies
printed for a reading at the Walker Art Center, April
1982. Translated by Alan Myers.

To Urania. New York: Farrar, Straus & Giroux, 1988. Cloth,
in slipcase as issued. One of 150 copies signed by the
author.

Verses on the Winter Campaign 1980. Translated by Alan
Myers. London: Anvil Press Poetry, 1981. Wrappers.
One of 500 copies.

Watermark. New York: Farrar, Straus & Giroux, 1992. Dust
jacket. Published at $15.00.

❧ PROSE

Less Than One: Selected Essays. New York: Farrar, Straus &
Giroux, 1986. Dust jacket. Published at $25.00.

Marbles: A Play in Three Acts. Translated by Alan Myers with
the author. New York: Farrar, Straus & Giroux, 1989.
Dust jacket. Published at $17.95 but soon raised to
$25.00. The translation contains several revisions and
additions to the original Russian text.

Amy Clampitt

Amy Clampitt (b. 1920) published her first full-length book of poetry, *The Kingfisher*, in 1983 at the age of sixty-three.[1] It received immediate critical acclaim for its inventive, playful rendering of experience. In "Beach Glass," Clampitt describes her poetic process as a kind of beach-combing, a hunting for luminous fragments by

> . . . *an intellect*
> *engaged in the hazardous*
> *redefinition of structures*
> *no one has yet looked at.*

Art and the ordinary continually transform into each other:

> *amber of Budweiser, chrysoprase*
> *of Almadén and Gallo, lapis*
> *by way of (no getting around it,*
> *I'm afraid) Phillips'*
> *Milk of Magnesia, with now and then a rare*
> *translucent turquoise or blurred amethyst*
> *of no known origin.*[2]

In its often complex syntax and metaphor as well as its themes, this poetry shows the perpetual transformations of the mind. Helen Vendler says that "Amy Clampitt writes a beautiful,

taxing poetry. In it, thinking uncoils and coils again, embody-
ing its perpetual argument with itself."[3]

Clampitt wishes to witness the poignancy of mute expe-
rience, "to tell it how it looks." In "Witness" she writes:

> An ordinary evening in Wisconsin
> seen from a Greyhound bus—mute aisles
> of merchandise the sole inhabitants
> of the half-darkened Five and Ten,
>
> the tables of the single lit café awash
> with unarticulated pathos. . . .[4]

In "Gooseberry Fool" we find, according to Mona Van Duyn,[5]
"not a gooseberry used to define adolescence . . . but adoles-
cence used to define a gooseberry":

> . . . the arrogant, shrinking,
> prickling-in-every-direction thorn-
> iness that loves no company except its.[6]

In two recent collections, Clampitt's concern with how
the mind processes experience is focussed on particular potent
images we construct. *Archaic Figure*, she says, centers on the
experience of women "as individuals and as a part of human
history." It explores the "experience of attachment," and "the
way experience otherwise scarcely bearable is reflected in art
and literature."[7] *Westward* explores the perpetual desire to
expand experience, to be at the frontier. The final long poem
of that collection, "The Prairie," interweaves two narratives:
that of her own pioneer ancestors on the American prairie, and
that of Anton Chekhov, her grandfather's exact contemporary,
who was born near the Russian steppe.

POETRY

Amy Clampitt. New York: DIA Art Foundation, 1988.
    Wrappers. "Readings in Contemporary Poetry,
    Number 7." The Reed Foundation Poetry Chapbook
    Series.

Archaic Figure: Poems. New York: Alfred A. Knopf, 1987. Dust jacket. Published at $15.95. "Knopf Poetry Series, 26."

A Homage to John Keats. New York: Sarabande Press, 1984. Wrappers, in slipcase as issued. One of 224 copies signed by the author in a total limitation of 250.

The Kingfisher: Poems. New York: Alfred A. Knopf, 1983. Dust jacket. Published at $11.95. "Knopf Poetry Series, 9."

Manhattan: An Elegy, and Other Poems. Woodcuts by Margaret Sunday. Iowa City: University of Iowa Center for the Book, 1990. Boards; glassine dust jacket. One of 130 copies signed by the author and the artist. There were also ten unnumbered proofs.

Multitudes, Multitudes. New York: Washington Street Press, 1973. Wrappers. The author's first book. This copy is signed by her and has two holograph corrections on page 25.

Westward: Poems. New York: Alfred A. Knopf, 1990. Dust jacket. Published at $18.95.

What the Light Was Like. New York: Alfred A. Knopf, 1985. Dust jacket. Published at $14.95. "Knopf Poetry Series, 18."

⪫ PROSE

Predecessors, Et Cetera: Essays. Ann Arbor: University of Michigan Press, 1991. Boards. Issued without dust jacket.

Alfred Corn

Alfred Corn (b. 1943), who has described himself as "late Symbolist,"[1] writes a colloquial, learned, cosmopolitan poetry in which his own experience, especially in love, is never far from the surface. Corn believes poetry is a practice of forming relations with others. In this self-preoccupied time, poetry should be contemplative: "I believe that those writers who wish to perform in the useful role of gadfly, a sting to intelligence and conscience, should at this moment in history, urge readers to *think* and not simply to lunge."

For Corn, as for James Merrill and John Ashbery, a narrative of homosexual loves is integral to a persistent existential questing. Being is being in relation to another. His book-length poem, *Notes from a Child of Paradise*, uses motifs from Dante and passages on the Lewis and Clark expedition in a narrative that traces his early marriage, coming of age in the 1960s, and discovery of his homosexuality. In "Songs for Five Companionable Singers,"[2] Corn pursues "A new way to imagine what love might be," and in "The Beholder," a reworking of the Narcissus myth, he explores surface and depth and the idea of searching for difference in likeness:

Deep lake, surfaced sky that a drop disrupts,
The beholder is one not wooed by stages.
Will he look for light in your flawed water?

Ideals nurtured in a far other air
Summon him to your persuasive body,
Deep lake, surfaced sky that a drop disrupts.[3]

Corn is concerned with our appetites, intellectual, visual, sexual, and how they mediate our experience, as in "Passages":

. . . thought itself may be
A disease when one decides perversely
And with a familiar sinking sensation
To get to the bottom of everything. . . .[4]

⪻ POETRY

All Roads At Once. New York: Viking Press, 1976. Dust jacket. Published at $5.95. The author's first book.

Autobiographies: Poems. New York: Viking Press, 1992. Dust jacket. Published at $19.00.

A Call in the Midst of the Crowd. New York: Viking Press, 1978. Dust jacket. Published at $8.95.

Navidad, St. Nicholas Ave. New York: Ampersand Books, 1984. Wrappers. One of 350 copies to be used as a holiday greeting by the author and the publisher.

The New Life. New York: Albondocani Press, 1983. Wrappers. One of 100 signed copies in a total limitation of 126. Published at $45.00. Flyer loosely inserted.

Notes from a Child of Paradise. New York: Viking Press, 1984. Dust jacket. Published at $14.95. Signed by the author on the title page.

The Pith Helmet: Aphorisms. With an introduction by the author. Omaha, Nebraska: Cummington Press, 1992. Wrappers. One of 150 copies.

Tongues on Trees. Illustrated by John Gundelfinger. Carmel, New York: Parenthèse Signatures, 1981. Portfolio, in printed green wrappers. One of 150 copies signed by the author and the artist.

The Various Light. New York: Viking Press, 1980. Dust jacket. Published at $12.95.

The West Door: Poems. New York: Viking Press, 1988. Dust jacket. Published at $17.95. With the author's presentation inscription "To John."

❧ PROSE

The Metamorphoses of Metaphor: Essays in Poetry and Fiction. New York: Viking Press, Elisabeth Sifton Books, 1987. Dust jacket. Published at $18.95.

Robert Creeley

Robert Creeley (b. 1926) writes short, everyday poems that are "structure[s] of . . . cognition."[1] A key figure of the Black Mountain School, Creeley taught at the experimental Black Mountain College and edited the *Black Mountain Review* during Charles Olson's rectorship of the college in the mid-1950s. He contributed one of the central tenets of Olson's ground-breaking essay, "Projective Verse": "Form is never more than an extension of content."[2] In the Preface to *For Love: Poems 1950–1960*, Creeley describes his humble, minimalist version of open form, or form that is not predetermined but emerges from the process of composition: "Wherever it is one stumbles (to get to wherever) at least some way will exist, so to speak, as and when a man takes this or that step—for which, god bless him."[3] Creeley's most recurring subject is relationship—poems about love (including explorations of the different stages of his three marriages), about the present moment and, in his more recent work, about the past and memory, all exploring the difficulties and joys of being where we are.

Creeley's poems often begin in the middle of a situation in progress: a conversation, an event, or an interior monologue. They bring us insistently, recurrently, back to the present. In "I Know a Man," the narrator relates a conversation:

> . . .—John, I
> sd, which was not his
> name, the darkness sur-
> rounds us, what
>
> can we do against
> it, or else, shall we &
> why not, buy a goddamn big car,
>
> drive, he sd, for
> christ's sake, look
> out where yr going.[4]

In poetry as on the road, it is necessary to navigate, to pay attention to where we are right now.

Creeley's short, syncopated line, with its unorthodox line breaks, owes much to bebop jazz as well as abstract expressionist and minimalist painting. It reaches its height of abstraction in *Pieces*, of which Louis Martz says, "It is impossible . . . to become more abstract without destroying the very presence of poetry. Yet Creeley manages to hold himself at the taut edge of poetic existence"[5]—as in "Echo Of":

> Can't myself
> let off this
> fiction. "You
> don't exist,
>
> baby, you're
> dead." Walk
> off, on—the
> light bulb
>
> overhead, beside,
> or, the bed, you
> think you laid
> on? When, what.[6]

In his recent work, Creeley takes on the past in the present, the presence or immediacy of memory. In "Prospect," the color green is a "subtle echo of itself . . . it is the color of life itself, / it used to be.[7]

⁓ POETRY

All That Is Lovely In Men. Drawings by Dan Rice. Asheville, North Carolina: Jonathan Williams, 1955. Wrappers, in dust jacket. Published at $2.50. "Jargon 10." One of 200 copies signed by the author and the artist. Postcard flyer for the book loosely inserted.

"America." Miami, Florida: Press of the Black Flag, 1970. Broadside. Limitation not stated.

As Now It Would Be Snow. Los Angeles: Black Sparrow Press, 1970. Glassine dust jacket. One of 50 copies in boards, signed by the author, in a total limitation of 579. A Christmas greeting from the publisher.

Autobiography. Madras, India, and New York: Hanuman Books, 1990. Wrappers, in dust jacket. A miniature book printed in Madras.

Away. Illustrations by Bobbie Creeley. Santa Barbara, California: Black Sparrow Press, 1976. Glassine dust jacket. One of 50 copies bound in boards by Earle Gray, containing an original color print by Bobbie Creeley, and signed by the author and the artist, in a total limitation of 3,306. Published at $30.

Backwards. Knotting, Bedfordshire, England: Sceptre Press, 1975. Wrappers. One of 100 copies in a total limitation of 150.

"The Birds, for Jane and Stan Brakhage." Berkeley, California: Arif Press, 1971. Broadside. One of 125 copies.

"Black Grackle." Durham, England: Pig Press, 1987. Single sheet folded to make four pages. Published on the occasion of Creeley's reading, May 1987.

"The Boy." Buffalo, New York: Gallery Upstairs Press, 1968. Broadside. Trade edition; there were also 50 signed copies.

"But." Buffalo, New York: Just Buffalo, 1975. Broadside, illustrated. Trade edition; there were also 50 copies signed by the author.

A Calendar: Twelve Poems. West Branch, Iowa: Morning Coffee Chapbook Five, 1984. Wrappers. One of 600 copies signed by the author. Accompanied by the broadside prospectus "Wyatt's May."

"Characteristically." Illustrated by Karyl Klopp. Cambridge, Massachusetts: Pomegranate Press, 1972. Broadside. One of 150 signed copies in a total limitation of 500.

The Charm: Early and Uncollected Poems. Mount Horeb, Wisconsin: Perishable Press, 1967. Boards. Not issued in dust jacket. One of 250 copies signed by the author. Not actually published until 1968.

The Charm: Early and Uncollected Poems. San Francisco: Four Seasons Foundation, 1969. Boards. One of 100 hardbound copies signed by the author. Expanded edition.

The Class of '47. Illustrated by Joe Brainard. New York: Bouwerie Editions, 1973. Wrappers. One of 100 copies in a total limitation of 328.

The Collected Poems, 1945–1975. Berkeley: University of California Press, 1982. Dust jacket. Published at $28.50.

The Company. Providence, Rhode Island: Burning Deck, 1988. Wrappers. One of 50 signed copies in a total limitation of 800.

Corn Close. Knotting, Bedfordshire, England: Sceptre Press, 1980. Wrappers. One of 75 signed copies in a total limitation of 250.

The Creative. Los Angeles: Black Sparrow Press, 1973. Wrappers. Published at 50 cents. "Sparrow 6."

A Day Book. Plates by R. B. Kitaj. Berlin, Germany: Graphis, 1972. Loose sheets laid into cloth portfolio as issued. One of 200 copies signed by the author and the artist in a total limitation of 295.

A Day Book. New York: Charles Scribner's Sons, 1972. Printed glassine dust jacket. Published at $6.95. First trade edition, the Berlin edition preceding.

Desultory Days. Knotting, Bedfordshire, England: Sceptre Press, 1978. Wrappers. One of 75 signed copies in a total limitation of 250.

"Distance." Drawing by Bobbie Creeley. Lawrence, Kansas: Terrence Williams, 1964. Broadside, printed on both sides. One of 500 copies.

Divisions & Other Early Poems. Madison, Wisconsin: Perishable Press, 1968. Wrappers. One of 100 copies in a total limitation of 110. This copy is inscribed by the author on the title page.

Dreams. New York: Periphery & The Salient Seedling Press, 1989. Boards. One of 50 copies signed by the author and the artist in a total limitation of 230. The title-page photograph is a letterpress reproduction of an original print by Duane Michals.

Echoes: Poems. West Branch, Iowa: Toothpaste Press, 1982. One of 200 hardbound copies signed by the author in a total limitation of 2,000.

The Finger. With collages by Bobbie Creeley. Los Angeles: Black Sparrow Press, 1968. One of 50 copies hand bound in boards, each with an original collage by Bobbie Creeley, signed by the author and the artist.

Published at $40.00. Accompanied by a copy of one of 250 copies in wrappers, signed by the author, and published at $10.00.

The Finger: Poems, 1966–1969. London: Calder & Boyars, 1970. Dust jacket. Published at £1.75. First English trade edition.

5 Numbers. New York: Poets Press, 1968. Wrappers. One of twenty starred copies signed by the author in a total limitation of 170.

"For Benny and Sabina." Brooklyn, New York: Samuel Charters, 1970. Broadside. One of 100 copies. "Portents 18."

"For Betsy and Tom." Detroit: Alternative Press, 1970. Broadside. Limitation not stated.

"For Joel." Rochester, Michigan: Perishable Press, 1966. Broadside. One of 85 copies. "For Joel and Helen Oppenheimer on the occasion of their marriage, 6 June 1966."

For My Mother: Genevieve Jules Creeley, 8 April 1887–7 October 1972. Rushden, Northamptonshire, England: Sceptre Press, 1973. Wrappers. One of 100 copies in a total limitation of 150.

"For the Graduation: Bolinas School, June 11, 1971." Bolinas, California: Privately printed, 1971. Small broadside pasted into illustrated wrappers. Number 17 of an unspecified number signed by the author. The unsigned copies were not issued in wrappers.

A Form of Women: Poems. New York: Jargon Books, 1959. Wrappers. Published at $1.50. One of 2,000 copies.

Le Fou. Columbus, Ohio: Golden Goose Press, 1952. Wrappers, glassine dust jacket. The author's first book.

Four Poems from A Form of Women. New York: Eighth Street Bookshop, 1959. Wrappers. Privately printed for friends of the Eighth Street Bookshop to celebrate the New Year.

Gnomic Verses. La Laguna, Tenerife: Zasterle Press, 1991. Wrappers. One of 500 copies.

Hello. Christchurch, New Zealand: Hawk Press Taylors Mistake, 1976. Wrappers. One of 750 copies in a total limitation of 800.

Hello: A Journal, February 29–May 3, 1976. New York: New Directions, 1978. Dust jacket. Published at $7.50. First trade, and first expanded, edition.

"Hero." Magnolia, Massachusetts: An Indianakatz Production, 1969. Single sheet folded to make four pages with tipped-in color illustration by Robert Indiana. One of 1,000 copies. With Creeley's presentation inscription.

His Idea. Photographs by Elsa Dorfman. Toronto: Coach House Press, 1973. Wrappers. First issue with unprinted wrappers. Accompanied by a copy of the second issue in gold-printed wrappers.

"Hotel Schrieder, Heidelberg." West Branch, Iowa: Toothpaste Press, 1984. Broadside. One of 150 signed copies. Issued on the occasion of a reading by the poet at the Walker Art Center, 21 February 1984.

If You: Poems. Illustrated by Fielding Dawson. San Francisco: Porpoise Bookshop, 1956. Folio. Loose sheets contained in wrappers. One of 200 copies. "Poems & Pictures: Number Eight."

In London. Bolinas, California: Angel Hair Books, 1970. Wrappers. One of 200 copies in a total limitation of 214.

Inside Out. Los Angeles: Black Sparrow Press, 1973. Wrappers. "Sparrow 14." Published at 50 cents.

The Island. New York: Charles Scribner's Sons, 1963. Wrappers. Paperback edition, preceding the cloth edition. First issue with transposed lines on page 145. Accompanied by a copy of the cloth edition in dust jacket, published at $3.50; also a first issue.

The Kind of Act Of. Palma de Majorca: Divers Press, 1953. Wrappers. Cover by René Laubies.

"Kitchen." Chicago: Wine Press, 1972. Broadside. One of 500 copies. Number 2 in the broadside series "Letters."

Later: A Poem. West Branch, Iowa: Toothpaste Press, 1978. Wrappers. One of 100 copies signed by the author and Louis J. Picek, who illustrated the wrappers. Total limitation was 900.

Later. New York: New Directions, 1979. Paperback; not published in cloth. Published at $4.95. Expanded from the West Branch, 1978, edition.

Lines on the Publication of The Collected Poems of Robert Creeley, 1945–1975. Buffalo, New York: Bolt Court Press, 1983. Wrappers. One of 100 signed copies in a total limitation of 126. Illustrated with photographs.

Listen. Monoprints by Bobbie Creeley. Los Angeles: Black Sparrow Press, 1972. Glassine dust jacket. One of 250 hardbound copies signed by the author in a total limitation of 1,805. Published at $15.00.

Mary's Fancy. New York: Bouwerie Editions, 1970. Wrappers. One of 100 signed copies in a total edition of 402. Color photograph by William Katz tipped in as a frontispiece.

Mazatlan: Sea. San Francisco: Poets Press, 1969. Wrappers. One of 50 copies signed by the author in a total limitation of 80.

"Mea Domina." Derry, Pennsylvania: Rook Society, 1976. Broadside. One of 100 copies signed by the author.

Memory Gardens. New York: New Directions, 1986. Dust jacket. Published at $15.95.

Mother's Voice. Drawings by Tom Clark. Santa Barbara, California: Am Here Books / Immediate Editions, 1981. Wrappers. Limitation not stated.

Myself. Knotting, Bedfordshire, England: Sceptre Press, 1977. Wrappers. One of 50 copies signed by the author in a total limitation of 250.

"Night in NYC: For Angus." Boulder, Colorado: Lodestar, ca. 1974. Broadside. From a portfolio entitled "The Lodestar Broadside Portfolio." Limitation not stated, but 150 copies were printed.

Notebook. New York: Bouwerie Editions, 1972. Wrappers. Robert Creeley's Notebook, 7 June 1970 to 19 June 1970. One of 250 copies in a total limitation of 350.

The Old Days. Tarzana, California: Ambrosia Press, 1991. Boards, not issued in dust jacket. One of 270 copies signed by the author in a total limitation of 360.

"On a Theme by Lawrence Hearing Purcell." Illustrated by T. Dreamer. Buffalo, New York: "Just Buffalo" Readings, 1978. Broadside. Limitation not stated.

"One day after another—." Detroit: Alternative Press, 1972. A poetry postcard. This copy is signed by Creeley.

1 2 3 4 5 6 7 8 9 0. Drawings by Arthur Okamura. Berkeley, California: Shambala, 1971. Illustrated glassine dust jacket. One of 200 hardbound copies signed by the author and the artist.

Pieces. New York: Charles Scribner's Sons, 1969. Dust jacket. Published at $4.50. Expanded edition.

Places. Paintings by Susan Barnes. Buffalo, New York: Shuffaloff Press, 1990. Wrappers. One of 50 copies signed by the author and the artist in a total limitation of 500.

"The Plan is the Body." Philadelphia: Middle Earth
   Bookstore, 1973. Broadside. One of 275 copies in a
   total limitation of 300.

"The Plan is the Body." Vancouver, British Columbia:
   Prester John, 1975. Broadside. Two versions, one
   printed on graph paper and the other on plain white
   paper. No limitations stated.

Poems 1950–1965. London: Calder & Boyars, 1966. Boards
   in slipcase as issued. One of 100 copies "in advance of
   the first edition" signed by the author. Actually, this
   limited edition did not appear until about two years
   after the trade edition.

Presences. New York: Charles Scribner's Sons, 1976. Dust
   jacket. Published at $7.95.

Selected Poems. New York: Charles Scribner's Sons, 1976.
   Dust jacket. Published at $7.95.

Selected Poems. Berkeley: University of California Press,
   1991. Dust jacket.

A Sense of Measure. London: Calder & Boyars, 1972. Dust
   jacket. "Signature 16."

7 & 6 (A Suite for Robert Therrien). Plates by Robert
   Therrien. Arrangements by Michel Butor. Albuquerque,
   New Mexico: Hoshour Gallery, 1988. Loose signatures
   in slipcase as issued. Fifteen hundred copies were
   printed but 700 were reportedly ruined.

"Sitting Here." Storrs: University of Connecticut Library,
   1974. Broadside. One of 350 copies issued on the
   occasion of a reading by the poet on March 28, 1974.

Some Time: A Selection, 1945–1987. New York: DIA Art
   Foundation, 1987. Wrappers. One of 500 copies.
   "Readings in Contemporary Poetry Number 2." The
   Reed Foundation Poetry Chapbook Series.

Thanks. Deerfield, Massachusetts: Deerfield Press, 1977.
   Dust jacket. One of 250 signed copies. Illustrated by

Timothy Engelland. Published simultaneously by the Deerfield Press and the Gallery Press, Ireland.

Thirty Things. Monoprints by Bobbie Creeley. Los Angeles: Black Sparrow Press, 1974. Glassine jacket. One of 250 hardcover copies signed by the author in a total limitation of 2,350. Published at $15.00.

"Time: For W.G.C." Vancouver, British Columbia: Slug Press, 1982. Broadside. One of 100 signed copies. "Contemporary Broadsides Number Five."

"Two Poems." Berkeley, California: Oyez, 1964. Broadside. Limitation not stated but 350 copies printed. First issue with white showing around the gold diamonds in the capital letter "T."

A Wall. With a serigraph by William Katz. New York: Bouwerie Editions, and Stuttgart: Edition Domberger, 1969. Wrappers, in portfolio. One of 125 copies signed by the author and the artist in a total limitation of 210.

The Whip. Worcester, England: Migrant Books, 1957. Stiff wrappers. One of 500 copies in a total limitation of 600.

Window. Paintings by Martha Visser't Hooft. Buffalo: State University of New York at Buffalo, 1988. Wrappers. Glassine dust jacket. Enclosed in an envelope with printed label. One of 100 unsigned copies in a total limitation of 200.

Windows. New York: New Directions, 1990. Dust jacket. Published at $19.95.

"Wishes." Santa Barbara, California: Cadmus Editions, 1982. Broadside. Block carved by Sally McQuillan. One of 100 signed copies in a total limitation of 126.

Words: Poems. New York: Charles Scribner's Sons, 1967. Dust jacket. Published at $4.95. Expanded edition.

"Wyatt's May": See *A Calendar: Twelve Poems*, 1984.

↜ PROSE

Charles Olson & Robert Creeley: The Complete Correspondence,
   ed. George F. Butterick and Richard Blevens. Santa
   Barbara, California: Black Sparrow Press, 1980–1990.
   Nine volumes. Glassine dust jackets. Volumes 1–3
   limited to 1,000 hardcover trade copies; 4–5 limited to
   750; 6–8 limited to 500; and volume 9 limited to 400.
   With volume 9 Richard Blevens takes over as editor.

The Collected Essays. Berkeley: University of California
   Press, 1989. Dust jacket. Review copy with slip loosely
   inserted.

The Collected Prose. New York: Marion Boyars, 1984. Dust
   jacket. Published at $26.00. The jacket drawing is by
   Kitaj.

Contexts of Poetry: Interviews, 1961–1971, ed. Donald Allen.
   Bolinas, California: Four Seasons Foundation, 1973.
   Paperback. Not issued in cloth. "Writing 30."

Contexts of Poetry at the Vancouver Conference, July 1963, by
   Robert Creeley and Allen Ginsberg. Buffalo, New York:
   Audit, 1968. Wrappers. Issued as *Audit* 5, no. 1 (Spring
   1968).

The Gold Diggers. Palma de Majorca: Divers Press, 1954.
   Wrappers. Published at $1.25.

The Gold Diggers and Other Stories. London: John Calder,
   1965. Dust jacket. Published at 25s. First English
   edition of the expanded edition following the Frankfurt
   edition; it precedes the Scribner's (paperback) edition
   issued the same year.

The Gold Diggers and Other Stories. New York: Charles
   Scribner's Sons, 1965. Paperback, not issued in cloth.
   Published at $1.65. Preceded by the English edition.
   With the author's presentation inscription to the poet
   Joel Oppenheimer.

Mabel, A Story, & Other Prose. London: Marion Boyars, 1976. Dust jacket. Copies were distributed in the United States with a printed dust jacket price of $10.00, later raised to $11.95.

A Quick Graph: Collected Notes & Essays, ed. Donald Allen. San Francisco: Four Seasons Foundation, 1970. Dust jacket. Published at $8.50. "Writing 22."

Was That A Real Poem or Did You Just Make It Up Yourself? Santa Barbara, California: Black Sparrow Press, 1976. Wrappers. "Sparrow 40." Published at 75 cents. Fifteen hundred and twenty copies printed.

Was That a Real Poem & Other Essays, ed. Donald Allen. With a chronology by Mary Novik. Bolinas, California: Four Seasons Foundation, 1979. Issued without dust jacket. Expanded edition. "Writing 39."

Guy Davenport

Guy Davenport (b. 1927), poet, translator, short-story writer, and essayist, whom George Steiner has characterized as "among the very few truly original, truly autonomous voices now audible in American letters,"[1] published *Thasos and Ohio: Poems and Translations 1950–1980* in 1985. The volume offers ample evidence of Davenport's playful, keenly attentive, and wide-ranging life of devotion to literature. For Davenport, translating and writing poetry are so intimate that they cannot be separated. Nearly two-thirds of the poems in *Thasos and Ohio* are translations, and many of the original poems constitute a loving dialogue with another poet or text, often placing the name of the other poet below the title just as the translations do. "Swan" plays off Mallarmé's famous sonnet, "Le vierge, le vivace et le bel aujourd'hui," sometimes offering a graceful rendition of the original—as in the first line, "Girlish, vivacious, and brash afternoon," whose repeated "sh" sounds capture the slightly savage, percussive quality of the alliterative French—but steering the poem on a different course from Mallarmé's, with beautiful lines like "The inward white of radiant space" that are all its own.

While Davenport's poetry ranges from limpid simplicity

("Ohio"; "For Lorine Niedecker") to dense, allusive parody ("The Resurrection in Cookham Churchyard"),[2] a characteristic feature is a surrender of human control to other orders and rhythms, as in "Springtime and Autumn":

> Out of complex hypocrisy (across blue eyes,
> The young's honest gaze, bobbing water's
> Ribboned refractions shift in plies)
> Guileless action comes, but at a loss,
>
> Without, indeed, an aim (raised arms
> Bunched a fluting of ribs to low relief)
> Unless the human parallel the force that
> Breaks the lean-limbed dogwood into leaf.[3]

This surrender of control permits the emergence of local processes and forms, the description of which becomes an end in itself. "The Medusa" is a look at a jellyfish in which scientific detail and mythic association form part of the same abundant reality:

> Their progeny is the ghost octopus
> with legs of smoke, the dozen-crotched-
> and-eyed Medusa Cyanea,
> fire in azure, quick to sting,
> a ferociousness of light
> in the cold dark of the seas.[4]

Davenport's short fiction is as suggestive and clean as any verse and certainly uses many of contemporary poetry's most important structural innovations. His stories use elements of parataxis, repetition, and, one suspects, chance assemblage to make his narrative space more fluid and porous. Narrative serves as a grounding to which clusters of association accrue. In "Wo Es War, Soll Ich Werden," "The hophornbeam explains its leaves. Lays them out flat to the sun. Human honesty should do no less."[5] Although conflicts, usually between adolescent boys, do occur in these stories, Davenport's sense of structure is more one of harmonious edges meeting in a still space under which pass the largely non-threatening histories of their objects than one of conflict resolved in a forward sweep of time. In consistently crisp and elegant prose, he places the homoerotic encounters and speculations of boys, beautiful and learned descriptions of flower and sky, the language of philosophy, and recreations of history in unstated connection. As Davenport says in "Badger" in the voices of a twelve-year-old cellist and his dog, respectively: "—The film of essences, one photon thick, is continuous. Everything apprehended is in the continuum of this film . . ." and "—the great thing is affability, not the kinship but the kindness of one thing to another."[6]

❧ POETRY

A Balthus Notebook. New York: Ecco Press, 1989. Dust jacket. Plates. Published at $17.95.

Belinda's World Tour. Illustrations by Deborah Norden. New York: Dim Gray Bar Press, 1991. Boards. One of 100 copies signed by the author and the illustrator.

The Bicycle Rider. New York: Red Ozier Press, 1985. Glassine dust jacket. One of 30 copies bound in boards in a total limitation of 150. Printed on buff paper with the paragraphs numbered in red.

The Bowmen of Shu. Illustrations by the author and Henri Gaudier-Brzeska. New York: Grenfell Press, 1983. Boards. One of 115 copies signed by the author in a total limitation of 125.

Do You Have a Poem Book on e.e. cummings? Penland, North Carolina: Jargon Society, 1969. Wrappers. One of 1,000 copies. Illustrated by the author. "Jargon 67."

The Drummer of the Eleventh North Devonshire Fusiliers. San Francisco: North Point Press, 1990. Dust jacket. Published at $19.95.

Flowers and Leaves. Poema vel Sonata. Highlands, North Carolina: Jonathan Williams, 1966. Wrappers, dust jacket. Published at $6.00. Illustrated by the author. "Jargon 46."

Goldfinch Thistle Star. Drawings by Lachlan Stewart. New York: Red Ozier Press, 1983. Boards. One of 45 hardbound copies signed by the author in a total limitation of 200. Accompanied by a copy of the issue in wrappers, one of 155 signed copies.

Jonathan Williams, Poet. Cleveland, Ohio: Asphodel Book Shop, 1969. Wrappers. Frontispiece portrait by Davenport. Published on the occasion of Jonathan Williams' fortieth birthday. This copy is signed by Davenport and Williams.

The Medusa. N.p.: Weng & Associates, 1984. One of 55 signed copies in boards. Accompanied by a copy of the trade issue, limited to 600 copies in wrappers.

"Posthumes," by Bradford Morrow. Illustrated by Guy Davenport. Santa Barbara, California: Cadmus Editions, 1982. Broadside. One of 100 copies signed by the author in a total limitation of 126. This copy is signed by Davenport.

The Resurrection in Cookham Churchyard. New York: Jordan Davies, 1982. Boards. One of 230 copies signed by the author in a total limitation of 255.

Thasos and Ohio: Poems and Translations 1950–1980. Manchester, England: Carcanet, 1985. Paperback; not published in cloth. Published at £5.95. Precedes the American edition, published by North Point Press in 1986.

Thasos and Ohio: Poems & Translations 1950–1980. San Francisco: North Point Press, 1986. Dust jacket. Published at $14.95. Preceded by the English edition.

"37, avenue Samson, Cimitière Montmartre." Lexington:
University of Kentucky, King Library Press, 1985.
Broadside. One of 150 copies signed by the author.

Trois Caprices. Louisville, Kentucky: Pace Trust, 1982.
Boards, glassine dust jacket. One of 75 copies signed by
the author. Accompanied by a copy of the trade edition
in wrappers.

❧ PROSE

Apples and Pears and Other Stories. San Francisco: North
Point Press, 1984. Dust jacket. Published at $20.00.
Illustrated by the author.

The Art of Lafcadio Hearn. Charlottesville: University of
Virginia Library, 1983. Wrappers. Illustrated exhibition
catalogue. Fifteen hundred copies were printed. Also
contains "On Collecting Lafcadio Hearn," by Clifton
Waller Barrett.

Da Vinci's Bicycle: Ten Stories. Baltimore, Maryland: Johns
Hopkins University Press, 1979. Dust jacket. Published
at $12.95. Illustrated by the author.

Eclogues: Eight Stories. Illustrated by Roy R. Behrens. San
Francisco: North Point Press, 1981. Dust jacket.
Published at $15.00.

Every Force Evolves a Form: Twenty Essays. San Francisco:
North Point Press, 1987. Dust jacket. Published at
$16.95. Illustrated.

Father Louie: Photographs of Thomas Merton, by Ralph
Eugene Meatyard. With an essay by Davenport. Edited
by Barry Magid. New York: Timken Publishers, 1991.
In cloth slipcase as issued. One of 100 copies signed by
Davenport and with an original photograph printed by
Christopher Meatyard from his father's negative laid in.

The Geography of the Imagination: Forty Essays. San Francisco: North Point Press, 1981. Dust jacket, with a drawing by the author. Published at $20.00.

The Intelligence of Louis Agassiz: A Specimen Book of Scientific Writing. Selected, with an introduction and notes, by Guy Davenport. Foreword by Alfred S. Romer. Boston: Beacon Press, 1963. Dust jacket. Illustrated. Davenport's first book.

Jonah: A Story. New York: Nadja, 1986. Wrappers. One of 100 signed copies in a total limitation of 126.

The Jules Verne Steam Balloon: Nine Stories. San Francisco: North Point Press, 1987. Dust jacket. Published at $21.95.

Pennant Key-Indexed Study Guide to Homer's Odyssey. Philadelphia: Educational Research Associates, 1967. Wrappers. Published at $1.00. Illustrated by the author.

Tatlin! Six Stories. New York: Charles Scribner's Sons, 1974. Dust jacket. Published at $7.95. Illustrated by the author.

❧ **TRANSLATIONS**

Anakreon: The Extant Fragments. Translated by Guy Davenport. University: University of Alabama, Parallel Editions, 1991. Wrappers. One of 90 copies signed by Davenport.

Archilochos, Sappho, Alkman: Three Lyric Poets of the Late Greek Bronze Age. Translated, with an introduction, by Guy Davenport. Berkeley: University of California Press, 1980. Dust jacket. A revised and extended edition of *Carmina Archilochi* and *Sappho: Poems and Fragments*, published in 1964 and 1965 respectively.

Carmina Archilochi: The Fragments of Archilochos. Translated from the Greek by Guy Davenport. Foreword by Hugh Kenner. Berkeley: University of California Press, 1964. Paperback issue. Published at $1.50. The text was revised and reissued as *Archilochos, Sappho, Alkman* in 1980.

Fragmenta Nova by Sappho. Frontispiece by Cheryl Miller. Berkeley, California: Arif Press, 1981. Boards; one of 100 copies. Greek text edited by Sir Denys Page. Loosely inserted is the prospectus with "A note on the text" by Guy Davenport.

Herakleitos. Berkeley, California: Peter Koch, 1990. Boards. One of 100 copies signed by Davenport in a total limitation of 113. Accompanied by the prospectus. Translations from the Greek, and in one case from the Latin. Greek / Latin / English text.

Herakleitos & Diogenes. Translated from the Greek by Guy Davenport. Bolinas, California: Grey Fox Press, 1979. Issued without dust jacket.

Maxims of the Ancient Egyptians. Translated from the hieroglyphs by Boris de Rachewiltz and from his Italian by Guy Davenport. Louisville, Kentucky: Pace Trust, 1983. Boards. One of 125 copies, this one signed by Davenport.

The Mimes of Herondas. Translated by Guy Davenport. San Francisco: Grey Fox Press, 1981. Boards, not issued in dust jacket.

Sappho: Poems and Fragments. Translated and with an introduction by Guy Davenport. Ann Arbor: University of Michigan Press, 1965. Dust jacket. Published at $3.95. The drawings in the text are by Davenport. The text was revised and reissued as *Archilochos, Sappho, Alkman* in 1980.

The Spirit Walks, the Rocks Will Talk: Eccentric Translations, by
Ronald Johnson. Vignettes by Guy Davenport. New
York and Penland, North Carolina: Jargon Society,
1969. Wrappers. One of 500 copies signed by Johnson
and Davenport.

Diane di Prima

Diane di Prima (b. 1934) began as a Beat poet, and her
early work is full of the slang and hip stances of the New
York City streets of the 1950s. Her work is characterized
by an emotional honesty. As Robert Creeley says in his
foreword to *Pieces of a Song: Selected Poems*, "She is an adept
and flexible provider of the real, which we eat daily or else we
starve."[1] Di Prima herself, in a 1978 interview with Anne
Waldman, puts it this way: "Poetry is not a place where you
can bluff. You speak directly to the hearts of people. People
are hungry for that directness ... whatever else we do, the first
thing is we reactivate the feeling, we reactivate the possibility
of living a life of emotion and of the flesh, as well as of the life
of the brain."[2]

Di Prima uses direct language and concrete details to
convey emotional subtlety, as in one of her "More or Less Love
Poems":

> *you are not quite*
> *the air I breathe*
> *thank god*
>
> *so go.*[3]

Always an activist poet, di Prima sees language as political.
In "Poetics" she rejects the role of preserving language, saying,
> let the language fend for itself.
> it turned over god knows enough carts in the city streets
> its barricades are my nightmares.[4]

She chooses rather to "enact the language as poetry"[5] so that
it becomes her element:
> I plunge in
> I suspect that I cannot drown
> like a fat brat catfish, smug
> > a hoodlum fish
> I move more and more gracefully
> > breathe it in,
> success written on my mug till the fishpolice
> corner me in the coral and I die.[6]

Di Prima is also a feminist poet. Her *Loba* cycle (1973–1978)
reworks mythic tradition to explore the feminine spirit. A
practicing Buddhist since 1962, di Prima sees that emptiness
and interdependence "describe the actual *structure* of the
world."[7] "Tassajara" was written the year after di Prima moved
west:
> Even Buddha is lost in this land
> the immensity
> takes us all with it, pulverizes, and takes us in
>
> Bodhidharma came from the west.
> Coyote met him.[8]

⟫ POETRY

"After Completion." Illustrated by "Frutkoff." San
  Francisco: Mongrel Press, 1972. Broadside. Limitation
  not stated.

"& we say 'casting the runes' . . ." San Francisco: Privately
  printed, 1983. Broadside. "A Solstice Greeting . . . by

Diane di Prima and Sheppard Powell." This copy is inscribed by di Prima.

Brass Furnace Going Out: Song, After an Abortion. Syracuse, New York: Pulpartforms, 1975. Wrappers. Published at $1.00. Cover illustration by Suzanne Benton.

The Calculus of Variation. San Francisco: Privately printed, 1972. Wrappers. One of 1,950 copies in a total limitation of 2,000.

Combination Theatre Poem & Birthday Poem for Ten People. New York: Brownstone Press, 1965. Loose sheets laid into paper wrappers. One of 100 copies.

Dinners & Nightmares. New York: Corinth Books, 1961. Wrappers. True first edition with $1.25 on top cover.

Earthsong: Poems, 1957–1959, chosen by Alan S. Marlowe. New York: Poets Press, 1968. Wrappers.

Freddie Poems. Point Reyes, California: Eidolon Editions, 1974. Wrappers. One of 500 copies in a total limitation of 600. Although the printed limitation states that there were 500 numbered and signed copies, there were only 100.

Haiku. Illustrated by George Herms. Topanga, California: Printed by the artist at the Love Press, 1966. Loose sheets in a leather pouch. One of 100 copies signed by di Prima in a total limitation of 112.

"Headlands: The Music." N.p., n.d. Broadside, signed by the author. Limitation not stated.

Hotel Albert: Poems. New York: Poets Press, 1968. Wrappers. One of 150 copies signed by the author.

"How shall I win you to me?" West Branch, Iowa: Toothpaste Press for Bookslinger, 1980. Broadside. One of 85 signed copies. Issued on the occasion of the author's reading at the Walker Art Center, 6 November 1980.

"Hymn." Pleasant Valley, New York: Kriya Press of Sri
Ram Ashram, 1967. Broadside. One of 90 copies in a
total limitation of 100.

"I am no good at pleading, . . ." San Francisco: The Tenth
Muse, 1971. Broadside. Limitation not stated.

"I feel myself fade. . . ." Photo by Peter Moore. Denver,
Colorado: Croupier Press, 1969. Poetry post card.
"Poetry Card Series #3."

Kerhonkson Journal, 1966. Berkeley, California: Oyez, 1971.
Wrappers. One of 1,000 copies. Photographic
frontispiece. Errata slip loosely inserted.

L.A. Odyssey. San Francisco: Poets Press, 1969. Wrappers
by George Heims. One of 100 copies signed by the
author.

"Last Travel Poem." Buffalo, New York: Allentown
Community Center, 1976. Broadside. Limitation not
stated.

Loba as Eve. New York: Phoenix Book Shop, 1975.
Wrappers. Limited to 126 signed copies, this one being
out of series.

Loba: Part I. Illustrated by Josie Grant. Santa Barbara,
California: Capra Press, 1973. One of 100 hardbound
copies signed by the author. "Yes! Capra Chapbook
Series 10."

Loba: Part II. Drawings by Josie Grant. Point Reyes,
California and Kathmandu, Nepal: Eidolon Editions,
1976. Boards. One of 50 hardbound copies signed by
the author and the artist in a total limitation of 550.
Printed in the Kingdom of Nepal.

The New Handbook of Heaven. San Francisco: Auerhahn
Press, 1963. Wrappers. One of 1,000 copies in a total
limitation of 1,030.

New Mexico Poem, June–July 1967. New York: Poets Press, 1968. Wrappers. One of 50 copies signed by the author in a total limitation of 62.

Revolutionary Letters. Ann Arbor: Artists Workshop / Trans-Love Energies, ca. 1968. Wrappers. The cover was designed to look like graffiti on a brick wall and has ragged holes deliberately poked in it and deliberately charred edges.

Revolutionary Letters Etc. San Francisco: City Lights Books, 1971. Wrappers. Published at $2.00. "The Pocket Poets Series Number 27." Expanded edition. Three thousand copies were printed.

Selected Poems, 1956–1975. Plainfield, Vermont: North Atlantic Books, 1975. Paperback. Not issued in cloth. Published at $5.00.

Selected Poems, 1956–1976. Plainfield, Vermont: North Atlantic Books, 1977. Wrappers. Published at $6.00. Adds to and corrects the author's *Selected Poems, 1956–1975* from the same publisher.

Seminary Poems. Point Reyes Station, California: Floating Island Publications, 1991. Wrappers. One of 2,000 copies.

"So Fine." Portland, Oregon: Yes! Press, 1971. Broadside. Limitation not stated.

This Kind of Bird Flies Backward. Introduction by Lawrence Ferlinghetti. New York: Totem Press, 1958. Wrappers. Published at 95 cents. The author's first book.

"Trajectory." Detroit: Alternative Press, 1974. Broadside. Limitation not stated.

"Whale Honey: A Poem / Play." San Francisco: Intersection Theatre, 1975. Poster for this poem / play by di Prima. Signed by the author.

Wyoming Series. San Francisco: Eidolon Editions, 1988.
   Oblong wrappers. One of 50 copies printed in two
   colors, signed by the author, and with her drawings.
   Accompanied by a copy of the trade edition, limited to
   250 copies.

⚛ PROSE

The Mysteries of Vision: Some Notes on H.D. Santa Barbara,
   California: Am Here Books, 1988. Wrappers.

⚛ TRANSLATION

Seven Love Poems from the Middle Latin. Translated by Diane
   di Prima. New York: Poets Press, 1965. Limitation not
   stated but this is one of twelve copies bound in boards
   and signed by the author. Accompanied by a copy of
   the trade editon in wrappers, published at $1.25. The
   cover drawing on the trade edition is by Brett Rohmer.

James Dickey

James Dickey (b. 1923) shares a penchant for exaggeration, the grotesque, and the mythologization of place and local history with the Southern fiction writers Flannery O'Connor, William Faulkner, and Eudora Welty. His use of narrative and robust tall-tale diction are "one way in which the Southern imagination can be turned to the possibilities of poetry."[1] Dickey, whose father was a lawyer and orator, spent six years working in advertising. In his poetry he speaks with a high pitch and energy, delighting in the powers and possibilities of talk.

Dickey is well known for his novel *Deliverance* (1970), a hair-raising tale of a group of middle-class businessmen who go on a camping trip and encounter the violence of a wilderness that they had thought benevolent. The novel is not an isolated case. Through much of Dickey's poetry there runs a streaking succession of sudden and violent acts:

> *Something far off   buried deep and free*
> *In the country   can always strike you dead*
> *Center of the brain. . . .*
>
> > *Whatever it does*
>
> *Again is worth waiting for*

and it is this which will "score off you" and send you "Beyond
speech-answer."[2] Dickey conceives of poetry, of language, as
the blinding deflection of a sudden and violent flash. He never
defines this flash, and has an ambiguous relationship with it.
It can be an orca like the one Dickey evokes in "Pursuit from
Under," which

> . . . *at the most uncertain of your ground*
> *Will shatter through, and lean,*
> *And breathe frankly in your face.*[3]

or it can be the black snake of "Cherrylog Road" with its
relation to a lurid sort of male sexuality and generation.
Dickey invites this extra-personal source of annihilation and
power, and forces us to recognize it, to see ourselves as
vehicles, even unwilling avatars, of a larger life that both
imperils and fulfills us: "Passing through many states, / Many
lives," he claims himself "Wild to be wreckage forever."[4]

However, Dickey is wary of this wild force and reluctant to
embrace or trust it fully. The destructive power of "Cherrylog
Road," the "Something far off buried deep and free / In the
country" smashes Southern racial boundaries and opens the
way to a freeing sexuality, but it also crashes planes, pulls
stewardesses to their deaths ("Falling"), and burns dollhouses
(*Puella*).[5] Dickey, who flew more than a hundred combat
missions in the Pacific during World War II, often writes
poems that involve flight. The fighter pilots in "Bread" aboard

> . . . *a B-25 sinking slowly*
> *into the swamps . . .*
> . . . *got out on the wings*
> *And lived there.*[6]

Dickey's speaker says of swamps,

> . . . *I who had not risen . . .*
> *knew always this was nothing*
> *Like home . . .*

and describes his fellow crashed pilots as "evolved drawn out
of the world's slime." This poem, with its frequent allusions to
the Last Supper, its preference for bread over lizards, and its

being "my own last war / Poem" seems to reach toward transcendence rather than toward an acceptance of the primal force in nature.

Dickey won the National Book Award in 1966 for *Buckdancer's Choice*.

❧ POETRY

Bronwen, the Traw, and the Shape-shifter: A Poem in Four Parts. Illustrated by Richard Jesse Watson. New York: Harcourt Brace Jovanovich / Bruccoli Clark, 1986. Dust jacket. Published at $13.95.

The Central Motion: Poems, 1968–1979. Middletown, Connecticut: Wesleyan University Press, 1983. Dust jacket. Published at $18.50.

"The Eagle's Mile." For William Douglas. Bloomfield Hills, Michigan: Bruccoli Clark, ca. 1990. Broadside. One of 250 copies, this one inscribed to the Princeton University Library by the author. A gift to the Milberg Collection from Matthew Bruccoli.

The Early Motion, Drowning with Others, and Helmets. Middletown, Connecticut: Wesleyan University Press, 1981. Dust jacket. Published at $15.00.

Falling, May Day Sermon, and Other Poems. Middletown, Connecticut: Wesleyan University Press, 1981. Dust jacket. Published at $10.00.

False Youth—Four Seasons. Dallas, Texas: Pressworks Publishing, 1983. Boards; glassine dust jacket. One of 200 signed copies in a total limitation of 226.

The Flash. Brockport: State University of New York, 1970. Wrappers. Issued for a reading by Dickey on 3 December 1970. This copy is signed by the poet.

"For a Time and Place." Columbia, South Carolina: Bruccoli Clark, 1983. Broadside. Commemorating the inauguration of Richard W. Riley to his second term as Governor of South Carolina, 12 January 1983. One of 250 copies signed by the author. A gift to the Milberg Collection from Matthew Bruccoli.

Four Poems. Winston-Salem, North Carolina: Privately printed, 1979. Wrappers. One of 25 copies signed by the author.

Head-Deep in Strange Sounds: Free-flight Improvisations from the unEnglish. Winston-Salem, North Carolina: Palaemon Press, 1979. Boards. One of 475 copies signed by Dickey in a total limitation of 525.

In Pursuit of the Grey Soul. Columbia, South Carolina: Bruccoli Clark, 1978. Wrappers, in slipcase as issued. One of 500 copies signed by the author. Dickey has also inscribed this copy.

"In the Child's Night." N.p.: Privately printed for James and Deborah Dickey, 1981. Broadside. One of 20 copies. Almost certainly printed in Winston-Salem by Stuart Wright.

"Mexican Valley." Winston-Salem, North Carolina: Palaemon Press, 1978. Broadside. One of 78 copies signed by the author. From *A Portfolio for Aaron Copland.*

Night Hurdling: Poems, Essays, Conversations, Commencements, and Afterwords. Columbia, South Carolina: Bruccoli Clark, 1983. Dust jacket. Signed by the author on the title page.

The Owl King. Illustrated by Ronald Keller. New York: Red Angel Press, 1977. Glassine dust jacket. One of 100 copies signed by the illustrator.

Poems. Melbourne, Australia: Sun Books, 1968. Wrappers.

Poems, 1957–1967. Middletown, Connecticut: Wesleyan University Press, 1967. Dust jacket. Published at $6.95.

Poems, 1957–1967. Middletown, Connecticut: Wesleyan University Press, 1967. Wrappers. One of 500 "miniature preview edition" copies for complimentary distribution. Only pages i–xvi and 1–15 are printed, the balance being blank.

The Poet Turns on Himself. Portree, Isle of Skye, Scotland: Aquila Publishing, 1982. Wrappers. Published at 60p. This copy is inscribed by the author on the front cover. A gift to the Milberg Collection from Matthew Bruccoli.

Puella. Garden City, New York: Doubleday, 1982. Dust jacket. Published at $10.95.

Scion. Illustrated by Timothy Engelland. Deerfield, Massachusetts: Deerfield Press, 1980. Dust jacket. One of 300 signed copies.

"The Shark at the Window." Winston-Salem, North Carolina: Palaemon Press, n.d., but after 1976. Broadside. One of 100 signed copies in a total limitation of 126. Original graphic by Robert Dance.

The Strength of Fields. Columbia, South Carolina: Bruccoli Clark, 1977. Wrappers. One of 350 copies signed by the author. Enclosed in the original printed envelope. A poem written for the inauguration of James Earle Carter as the thirty-ninth President of the United States.

The Strength of Fields. Garden City, New York: Doubleday, 1979. Dust jacket. Published at $6.00. Review copy with slip loosely inserted.

"Summons." Columbia, South Carolina: Bruccoli Clark,

1988. Broadside. One of 100 signed copies in a total limitation of 120.

Varmland: Poems Based on Poems. Winston-Salem, North Carolina: Palaemon Press, 1982. Wrappers. One of 150 copies signed by the author (of which only 45 were for sale).

Wayfarer: A Voice from the Southern Mountains. Photographs by William A. Bake. Birmingham, Alabama: Oxmoor House, 1988. Dust jacket. Published at $40.00, later raised to $50.00.

The Whole Motion: Collected Poems, 1945–1992. Middletown, Connecticut: Wesleyan University Press, 1992. Dust jacket.

The Zodiac. Garden City, New York: Doubleday, 1976. Dust jacket. One of an unknown number of copies signed on an inserted leaf and enclosed in a slipcase.

➣ PROSE

All is Brillig (or ought to be), by Allen Tate. Preface by James Dickey. Winston-Salem, North Carolina: Palaemon Press, 1979. Wrappers. Previously published as a broadside, this is the first edition to contain the Dickey preface. One of 50 copies signed by Dickey in a total limitation of 200.

Alnilam. Garden City, New York: Doubleday, 1987. One of 150 specially bound and slipcased copies signed by the author.

Deliverance. Carbondale: Southern Illinois University Press, 1982. Dust jacket. Screenplay for the film starring Jon Voight and Burt Reynolds.

"Firing Line." Columbia, South Carolina: Southern

Educational Communications Association, 1971.
Transcript of a television interview with Dickey hosted
by William F. Buckley, Jr., 22 April 1971, in New
Orleans. This copy is signed by Dickey.

God's Images: The Bible, A New Version. Illustrated by Marvin
Hayes. Birmingham, Alabama: Oxmoor House, 1977.
Dust jacket. Published at $24.95.

"How to Enjoy Poetry." New York: International Paper
Company, 1982. Broadside, illustrated with a
photograph of the author, and printed on both sides.
Limitation not stated.

*James Dickey: The Expansive Imagination. A Collection of
Critical Essays*, ed. Richard J. Calhoun. Deland, Florida:
Everett / Edwards, 1973. Cloth boards; not issued in
jacket. Contains "A Conversation with James Dickey,"
by Carolyn Kizer and James Boatwright, and a checklist
of his publications.

Jericho: The South Beheld, by Hubert Shuptrine and James
Dickey. Birmingham, Alabama: Oxmoor House, 1974.
Dust jacket. Published at $60.00. Text by Dickey, plates
by Shuptrine.

"National Book Award in Poetry, 1966. Acceptance
Speech." N.p.: Privately published, 1966. Three
mimeographed sheets. Inscribed by the author "To
Stuart [Wright]."

"Some Contemporaries." Detroit, Michigan: Gale
Research, 1980. Single sheet folded twice to make four
pages. One of 500 signed copies. Offprint of the
"Foreword" to *Dictionary of Literary Biography: American
Poets Since World War II*. A gift to the Milberg
Collection from Matthew Bruccoli.

*Spinning the Crystal Ball: Some Guesses at the Future of
American Poetry*. Washington, D.C.: Library of Congress,
1967. Wrappers. A lecture delivered at the Library of
Congress on 24 April 1967.

The Starry Place Between the Antlers: Why I Live in South Carolina. Bloomfield Hills, Michigan: Bruccoli Clark, 1981. Wrappers. One of 500 copies signed by the author, this copy is also inscribed by the author to Stuart Wright.

The Water-Bug's Mittens: Ezra Pound—What We Can Use. Bloomfield Hills, Michigan: Bruccoli Clark, 1980. Wrappers. One of 50 copies reserved for the author and publisher in a total limitation of 350. All copies are signed by the author.

Edward Dorn

Edward Dorn (b. 1929), who studied at Black Mountain College with Charles Olson, is perhaps best known for his comic epic poem in four parts, *Slinger*, in which the poet-narrator, a god-like cowboy, a dance-hall madam, and a talking horse sometimes called Claude Lévi-Strauss and sometimes Heidegger, set off to find Howard Hughes in Las Vegas. Begun in the late 1960s and first published in its entirety in 1975,[1] *Slinger*, says Marjorie Perloff, was ahead of its time, "with its amalgam of 'theory' and lyric, of prose narrative and sound-text, and especially of citation embedded in or superimposed upon the speech of a particular self."[2] Dorn expands the boundaries of the lyric and the lyric "I": the narrator of the poem disappears half-way through Book II. As Donald Wesling says, the poem is also "about how a self or voice can be differentiated into a cluster of other selves."[3]

    Slinger is also thoroughly a Western, with its laconic wit and sensitivity to the Western landscape:

> *And why do you have such a horse*
> *Gunslinger? I asked. Don't move*
> *he replied*

> *the sun rests deliberately*
> *on the rim of the sierra.*[4]

Dorn thinks of himself as a "poet of the West—not by nativity but by orientation."[5] *Slinger* mixes pop-culture images of the West with Western philosophy and the English literary tradition to create an off-beat, shifting mythology of our time. Perloff calls Slinger's farewell speech in Book IIII "a slightly offbase iambic pentameter sonnet that splices together bits of Keats, Shakespeare, and Sci-Fi":[6]

> *. . . Keen, fitful gusts are whispering here and there*
> *The mesas quiver above the withdrawing sunne*
> *. . . The smallest things now have their time*
> *. . . But now niños, it is time for me to go inside*
> *I must catch the timetrain*
> *The parabolas are in sympathy*
> *But it grieves me in some slight way*
> *because this has been such fine play*
> *and I'll miss this marvellous accidentalism*[7]

Dorn's playfulness is a serious critique of profit-oriented, imperialist American culture; as the "I" in *Slinger* says, after returning from the dead:

> *Entrapment is this society's*
> *Sole activity, I whispered*
> *and Only laughter,*
> *can blow it to rags*
> *But there is no negative pure enough*
> *to entrap our Expectations*[8]

In *Slinger* and in shorter poems, Dorn makes the lyric political, exhorting us to awareness and response: the duty of the poet in our times

> *is to maintain the plant*
> *to the end that the mumbling horde*
> *bestirs its prunéd tongue.*"[9]

Dorn won the American Book Award in 1980 for *Hello, La Jolla.*

✻ POETRY

Abhorrences. Santa Barbara, California: Black Sparrow Press, 1990. Glassine dust jacket. One of 150 hardcover copies signed by the author.

(Bean News). San Francisco: Hermes Free Press, 1972. Written anonymously by Edward Dorn and Jeremy Prynne. Tabloid newspaper format, this copy on white paper. There was also another issue printed on newsprint.

By the Sound. With a new preface by the author. Santa Rosa, California: Black Sparrow Press, 1991. Glassine dust jacket. One of 150 hardcover copies signed by the author.

Captain Jack's Chaps; or, Houston / MLA. Illustrated by Jim Lee. Madison, Wisconsin: Black Mesa Press, 1983. Wrappers. One of 260 copies.

The Collected Poems 1956–1974. Bolinas, California: Four Seasons Foundation, 1975. Boards. Issued without dust jacket. Accompanied by a copy of the second edition, revised.

"The Contract." East Lansing, Michigan: East Lansing Arts Workshop Press, 1973. Broadside. Printed for distribution at the National Poetry Festival, Thomas Jefferson College. Limitation not stated.

"The Cosmology of Finding Your Spot." Lawrence, Kansas: Cottonwood, 1969. Broadside. "Presented april 10, 1969 at the united campus christian fellowship benefit reading for the draft resisters league." Published at 15 cents.

The Cycle. West Newbury, Massachusetts: Frontier Press, 1971. Wrappers. Illustrated in color.

From Gloucester Out. Illustrated by Barry Hall. London: Matrix Press, 1964. Wrappers. One of 335 copies in a total limitation of 350.

"From *Hello, La Jolla*." Silkscreen design by Darcie Sanders. Evanston, Illinois: Whole Earth Center, 1976. Broadside. One of 150 copies signed by the author.

Geography. London: Fulcrum Press, 1965. Dust jacket. One of 950 copies in a total limitation of 1,000. An expanded edition was published in 1968.

Gunslinger, Book I. Los Angeles: Black Sparrow Press, 1968. Glassine dust jacket. One of 100 hardbound copies signed by the author in a stated total limitation of 726, but only 668 copies were actually printed. Published at $15.00.

Gunslinger, Book II. Los Angeles: Black Sparrow Press, 1969. Glassine dust jacket. One of 250 hardcover copies signed by the author in a total limitation of 1,290. Published at $10.00.

Gunslinger: Book III. West Newbury, Massachusetts: Frontier Press, 1972. Wrappers. The half-title reads "The Winterbook, prologue to the great Book IIII, Kornerstone."

"The Hamadryas Baboon at the Lincoln Park Zoo." Chicago: Wine Press, 1972. Broadside. One of 500 copies.

Hands Up! New York: Totem Press, 1964. Wrappers. The correct first edition with $1.25 on the top of the cover.

Hello, La Jolla. Berkeley, California: Wingbow Press, 1978. Tissue dust jacket. One of 100 hardbound copies signed by the author. Accompanied by a copy of the hardbound unsigned edition limited to 300 copies. There was also a trade edition in wrappers.

Idaho Out. London: Fulcrum Press, 1965. Wrappers. Second printing. Published at 10s. Cover drawing by Fielding Dawson.

"In Defense of Pure Poetry." West Branch, Iowa: Toothpaste Press for Truck Press, 1978. Broadside. One of 26 signed copies in a total limitation of 200. This copy is inscribed for Allan Kornblum.

"The Kultchural Exchange." Lisbon and the Orcas Islands: Toothpick Press, 1971. Single sheet folded to make four pages. From *Gunslinger, Book IIII.*

Manchester Square, by Edward Dorn and Jennifer Dunbar. London: Permanent Press, 1975. Wrappers. One of 500 copies in a total limitation of 600. Photographic frontispiece.

"Maximum Ostentation." Madison, Wisconsin: Black Mesa Press, 1984. Broadside. Signed by the author. Limitation not stated. "Printed by Black Mesa Press for Woodland Pattern Book Center. . . ."

"The Midwest is That Space Between the Buffalo Statler and the Lawrence Eldridge." Lawrence, Kansas: Terence Williams, 1968. Broadside. Limitation not stated.

The Newly Fallen. New York: Totem Press, 1961. Wrappers.

The North Atlantic Turbine. London: Fulcrum Press, 1967. Dust jacket. One of 100 signed copies. Accompanied by a copy of the hardcover trade edition in dust jacket. There was also an issue in wrappers.

"The Octopus Thinks with Its Third Arm." Illustrated by Michael Myers. San Francisco: Zephyrus Image, 1973. Broadside. Illustration printed in blue; some were printed in orange. Limitation not stated.

"The Poem Called Alexander Hamilton." Lawrence, Kansas: Tansy / Peg Leg Press, 1971. Broadside. One of 1,000 copies in a total limitation of 1,050.

The Poet, The People, The Spirit. Vancouver, British Columbia: Talonbooks, 1976. Wrappers.

Recollections of Gran Apacheria. San Francisco: Turtle Island, 1974. Boards.

The Rites of Passage: A Brief History. Buffalo, New York: Frontier Press, 1965. Wrappers. This copy is signed by the author.

"A Robert Service Bear Flies Imitation." Santa Barbara, California: Cadmus Editions, 1982. Broadside. One of 100 copies signed by the author and by the illustrator, "Trixie," in a total limitation of 126.

Selected Poems. Preface by Robert Creeley. Bolinas, California: Grey Fox Press, 1978. Wrappers. Published at $3.50.

"A Selection from His Book Entitled Abhorrences." Madison: University of Wisconsin, Silver Buckle Press, 1984. Broadside. Limitation not stated.

"Shufflin Off to Buffalo." Buffalo, New York: Just Buffalo, 1975. Broadside. One of 500 copies in a total limitation of 550. This copy bears the author's presentation inscription.

Slinger. Berkeley, California: Wingbow Press, 1975. Tissue dust jacket. One of 50 hardcover copies signed by the author.

Some Business Recently Transacted in the White World. West Newbury, Massachusetts: Frontier Press, 1971. Wrappers. Published at $2.00.

Songs: Set Two, A Short Count. Buffalo, New York: Frontier Press, 1970. Wrappers. Limitation not stated.

Spectrum Breakdown. LeRoy, New York: Athanor Books, 1971. Eight-page pamphlet, not bound, originally laid into *Athanor I* (Winter / Spring 1971).

Twenty-four Love Songs. Buffalo, New York: Frontier Press, 1969. Yapp wrappers.

Yellow Lola: Formerly Titled Japanese Neon (Hello La Jolla, Book II). Frontispiece by David Hockney. Santa Barbara, California: Cadmus Editions, 1981. Hardbound. One of 161 signed copies.

☞ PROSE

The Camp. San Francisco: Four Seasons Foundation, 1964. Wrappers. "Prose I, Writing 2." "The Camp" is chapter two from the novel *Rites of Passage*. Other contributors are Michael Rumaker and Warren Tallman.

Interviews, ed. Donald Allen. Bolinas, California: Four Seasons Foundation, 1980. Wrappers. Published at $5.00. "Writing 38."

Roadtesting the Language: An Interview with Edward Dorn, by Stephen Fredman. San Diego: University of California Press, 1978. Wrappers. "Documents for New Poetry I."

The Shoshoneans: The People of the Basin-Plateau. Photographs by Leroy Lucas. New York: Morrow, 1966. Dust jacket. Published at $6.95.

☞ TRANSLATION

Our Word: Guerrilla Poems from Latin America. Translated by Edward Dorn and Gordon Brotherston. New York: Grossman, in association with Cape Goliard, London, 1968. Wrappers. Bilingual text.

Richard Eberhart

Richard Eberhart (b. 1904), a visionary poet in the tradition of Blake, often writes about inspiration and its paradoxes: "I am a vehicle of the spirit moving in me. All the intellect in the world cannot make a perfect poem. But the poet may . . . become a sensitive vane or instrument through which a spirit blows beyond his will, a psychic draft of absolute reality may move his hand."[1] Eberhart's style is one of deliberate awkwardness, of sudden catches or hesitations in rhythm, of surprising diction, as if to emphasize the unexpectedness of inspiration, the rawness and inadequacy of human expression. As he wrote in "A Commitment":

> *I am committed*
> *To the spirit that hovers over the graves.*
>
> *All greatness flails.*
> *Even evangelical Aristotle*
>
> *Deploys his systems into mystification,*
> *Obfuscating his clarity of sight.*[2]

Eberhart persistently narrates the human attempt to move beyond our limits, whether through an awareness of death, an experience of war, or a connection with a specific natural place—his native Minnesota or his adopted New Hampshire, where he began teaching at Dartmouth College in 1956. As Jean Garrigue says, his "is a poetry of conflict, for his sensory world is usually haunted by some great ghost of its original maker. Or by powers or mysteries that ultimately rule us. This largeness and darkness of reference is essential for his airiness of style when he is airy, his delicacy, his gusto and his élan. And all this is set to a surge of sound, a metered and yet roughened beat."[3] In a series of poems beginning with "The Ground-hog," an encounter with death moves the poet beyond himself. In this early poem, Eberhart finds a decaying groundhog: "my sense shook, / And mind outshot our naked frailty."[4] His experience as a Naval Reserve officer teaching aerial gunnery in World War II leads to poetic meditations on the possibility of making sense out of war:

> You would think the fury of aerial bombardment
> Would rouse God to relent; the infinite spaces
> Are still silent. He looks on shock-pried faces.
> History, even, does not know what is meant.[5]

Eberhart shared the Bollingen Prize in Poetry in 1962. Four years later he won the Pulitzer Prize for *Selected Poems*, and in 1977 the National Book Award for *Collected Poems*.

≈ POETRY

"Better Management." Winston-Salem, North Carolina: Stuart Wright, 1980. Broadside. One of 30 copies privately printed.

A Bravery of Earth. London: Jonathan Cape, 1930. Dust jacket. Published at 5s. The author's first book.

A Bravery of Earth. New York: Jonathan Cape & Harrison Smith, 1930. Dust jacket. Published at $2.00. First American edition of the author's first book, on English sheets.

Burr Oaks. London: Chatto & Windus, 1947. Dust jacket. Published at 6s.

Burr Oaks. New York: Oxford University Press, 1947. Dust jacket. First American edition, preceded by the English edition.

Chocorua. New York: Nadja, 1981. Wrappers. One of 50 signed copies in a total limitation of 76.

Collected Poems 1930–1960: Including 51 New Poems. New York: Oxford University Press, 1960. Dust jacket.

Collected Poems 1930–1976: Including 43 New Poems. London: Chatto & Windus, 1976. Dust jacket. Published at £8.00.

Collected Poems 1930–1986. New York: Oxford University Press, 1988. Dust jacket. Published at $29.95.

Collected Verse Plays. Chapel Hill: University of North Carolina Press, 1962. Tissue dust jacket. One of 100 specially bound copies signed by the author.

Fields of Grace. New York: Oxford University Press, 1972. Dust jacket. Published at $5.95. With the author's presentation inscription to John Pauker, the late Washington, D.C., poet.

Four Poems. Winston-Salem, North Carolina: Stuart Wright, 1980. Glassine dust jacket. One of 125 copies signed by the author in a total limitation of 165.

Hour:::Gnats. New Poems. Illustrated by Carolyn S. Shine. Davis, California: Putah Creek Press, 1977. Wrappers. One of 200 copies signed by the author and the artist.

"John Finley." Winston-Salem, North Carolina: Stuart Wright, 1980. Broadside. One of 40 copies signed by the author.

The Long Reach: New & Uncollected Poems, 1948–1984. New York: New Directions, 1984. Dust jacket. Published at $16.00.

New Hampshire: Nine Poems. Roslindale, Massachusetts: Pym-Randall Press, 1980. Wrappers. One of 450 copies in a total limitation of 500.

"The Play." Washington, D.C.: Folger Library, 1977. Broadside. "The Folger Evening Poetry Series 1977/ 78."

Poems New and Selected. Norfolk, Connecticut: New Directions, 1944. Boards, dust jacket. "The Poets of the Year" series.

Poems to Poets. Engravings by Michael McCurdy. Lincoln, Massachusetts: Penmaen Press, 1975. Glassine dust jacket. One of 300 hardbound copies signed by the author.

The Quarry: New Poems. New York: Oxford University Press, 1964. Dust jacket. Published at $4.75.

"Rain." Winston-Salem, North Carolina: Stuart Wright, 1982. Single sheet folded to make four pages. Invitation to a reading on 7 October 1982. One of only 50 copies.

Reading the Spirit. London: Chatto & Windus, 1936. Tissue dust jacket. Although not so noted, this is Reed Whittemore's copy with his pencilled notes on several pages. Signed by Eberhart on the front endpaper.

"Recapitulation of a Poem Taken by *The New Yorker.*" Winston-Salem, North Carolina: Palaemon Press, 1984. Broadside, signed by the author. Limitation not stated.

Selected Poems. London: Chatto & Windus, 1951. Dust jacket. Published at 6s.

Selected Poems. New York: Oxford University Press, 1951. Dust jacket. Preceded by the English edition.

Selected Poems, 1930–1965. New York: New Directions, 1965. Paperback, published at $1.75. Not published in cloth.

Shifts of Being: Poems. New York: Oxford University Press, 1968. Dust jacket. Published at $3.75. With the author's presentation inscription to Kimon Friar.

Song and Idea. New York: Oxford University Press, 1942. First American edition on English sheets. Published at $1.50.

"Spite Fence." Charleston, West Virginia: Mountain State Press, 1984. Broadside. One of 78 copies signed by the author. Issued in celebration of the author's eightieth birthday.

Survivors. Brockport, New York: BOA Editions, 1979. Wrappers. One of 25 copies bound in French papers over boards by Gene Eckert, signed by the poet and with a poem in his hand. Accompanied by one of 400 copies in wrappers. The total limitation was 500.

Ten Poems. Winston-Salem, North Carolina: Privately printed for Stuart Wright, 1984. Boards. Not issued in dust jacket. "Ten copies have been printed to honor Richard Eberhart on the occasion of his eightieth birthday, 5 April 1984." Signed by the author on the title page.

Thirty One Sonnets. New York: Eakins Press, 1967. Glassine dust jacket and cloth slipcase as issued. One of 99 specially bound copies signed by the author. Accompanied by a copy of the trade edition in dust jacket, published at $4.95. This copy is signed by the author.

Three Poems: On the Occasion of The English Department Dinner at the Coolidge Hotel, White River Junction, Vermont, June 1, 1968. Cambridge, Massachusetts: Pym-Randall Press, 1968. Wrappers. One of 200 copies signed by the author.

Two Poems. West Chester, Pennsylvania: Aralia Press, 1975. Wrappers, glassine dust jacket. One of 200 copies signed by the author in a total limitation of 326.

Ways of Light: Poems, 1972–1980. New York: Oxford University Press, 1980. Dust jacket. Published at $11.95.

A World-View. Medford, Massachusetts: Tufts College Press, 1941. Wrappers. One of 200 copies reprinted from *The Tuftonian.* Tufts College Phi Beta Kappa Poem, 1941.

⁂ PROSE

Of Poetry and Poets. Urbana: University of Illinois Press, 1979. Dust jacket. Published at $15.00. Foreword by James Dickey.

Allen Ginsberg

Allen Ginsberg (b. 1926) published *Howl and Other Poems* in 1956, breaking new poetic ground for the Beats and future generations trying

> to recreate the syntax and measure of poor human prose
>> and stand before you speechless and intelligent
>> and shaking with shame, rejected yet confessing
>> out the soul to conform to the rhythm of thought
>> in his naked and endless head,
> the madman bum and angel beat in Time, unknown, yet
>> putting down here what might be left to say in
>> time come after death.[1]

Ginsberg says of his long-line form, "The lines are the result of long thought and experiment as to what unit constitutes *one speech-breath-thought*," and thus the language enacts the flow of consciousness. Richard Eberhart called the poem "a howl against everything in our mechanistic civilization which kills the spirit,"[2] but "Howl" also provides a liberation, a validation of visionary experience and "expression of natural ecstasy."[3] The poem went on trial in San Francisco for its raw language and frank sexuality in the famous obscenity trial against City Lights publisher Lawrence Ferlinghetti, which ended in a verdict of not guilty. Judge Clayton Horn said in his conclusion, "An author should be real in treating his subject and be allowed to express his thoughts and ideas in his own words."[4]

Ginsberg, who has called himself a Buddhist Jew, had an early visionary experience in which he heard Blake reciting "Ah! Sunflower."[5] He has continued to evolve a religious and politically engaged poetics, using mantras (rhythmic chants for spiritual effects) in poems like "Wichita Vortex Sutra," which willed the end of the Vietnam war through its own act of being,[6] and more recently following the idea of the spontaneous flow of thought, begun in "Howl," to an improvisatory poetry which assumes, "first thought, best thought."[7]

Ginsberg won the National Book Award in 1974 for *The Fall of America: Poems of These States*, but in a recent chant poem, "Going to the World of the Dead,"[8] he asks us (and himself) to let go of everything:

> *Let go of your money   Ho Ho Ho*
> *Let go your Big Poetry   Let go Let go*

❧ POETRY

Careless Love. Madison, Wisconsin: Red Ozier Press, 1978. Wrappers. One of 280 signed copies in a total limitation of 290. Printed for the benefit of the Jack Kerouac School of Disembodied Poetics at Boulder, Colorado.

"Cherry Blues." London: Turret Bookshop, 1992. Broadside. Published by Bernard Stone and Raymond Danowski, August 1992. Not for sale.

Collected Poems 1947–1980. New York: Harper & Row, 1984. Dust jacket. Published at $27.50.

Composed on the Tongue, ed. Donald Allen. Bolinas, California: Grey Fox Press, 1980. Wrappers. Published at $5.95.

Empty Mirror: Early Poems. Introduction by William Carlos Williams. New York: Totem Press, 1961. Wrappers. Published at $1.25.

"Entering Kansas City High." Lawrence, Kansas: Terrence Williams, 1967. Broadside. "Tansy Series No. 1." Limitation not stated.

The Fall of America: Poems of These States 1965–1971. San Francisco: City Lights Books, 1972. Wrappers. Published at $3.00. "The Pocket Poets Series No. 30." Ten thousand copies were printed.

First Blues: Rags, Ballads & Harmonium Songs, 1971–74. New York: Full Court Press, 1975. Dust jacket. Published at $7.95. This copy is signed by the author on the title page.

Howl: Original Draft Facsimile, Transcript & Variant Versions, Fully Annotated by the Author, ed. Barry Miles. New York: Harper & Row, 1986. Cloth slipcase as issued. One of 250 specially bound copies signed by the author. Accompanied by a copy of the trade edition in dust jacket, published at $22.50.

Howl and Other Poems. Introduction by William Carlos Williams. San Francisco: City Lights Books, 1956. Wrappers. "Pocket Poets Series Number Four." Correct first edition with "75 cents" on the back cover. This copy is signed by the author.

"Hum Bom!" Bixby Canyon, California, 1971. Broadside. "U.S. Shiva Mantra Bixby Canyon Sabdh, May 1971."

Improvised Poetics. Edited with an introduction by Mark Robison. San Francisco: Anonym, 1972. Boards, not issued in dust jacket. One of 1,900 copies in a total limitation of 2,000.

Indian Journals, March 1962 – May 1963. San Francisco: City Lights Books / David Haselwood Books, 1970. Dust jacket. Published at $6.50. Drawings by the author. One thousand copies were printed.

Iron Horse. San Francisco: City Lights Books, 1974. Wrappers. Published at $3.00. Ten thousand copies were printed.

Iron Horse. Bonn, Germany: Expanded Media Editions, 1978. Wrappers. German text, translated by Carl Weissner.

Journals: Early Fifties Early Sixties, ed. Gordon Ball. New York: Grove Press, 1977. Dust jacket. Published at $10.00. Review copy with promotional material loosely inserted.

Kanreki: A Tribute to Allen Ginsberg, Pt. 2, ed. Bill Morgan. New York: Lospecchio Press, 1986. Issued without dust jacket. One of 26 lettered copies signed by Ginsberg and the editor in a total limitation of 176.

Many Loves. Drawings by Roberta L. Collier. New York: Pequod Press, 1984. Wrappers. One of 500 copies. Published at $6.00.

Mind Breaths: Poems 1972–1977. San Francisco: City Lights Books, 1977. Dust jacket. Published at $7.50. "The Pocket Poets Series Number Thirty-five." There were 300 hardcover copies printed and 10,000 bound in wrappers.

"Moloch." Wood engraving by Lynd Ward. Lincoln, Massachusetts: Penmaen Press, 1978. Broadside. One of 300 copies in a total limitation of 600.

Mostly Sitting Haiku. Paterson, New Jersey: From Here Press, 1978. Wrappers. Published at $1.50.

Open Head. Melbourne, Australia: Sun Books, 1972. Wrappers. Printed dos-à-dos with Lawrence Ferlinghetti's *Open Eye* and inscribed by both authors.

Photographs. Altadena, California: Twelvetrees Press, 1990. Dust jacket. One of 5,000 copies in a total limitation of 5,100. Illustrated with photographs.

Planet News 1961–1967. San Francisco: City Lights Books, 1968. In publisher's slipcase as issued. One of 500 copies signed by the author. Published at $15.00.

Plutonian Ode. Plutonische Ode. Heerlen, Holland: Rob Vermeulen, 1980. Wrappers. Bilingual text, the Dutch translation by Simon Vinkenoog.

Plutonian Ode: Poems, 1977–1980. San Francisco: City Lights Books, 1982. Dust jacket. One of 150 signed copies in slip case as issued. Published at $35.00. "Pocket Poets Series Number Forty." Accompanied by a copy of the trade edition in dust jacket, published at $10.95.

Poems All Over the Place, Mostly 'Seventies. Cherry Valley, New York: Cherry Valley Editions, 1978. Wrappers, trade edition. Published at $3.00.

"Punk Rock Your My Big Crybaby." Grindstone City, Michigan: Alternative Press, 1977. Broadside. Limitation not stated.

"Rain-wet Asphalt Heat, Garbage Curbed Cans Overflowing." Detroit, Michigan: Alternative Press, 1969. Broadside. Limitation not stated.

"Returning to the Country for a Brief Visit." East Lansing, Michigan: East Lansing Arts Workshop Press, 1973. Broadside. Printed for distribution at the National Poetry Festival, Thomas Jefferson College. Limitation not stated.

"Returning to the Country for a Brief Visit." Oakland, California: Stone Press Weekly, 1975. Poem card.

"The Rune." New York: Hardly Press, 1978. Poem card. From "Contest of Bards."

Sad Dust Glories: Poems During Work Summer in Woods.
Berkeley, California: Workingmans Press, 1975.
Wrappers. Published at $2.00.

T. V. Baby: Poems. London: Cape Goliard Press, 1967. Dust
jacket. Published at 21s. One of 400 casebound copies
in a total limitation of 2,000. Precedes the American
edition.

T. V. Baby: Poems. San Francisco: Beach Books, Texts &
Documents, 1968. Wrappers. First American edition.

Wales: A Visitation, July 29, 1967. London: Cape Goliard
Press, 1968. Wrappers, not for sale. Limitation not
stated. Accompanied by a copy of the trade edition in
dust jacket, limited to 300 copies.

"What's Dead?" West Branch, Iowa: Toothpaste Press for
Bookslinger, 1980. Broadside. One of 125 signed copies
in a total limitation of 151. Printed on the occasion of
the author's reading at Coffman Union, 8 April 1980, as
part of the Walker Art Center's Reading Series.

White Shroud: Poems, 1980–1985. New York: Harper & Row,
1986. Dust jacket. Published at $14.95.

Wichita Vortex Sutra. London: Peace News, 1966. Wrappers.
Precedes the American edition.

Wichita Vortex Sutra. San Francisco: Coyote Books, 1966.
Wrappers. One of 500 copies. First American edition.
Published at 85 cents.

Your Reason & Blake's System. Madras, India, and New York:
Hanuman Books, 1988. Wrappers in dust jacket. A
miniature book printed in Madras.

⪻   PROSE

Allen Verbatim: Lectures on Poetry, Politics, Consciousness, ed.
Gordon Ball. New York: McGraw-Hill, 1974. Dust
jacket. Published at $8.95. Signed by the author on the
title page.

As Ever: The Collected Correspondence of Allen Ginsberg and Neal Cassady. Foreword by Carolyn Cassady. Edited with an introduction by Barry Gifford. Afterword by Allen Ginsberg. Berkeley, California: Creative Arts Book Company, 1977. Tissue dust jacket.

Best Minds: A Tribute to Allen Ginsberg, ed. Bill Morgan and Bob Rosenthal. New York: Lospecchio Press, 1986. Cloth boards; not issued in jacket. One of 200 copies signed by the editors in a total limitation of 226. Ginsberg contributes a poem, a short paragraph, and an illustration.

Chicago Trial Testimony. San Francisco: City Lights Books, 1975. Wrappers. Published at $2.50. Ten thousand copies printed.

Contexts of Poetry: Interviews, 1961–1971, ed. Donald Allen. Bolinas, California: Four Seasons Foundation, 1973. Paperback. Not issued in cloth. "Writing 30."

"'The Fall of America' Wins a Prize." New York: Gotham Book Mart, 1974. Single sheet folded twice to make four pages. One of 100 signed copies in a total limitation of 126. The text of Ginsberg's National Book Award speech delivered by Peter Orlovsky, 18 April 1974, at Alice Tully Hall, Lincoln Center.

Gay Sunshine. Interview with Allen Young. Bolinas, California: Grey Fox Press, 1976. Wrappers. Published at $1.95. Second printing.

"National Book Award Acceptance Speech." New York: Alice Tully Hall, Lincoln Center, 1974. Two mimeographed sheets.

To Eberhart from Ginsberg: A Letter about Howl 1956. Foreword by Richard Eberhart. Etchings by Jerome Kaplan. Lincoln, Massachusetts: Penmaen Press, 1976. Glassine jacket. One of 300 copies signed by Eberhart and Ginsberg in a total limitation of 1,500.

Accompanied by a copy of the trade edition in glassine
dustjacket, one of 1,200 copies.

The Visions of the Great Rememberer. With letters by Neal
Cassady and drawings by Basil King. Amherst,
Massachusetts: Mulch Press, A Haystack Book, 1974.
Paperback. Published at $3.50.

Louise Glück

Louise Glück (b. 1943) attained critical acclaim with her first book, *Firstborn* (1968), whose stark view of the world and dreamy, highly-crafted lyricism showed influences of Confessional poets like Robert Lowell, Sylvia Plath, and Anne Sexton, and yet evidenced a unique voice. These early poems speak insistently of loss, desertion, and abortion, and Glück's work has continued to chart a distinctly feminine world of pain, and, occasionally, liberation. Her reworking of myth, fairy tale, and biblical story have a rare psychological depth, in which woman and artist struggle with a father, male creative figure, or both. Helen Vendler has described the style of her more recent work as "veiled and almost disembodied . . . at once austere and sensuous."[1] In "Mythic Fragment," the nymph Daphne is transformed into a laurel tree by her father, a river spirit, so she can avoid Apollo's pursuit. Caught between being the subject of male song ("I saw captivity in praise") and the object of her father's all-encompassing protection, she is paralyzed, without access to any inner source of creativity or eroticism:

as
I stiffened in the god's arms,

of his encompassing love
my father made
no other sign from the water.²

Male song, male language, male mythic tradition, allow no
space, and preclude female wholeness. In "Lamentations," a
series of retellings of the biblical creation account, God (the
Logos, the Creator) is the source of female division, which
seems to be simultaneous with human creation and with the
birth of the symbolic:

Then the angels saw
how He divided them:
the man, the woman, and the woman's body.³

In "Pomegranate," her reworking of the Persephone myth,
Glück forges a more positive female imagery, offering an
uneasy acceptance of a male creative gift, and its transforma-
tion into female power. The seedy fruit becomes female, and
the god partakes of it:

At which
he cut one open & began
to suck. When he looked up at last
it was to say My dear
you are your own woman, finally, but examine
this grief your mother
parades over our heads
remembering
that she is one to whom
these depths were not offered.⁴

This poem also gives us a healing acknowledgement of a
generational difference in women's experience.

Glück won the Pulitzer Prize in 1993 for *The Wild Iris*.

⇗ **POETRY**

Ararat. New York: Ecco Press, 1990. Dust jacket. Published
at $17.95.

Descending Figure. New York: Ecco Press, 1980. Dust jacket. Published at $9.95. "The American Poetry Series, volume 20."

Firstborn. New York: New American Library, 1968. Dust jacket. Published at $4.00. The author's first book.

Firstborn. Northwood, Middlesex, England: Anvil Press Poetry, 1969. Dust jacket. First English edition. One of 50 copies printed on rose-colored paper and signed by the author.

The Garden. New York: Antaeus Editions, 1976. Wrappers. One of 50 signed copies in a total limitation of 500.

The House on Marshland. New York: Ecco Press, 1975. Dust jacket. Published at $6.95. "The American Poetry Series, 5."

"Summer." Berkeley, California: Black Oak Books, 1987. Broadside. Issued on the occasion of a reading by the author. Limitation not stated.

The Triumph of Achilles. New York: Ecco Press, 1985. Dust jacket. Published at $13.50.

The Wild Iris. New York: Ecco Press, 1992. Dust jacket. Published at $19.95.

Jorie Graham

Jorie Graham (b. 1951) writes a metaphysical and sensu-
ous poetry that moves associatively and interrogates the
way we construct reality and tell stories. For Graham,
language and the material world are very close neighbors, and
she uses each to unsettle the other. Clearly influenced by post-
structuralist theories that see reality as textual, Graham insis-
tently uses language and narrative as metaphors to describe the
natural world and our attempts to understand it and function
in it. In "Syntax," for example, starlings are "a regular syntax
on wings."[1] Yet her philosophical questioning and sometimes
abstract use of language and image are grounded in a desire to
"help [poetry] reconnect itself to mystery and power," for
poetry "is an extraordinary medium for spiritual undertak-
ing."[2]

Raised and educated in Italy and France by American
parents, Graham returned to the United States in 1969, one
year after participating in the student uprisings in Paris. As a
child Graham played among the paintings of the Italian
Renaissance. In poems about painters and painting ("For
Mark Rothko," "Masaccio's Expulsion," "Pollock and Can-
vas"[3]), poems about nature, and poems that rework myth and

history, Graham explores the forces, the desires and compulsions, that drive us to create. In "I Watched a Snake," it is hunger and necessity,

> *. . . this going where we must,*
> *leaving a not*
> *unpretty pattern by default. But going*
> *out of hunger*
> *for small things—flies, words—going*
> *because one's body*
>
> *goes . . .*
>
> *. . . Desire*
>
> *is the honest work of the body,*
> *its engine, its wind,*
> *It too must have its sails—wings*
> *in this tiny mouth, valves*
> *in the human heart, meanings like sailboats*
> *setting out*
>
> *over the mind.*[4]

At other times it is the imperative of responding to historical tragedy, to human cruelty, the need to remember, to find a way to make images, to allow human beings to exist. In "From the New World," a little girl who emerges from the gas chamber asking for her mother makes Graham question how she should write poetry: "God knows I too want the poem to continue," she says, but this is not a matter of easy craft, but a struggle, a search, "to make the bodies come on, to make / room. . . ."[5] Graham's poetry is full of questions. She works interrogatively, in a search for answers that does not rely on rational processes.

❧ POETRY

The End of Beauty. New York: Ecco Press, 1987. Dust jacket. Published at $16.50.

Hybrids of Plants and of Ghosts. Princeton: Princeton University Press, 1980. Dust jacket. The author's first book.

Region of Unlikeness. New York: Ecco Press, 1991. Dust jacket. Published at $17.95.

Emily Grosholz

Emily Grosholz (b. 1950), a professor of philosophy at the Pennsylvania State University, is haunted by the losses and gains we accrue with the passing of time. For her, writing is a return to one's past experience as a way of understanding both where one was and where one is, as in the title poem from her first collection, *The River Painter*:

> *In the winter, after the new year,*
> *Chao Meng-Fu paints the river*
> *to recollect himself . . .*
> *He tries to call back who he was*
> *at the last stopping place,*
> *what face he discerned in the water;*
> *his eyes change color*
> *from blue to gray to green . . .*

But it is also a way of losing the self by merging into the present moment:

> *He becomes, like a god, at one*
> *with his desire, and the line,*
> *like the trace of a god,*
> *is only himself, thrown off*
> *with a god's abundance.*

Return is crucial to Grosholz's poetics. It is because, as she explains Nietzsche,

> *we always come*
> *back to this very moment;*
> *this moment will always happen*
> *again and again and again,*
> *as the universe combines*
> *and recombines its atoms.*[1]

Each moment is the recurrence of each past moment, with its elements recombined. Thus as an adult she can see the sycamores she missed as a child blinded by painful family drama; or she can cherish the family furniture she had to resist as a younger woman wanting "existence / pure as Sartre's or Weil's":

> *Worlds are multiple and have their seasons,*
> *it seems, no less materially sketched out*
> *than Bedouin settlements. Dark tents and fires.*[2]

There are an endless number of Edens; paradises continually lost, continually regained. The undifferentiation of early, wordless childhood or of making love is one Eden, and the return into self another.

"Dream-Tree and Moon" is about the nature of commitment, that process of making choices and eliminating alternatives, letting go of the promise of endless possibility past and future. On vacation in Europe with her family, the poet wakes to "the scent of my lost youth, dispelled." She has let go of it to be where she is now, unlike the fishermen beneath her terrace, whose "trade is dying out: they fish too hard, / hold back too many fingerlings, their tithe." In the enticing, exotic night air, evoking possibility, she is able to say, "There's no alternative / beside the one I love."[3]

🖝 POETRY

Eden. Baltimore, Maryland: Johns Hopkins University
   Press, 1992. Dust jacket.

The River Painter: Poems. Urbana: University of Illinois
     Press, 1984. Paperback; not published in cloth. The
     author's first book.

Shores and Headlands. Princeton: Princeton University
     Press, 1988. Dust jacket. "Princeton Series of
     Contemporary Poets."

Barbara Guest

Barbara Guest's concern with poetic construction stems
from her lifelong attention to painting and music. Guest
(b. 1920) writes with a disjunctive syntax that makes her
the most abstract of the original New York School poets, and
the one with the closest relation to the work of the Language
poets. Unlike John Ashbery or Frank O'Hara, whose typical
unit of disjunctiveness is the sentence, thought, or paragraph,
Guest moves paratactically from one word or phrase to an-
other, using abrupt shifts in sense and qualities of music and
color as structural elements. More than any of the other New
York School poets, Guest is interested in the physical poem,
both the space on the page and the relation between the
environment and conditions at the moment of composition
and the resulting work. In "The View from Kandinsky's
Window," the view is searched for clues to the events in
Kandinsky's life:

> The park shows little concern with Kandinsky's history
> these buildings are brief about his early life,
> reflections of him seen from the window
> busy with preparations for exile
> the relevance of the geranium color.

The life and the work both reflect a movement of exile, in which definite forms disappear, replaced by rhythm or gesture.

The stroke of difficult white finds an exit
the canvas is clean, pure and violent
a rhythm of exile in its vein . . .[1]

As Guest says, ". . . the poem gathers itself (becomes embodied) the way a narrative diffuses and is sustained by movements, auditory and visual, transcending their own context as they echo and foreshadow other moments in the poem, deploying their own patterns and lyric arrangements."[2]

For Guest, violence is a necessary component of poetry, creating tension in her composition and countering a pure lyric, musical impulse. Thus in "The Advance of the Grizzly," the grizzly is a violent prose force (". . . the ragged prose clump / clump on the cold landscape") that breaks into the "plush interior"; indeed, the romantic itself is a voracious destroyer, consuming nature:

dendrophagous *"feeding on trees"*
to sustain the romantic vision route over snow
the sudden drop into pines:

      "feeding on trees"
new mouths red of Okeechobee.[3]

Guest has created several works in collaboration with visual artists, including the long poem "The Altos," in which Richard Tuttle's etchings and Guest's irregularly spaced words form a dialogue about the use of space.[4]

POETRY

Biography. Providence, Rhode Island: Burning Deck, 1980.
    Wrappers. One of 500 copies in a total limitation of
    526. Review copy with slip loosely inserted.

The Blue Stairs. New York: Corinth Books, 1968. Wrappers.
    One of 100 copies signed by the author.

The Countess from Minneapolis. Providence, Rhode Island: Burning Deck, 1976. Wrappers. One of 950 copies in a total limitation of 1,000. Published at $3.50.

Fair Realism. Los Angeles: Sun & Moon Press, 1989. Dust jacket.

Moscow Mansions: Poems. New York: Viking Press, A Richard Seaver Book, 1973. Dust jacket. Published at $6.95. Review slip loosely inserted.

Poems: The Location of Things; Archaics; The Open Skies. Garden City, New York: Doubleday, 1962. Dust jacket. Published at $2.95. The author's first commercially published book. This copy bears the author's signed presentation inscription.

Quilts. New York: Vehicle Editions, 1980. Wrappers. One of 50 copies numbered and signed by the author and by the designer of the cover, Deborah S. Freedman, in a total limitation of 100.

The Türler Losses. Montreal: Mansfield Book Mart, 1979. Wrappers. "M.B.M. Monograph Series number five."

☙ PROSE

Goodnough. B. H. Friedman, co-author. Paris: The Pocket Museum, Éditions Georges Fall, 1962. Wrappers. Plates in color and black-and-white.

Seeking Air. Santa Barbara, California: Black Sparrow Press, 1978. Boards; glassine jacket. One of 26 lettered and signed copies in a total hardbound edition of 776. There was also an edition in wrappers.

Donald Hall

Whether in his early, formal wrestling with W. H. Auden's influence, or in the later, meditative writings of his maturity, time, as the patterning of sound and as subject, seems the unifying obsession of Donald Hall's poetic career. Long-time poetry editor of the *Paris Review*, Hall (b. 1928) also edited (with Robert Pack and Louis Simpson) *The New Poets of England and America*, an anthology defending the formalist academic tradition. His early preoccupation with cultivated wit and formal elegance gave way to surrealist or Deep Image experiments, as it did for many poets of his generation. Perhaps this is reflected in the progression of images of wrecked planes and abandoned airfields of World War II in his pivotal volume, *The Alligator Bride*. It is as if he confronted the wreckage of a limited tradition upon which he depended and turned inward to find the source and patterns of his art in the idiosyncratic, the archetypal, and the wild.

In "An Airstrip in Essex, 1960," Hall calls the airstrip "a lost road into the air," and later says, "Goodnight, old ruined war." In "The Old Pilot," a man "discovers himself on an old airfield," and feels he has been there before, "but rain has washed out the lettering of a sign." These are the bleak

landscapes of European illegibility, of an irrecoverable tradi-
tion. The pilot "pulls himself into the narrow cockpit / . . .
and sits like an egg." From under the effaced sign, from the
"pit," he waits for another moment and culture to begin to
articulate itself like the bones of an embryonic bird.[1]

What rises is an acceptance of the mind's wilderness and
seeming chaos. Poems like "Swan" and "Apples" join tenu-
ously, even idiosyncratically, associated fragments as Hall
searches out wilder, more frightening, methods of poetic
construction.[2] In "Swan," we see, from the fog,

> . . . a thudding
> white shape in the whiteness,
> running huge and frightened, lost
> from its slow stream . . .

This swan, if that is what it is, is placed in the company of
burnt fields that are "'Putting / the goodness back / into the
soil,'" of farm labor, mills, and, explicitly, the bound roots of
a plant.

This may have prepared Hall for his later work exploring
his connection to the New Hampshire farm inherited from his
grandparents, where he writes in a gentle and elegiac tone
about the farm's landscape, history, and animals:

> I brought grain to raise your spirits.
> and ten thousand years
> wound us through pasture and hayfield together,
> threads of us woven
> together, three hundred generations
> from Africa's hills to New Hampshire's.[3]

Here time is no longer a frightening instrument of destruction
or chaos, but the vehicle of the mysterious and inevitable
connections in which we discover our place and nativity, our
intimacy.

✺ POETRY

The Alligator Bride. Menomonie, Wisconsin: Ox Head Press,
  1968. Wrappers. One of 350 copies. Second issue with

the title and the author's name at the top of the wrappers. The first issue had the author's name at the bottom of the wrappers.

The Alligator Bride. Poems New and Selected. New York: Harper & Row, 1969. Dust jacket. Expanded edition.

"Birch Maple Ash." Concord, New Hampshire: William B. Ewert, 1985. Greeting card; one page folded twice to make four pages. One of 36 copies signed by the author in a total limitation of 336.

A Blue Wing Tilts at the Edge of the Sea: Selected Poems, 1964–1974. London: Secker & Warburg, 1975. Dust jacket. Published at £2.90. There was no American edition. This copy is signed by the author on the title page.

"Brief Lives: Seven Epigrams." Concord, New Hampshire: William B. Ewert, 1983. Loose cards contained in a printed envelope and enclosed in a cloth folder. One of 26 copies signed by the author and with a holograph epigram in a total limitation of 136. Accompanied by a copy of the issue limited to 110 signed copies.

Carol. Woodcut by J. J. Lankes. Concord, New Hampshire: William B. Ewert, 1988. Wrappers. One of 26 lettered and signed copies in a total limitation of 436. Issued as a Christmas greeting.

Day Lilies on the Hill: A Poem. Illustrated by Mary Azarian. Concord, New Hampshire: William B. Ewert, 1992. Boards. One of 25 hardbound copies in a total limitation of 100, each signed by the author and the artist.

"The December Stove." Concord, New Hampshire: William B. Ewert, 1984. Greeting card format. One of 500 copies in a total limitation of 536. In the original unprinted mailing envelope.

Exile: The Newdigate Prize Poem, 1952. Swinford, Eynsham, Oxon, England: Fantasy Press, 1952. Wrappers. The author's first book. Privately printed for the author by Oscar Mellor.

Exiles & Marriages. New York: Viking Press, 1955. Dust jacket. Published at $3.00. With the author's presentation inscription on the free front endpaper.

Great Day in the Cows' House. Photographs by T. S. Bronson. Mount Carmel, Connecticut: Ives Street Press, 1984. Boards. One of 130 copies signed by Hall. The photographs are circa 1900. A copy of the prospectus is loosely inserted.

Here at Eagle Pond. Illustrations by Thomas W. Nason. New York: Ticknor & Fields, 1990. Boards, in slipcase as issued. Not issued in dust jacket.

"In November, In Advent, Waiting." Concord, New Hampshire: William B. Ewert, 1991. Broadside. One of 36 copies signed by the author. Issued as a holiday greeting. Accompanied by one of 300 copies issued in a folded format.

"Jane at Pigall's." Highland Park, Michigan: Red Hanrahan Press, 1973. Broadside, this copy signed by the author. For free distribution; limitation not stated.

Kicking the Leaves. Mount Horeb, Wisconsin: Perishable Press, 1975. Wrappers. One of 125 copies signed by the author. The colophonic boxwood engraving is by Reynolds Stone.

Kicking the Leaves: Poems. New York: Harper & Row, 1978. Dust jacket. Published at $8.95.

Measure. Wood engraving by J. J. Lankes. Concord, New Hampshire: William B. Ewert, 1983. Wrappers. One of 36 signed copies hand-sewn in paper wrappers.

The Museum of Clear Ideas. New York: Ticknor & Fields, 1993. Dust jacket. Published at $18.95.

"O Cheese." Lexington, Kentucky: King Library Press, 1979. Folded broadside. Printed for the annual meeting of members of the University of Kentucky Library Associates, 27 March 1979. This copy is signed by the author.

" 'Oh,' said Kate, . . ." Austin, Texas: Cold Mountain Press, 1973. "Cold Mountain Press Poetry Post Card, Series I, Number 5." This copy is signed by the author.

Old and New Poems. New York: Ticknor & Fields, 1990. Dust jacket. Published at $24.95. Review copy with a printed letter from the publisher loosely inserted.

"Old Roses." Original woodcut by Mary Azarian. Concord, New Hampshire: William B. Ewert, 1992. Broadside. One of 50 copies signed by the author. There were also 400 copies issued as a printed card.

The One Day: A Poem in Three Parts. New York: Ticknor & Fields, 1988. Dust jacket. Published at $16.95.

"The Onset." Concord, New Hampshire: William B. Ewert, 1986. Greeting card in wrappers. One of 26 specially bound copies, signed by the author, in a total limitation of 330 copies.

"Ox Cart Man." Calligraphy by Douglas Strickler. Durham: University of New Hampshire, 1983. Broadside. One of 100 copies printed for Friends of the Library at a reading on 14 November 1983. This copy is signed by the author.

"Ox Cart Man." Philadelphia: American Poetry Center, 1987. Single sheet folded once to make four pages. Program for a reading at the Please Touch Museum for Children, 9 March 1987. This copy is signed by the poet.

"Passage." Grindstone City, Michigan: Alternative Press, n.d. Poetry post card. Undated, but published in the late 1970s.

A Roof of Tiger Lilies: Poems. New York: Viking Press, 1964. Dust jacket. Published at $3.50. First American edition; preceded by the English edition.

Seasons at Eagle Pond. Illustrations by Thomas W. Nason. New York: Ticknor & Fields, 1987. Boards, in slipcase as issued. Not issued in dust jacket.

"Stoves & Kettles." Concord, New Hampshire: William B. Ewert, 1990. Broadside. One of 36 copies signed by the author in a total limitation of 286.

To the Loud Wind, and Other Poems. Cambridge, Massachusetts: Harvard Advocate, 1955. Wrappers. Published at 65 cents. "Pegasus Publications Series, Volume I, No. 1."

The Town of Hill. Boston: David R. Godine, 1975. Boards, issued without dust jacket. Published at $4.00.

The Toy Bone. Brockport, New York: BOA Editions, 1979. Wrappers. Published at $2.00. "BOA Pamphlets, Series A, No. 2."

The Twelve Seasons. Illustration by Timothy Engelland. Deerfield, Massachusetts: Deerfield Press, 1983. Issued without dust jacket. One of 300 copies handcolored by the illustrator and signed by the author.

The Yellow Room: Love Poems. New York: Harper & Row, 1971. Dust jacket. Published at $4.95. Review copy with slip loosely inserted.

❧ PROSE

Anecdotes of Modern Art: From Rousseau to Warhol, by Donald Hall and Pat Corrington Wykes. New York: Oxford University Press, 1990. Dust jacket. Published at $21.95.

The Ideal Bakery: Stories. San Francisco: North Point Press, 1987. Dust jacket. Published at $14.95.

Marianne Moore: The Cage and the Animal. New York: Pegasus, 1970. Dust jacket.

1 2 3 4 Stories. Sweden, Maine: Ives Street Press, 1989. One of 155 copies signed by the author.

Remembering. Poets' Reminiscences and Opinions: Dylan Thomas, Robert Frost, T. S. Eliot, Ezra Pound. New York: Harper & Row, 1978. Dust jacket. Published at $10.00. Illustrated with portraits.

String Too Short to be Saved: Memories of a Disappearing New England. Illustrated by Mimi Korach. New York: Viking Press, 1961. Dust jacket. Published at $5.00.

Their Ancient Glittering Eyes: Remembering Poets and More Poets. New York: Ticknor & Fields, 1992. Dust jacket. Published at $22.95.

Daniel Halpern

Daniel Halpern (b. 1945) has a multifaceted devotion to literature. He is a poet, and also editor of *Antaeus*, editor in chief of Ecco Press, and a professor in the graduate writing program of Columbia University. In his poetry, Halpern is concerned with "accessibility to experience"; his calm, graceful voice searches out the intensity of ordinary life. As Derek Walcott says of *Tango*, Halpern's poems are "remarkable for their quiet—the intimacy of a man talking honestly to himself. . . . His lines break with the gentle snap of a twig with natural poignancy."[1]

From his first volume, *Traveling on Credit*, to his most recent, *Foreign Neon*, Halpern has been looking for connections between the exotic and the local or ordinary. The opening poems of each volume are illustrative. "The Ethnic Life" begins, "I've been after the exotic / for years," and ends,

> For years I've lived simply,
> Without luxury—
> With the soundness of the backward
> Where the senses can be heard.[2]

The desire for discovery and exploration, and the recognition that *where one is* provides amply fertile ground, are subtly expressed in "Foreign Neon," where

You like to think there's something endless
in what's still to be discovered.

The foreign neon can be found elsewhere in "high-contrast cities," or, better, in the color of the face of the woman by his side as he writes,

the rising sun
tattooing the noticeably smooth surface of
her cheek . . .[3]

Often concerned with loneliness and the solitary condition, Halpern has a keen sense of how tenuous and precious relationships are, which he expresses in sad, wry poems like "Aubade"[4] and "Señor Excellent," in which the interaction at a farmer's market between a myna bird and the people who come to talk to it becomes an image for communication and for poetry:

. . . Have you ever listened carefully

to what people say to talking birds
when they think they are alone? Señor Excellent
just looked at us, his expression one of agony
and disgust. I can picture him . . .

and I know that his was a life not so different,
witnessing the utterances of the human race.[5]

⮞ POETRY

Foreign Neon: Poems. New York: Alfred A. Knopf, 1991. Dust jacket. Published at $19.00.

The Lady Knife-Thrower. Binghamton, New York: Bellevue Press, 1975. Wrappers. One of 300 copies in a total limitation of 350.

Life Among Others. New York: Viking Press, 1978. Dust jacket. Published at $8.95.

Seasonal Rights: Poems. New York: Viking Press, 1982. Dust jacket. Published at $12.95.

Street Fire. New York: Viking Press, 1975. Dust jacket. Published at $5.95. Review slip loosely inserted.

Tango: Poems. New York: Viking Press, Elisabeth Sifton Books, 1987. Dust jacket. Published at $17.95. Review copy with informational inserts.

✎ PROSE

The Good Food: Soups, Stews, and Pastas, by Daniel Halpern and Julie Strand. New York: Viking Press, 1985. Dust jacket. Published at $17.95. A cookbook.

✎ TRANSLATION

Songs of Mririda, Courtesan of the High Atlas, by Mririda n'Ait Attik. Translated by Daniel Halpern and Paula Paley. Greensboro, North Carolina: Unicorn Press, 1974. Wrappers. Introduction by Halpern. Volume six in the "Unicorn Keepsake Series."

Michael S. Harper ✦

Michael S. Harper (b. 1938) is a poetic healer who seeks to expose the wounds in American history in order to "illuminate . . . black experience," as David Lehman says, and move toward a vision of wholeness. He forges links of kinship with family, black ancestors, and key black figures like John Coltrane, Jackie Robinson, and Malcolm X. For Harper, history dwells in and arises from the human body:

> *yellow in the canned*
> *sunshine of gauze,*
> *stitching, bedsores,*
> *each tactoe cut*
> *sewn back*
> *is America:*
> *I am telling you this:*
> history is your own heartbeat.[1]

Harper seeks to "operate on historical legacies" by using "a clinical imagery to draw attention, to shock a reader with a detailed, medical closeness and approximation."[2]

The "national wounds kept / secretly bound" include the wounded of his own family: two dead infant sons, his grandfather who faced an angry mob threatening to burn his home,

his wife in childbirth, his wife and himself mourning the dead.
The wounded also include figures from history—slaves and
Native Americans killed for land, black artists, athletes, and
heroes suffering persecution and early death, like John Henry
Louis, who won the Congressional Medal of Honor for his
service in Vietnam, and was killed by a Detroit shopkeeper
who owed him money. Often these figures try to forge out of
their pain something that endures, like his photographer wife,
who bakes bread and develops photographs of their daughter
after her father dies, even though

> *your hands throb the images*
> *with old chemicals that won't*
> *work their magic*
> *of bringing back his face.*[3]

Harper's poetry is steeped in jazz and blues rhythms and
themes, from his first volume, *Dear John, Dear Coltrane* (1970),
to recent pieces improvising on Coltrane, McCoy Tyner,
Thelonious Monk and others. Harper's poems do what he
describes the blues as doing: "They always say *yes* to life, meet
life's terms but never accept them."[4] Modal jazz serves as the
structural element for making arrangements of events and
moods in time. Harper sums up his philosophy and practice in
"Here Where Coltrane Is":

> *Soul and race*
> *are private dominions,*
> *memories and modal*
> *songs, a tenor blossoming,*
> *which would paint suffering*
> *a clear color but is not in*
> *this Victorian house*
> *without oil in zero degree*
> *weather and a forty-mile-an-hour wind;*
> *it is all a well-knit family,*
> *a love supreme.*[5]

❧ POETRY

"The Beauty Shell." Providence, Rhode Island: Bernard E. Bruce, 1992. Broadside. "In memoriam, Bernice Lewis Clark, 1914–1990, for Bernard Bruce, Sr." This copy is signed by the author.

Debridement. Garden City, New York: Doubleday, 1973. Dust jacket. Published at $5.95.

Healing Song for the Inner Ear: Poems. Urbana: University of Illinois Press, 1985. Dust jacket.

"Homage to the New World." San Francisco: Hermes Free Press, n.d., but between 1970 and 1980. Broadside. Limitation not stated.

Images of Kin: New and Selected Poems. Urbana: University of Illinois Press, 1977. Dust jacket. Published at $8.95.

"Nightmare Begins Responsibility." Providence, Rhode Island: Burning Deck Press, 1974. Broadside. One of 200 copies signed by the author.

Nightmare Begins Responsibility. Urbana: University of Illinois Press, 1975. Dust jacket. Published at $6.95.

Photographs: Negatives: History as Apple Tree. San Francisco: Scarab Press, 1972. Dust jacket. Published at $7.50. One of 500 copies signed by the author.

Rhode Island: Eight Poems. Roslindale, Massachusetts: Pym-Randall Press, 1981. Wrappers. One of 450 copies in a total limitation of 500.

Song: I Want a Witness. Pittsburgh: University of Pittsburgh Press, 1972. Dust jacket. Published at $5.95.

Songlines: Mosaics. Providence, Rhode Island: Brown / Ziggurat Press, 1991. Wrappers, in cloth box as issued. One of 50 copies, total limitation, signed by Harper and Walter Feldman, the artist and pressman.

Robert Hass

For Robert Hass (b. 1941), poetry is a means of exploring how to care about the world. He writes movingly about desire: Our separation from the natural world, from each other, from a lover is what enables our delight in the other and our repeating, sometimes painful movement toward union. In "Misery and Splendor," a couple making love

> are trying to become one creature,
> and something will not have it . . .
> . . . They feel
> they are an almost animal,
> washed up on the shore of a world —.[1]

Hass moves naturally from idea to perception to idea, in rhythms that give each word a proper weight. Stanley Kunitz says of this naturalness, "Reading a poem by Robert Hass is like stepping into the ocean when the temperature of the water is not much different from that of the air. You scarcely know, until you feel the undertow tug at you, that you have entered into another element. Suddenly the deep is there, with its teeming life."[2]

Hass' first volume, *Field Guide*,[3] reflects his concerns about history and his place in it. Written in the turbulent late 1960s and early 1970s, these poems articulate a political position, that "feeling human was a useful form of political subversion."[4] For Hass, history is a complex of interactions between individuals and their environment. Human history and natural history create each other. In "On the Coast near Sausalito," set like many of Hass' poems on his native California coast, the poet catches a cabezone, a primitive fish, and

> the fierce quiver of surprise
> and the line's tension
> are a recognition.

This recognition is what he desires and must be responsible for:

> Holding the spiny monster in my hands
> his bulging purple eyes
> were eyes and the sun was
> almost tangent to the planet
> on our uneasy coast.
> Creature and creature,
> we stared down the centuries.[5]

Praise and *Human Wishes* are marked by an increased attention to the ways in which language mediates experience, creating separation and enabling approach. The language of these volumes moves between transparency and self-referential materiality, while retaining Hass' characteristic naturalness of tone and what Charles Molesworth calls his "loving tentativeness."[6] We tentatively create and that act itself becomes our solid ground:

> . . . the interval created by if, to which mind and breath
>   attend, nervous
> as the grazing animals the first brushes painted,
>
> has become habitable space, lived in beyond wishing.[7]

🖎 POETRY

Human Wishes. New York: Ecco Press, 1989. Dust jacket. Published at $17.95.

"Misery and Splendor." Berkeley, California: Black Oak Books, 1989. Broadside. Limitation not stated. Issued on the occasion of a reading by the author.

Praise. New York: Ecco Press, 1979. Dust jacket. Published at $7.95.

"When my oldest child was two or so . . ." Berkeley, California: Black Oak Books, 1984. Broadside. Limitation not stated.

🖎 PROSE

Twentieth Century Pleasures: Prose on Poetry. New York: Ecco Press, 1984. Dust jacket. Published at $17.95.

🖎 TRANSLATIONS

Provinces, by Czeslaw Milosz. Translated by the author and Robert Hass. New York: Ecco Press, 1991. Dust jacket. Published at $19.95. Dust jacket states "Poems 1987–1991."

The Separate Notebooks: Poems, by Czeslaw Milosz. Translated by Robert Hass and Robert Pinsky with the author and Renata Gorczynski. New York: Ecco Press, 1984. Dust jacket. Published at $17.50.

Unattainable Earth, by Czeslaw Milosz. Translated by the author and Robert Hass. New York: Ecco Press, 1986. Dust jacket. Published at $17.95.

Anthony Hecht

For Anthony Hecht (b. 1923), form in poetry is refinement and responsibility, a necessary submission to fate or order that constitutes our moral development. The discipline of writing is

> Governed by laws which stand for other laws,
> Both of which aim, through kindred disciplines,
> At the soul's knowing and habiliment.[1]

As Peter Sacks points out, in Hecht "empowerment exists only in tension with a kind of submission."[2] Firmly rooted in the English tradition, Hecht is a Jewish poet haunted by the atrocities of the Holocaust and a contemporary bemused by "the grotesqueness of modern life."[3] Born in New York City, Hecht fought in Europe and Japan during World War II, of which he says, "the cumulative sense of these experiences is grotesque beyond anything I could possibly write." Hecht's form is baroque in its profusion of details, Marvellian in its sense of "controlled disorder . . . where the tension lectures / Us on our mortal state."[4] This tension is not merely artificial, but reflects the quality of nature: "The poem wishes to pay its homage to the natural world, from which it derives and strives to imitate. And there is in nature a superfluity, an excess of texture."[5]

After his highly ornate first volume, *A Summoning of Stones*, Hecht made a radical break with *The Hard Hours*, which tempers his formal verse into "starkly undecorative — and unpretentious — writing,"[6] and takes on grief, madness, and human courage and atrocity. In "More Light! More Light!" (Goethe's dying words), Hecht explores the vulnerability of human light and dignity by juxtaposing two stories: the burning of a Christian at the stake, and a Nazi ordering a Pole to bury two Jews alive:

> Not light from the shrine at Weimar beyond the hill
> Nor light from heaven appeared. But he did refuse.[7]

Hecht has continued to write about human efforts to overcome despair and remain responsible. He writes wittily about struggles with weather and conscience. "Sestina d'Inverno" is about trying to survive winter in Rochester, New York, where he taught for many years:

> Under our igloo skies the frozen mind
> Holds to one truth: it is grey, and called Rochester.[8]

And "The Ghost in the Martini" is a seduction poem in which he gets the better of his conscience:

> The martini does its job,
> God bless it, seeping down to the dark old id.[9]

Later long poems like "The Venetian Vespers" and "See Naples and Die" show Hecht coming to terms with failure and affirming the possibility of human beauty.[10] He won the Pulitzer Prize in 1968 for *The Hard Hours*, and shared the Bollingen Prize in Poetry with John Hollander in 1983.

❧ POETRY

Æsopic: Twenty Four Couplets . . . to Accompany the Thomas Bewick Wood Engravings for "Select Fables." With an afterword on the blocks by Philip Hofer. Northampton,

Massachusetts: Gehenna Press, 1967. Boards. One of
500 copies.

The Book of Yolek. Atlanta, Georgia: Emory University,
1990. Wrappers. Printed at the Shadowy Waters Press to
mark the 1990 Richard Ellmann Lectures in Modern
Literature.

Collected Earlier Poems. New York: Alfred A. Knopf, 1990.
Dust jacket. Published at $22.95. Contains the complete
texts of "The Hard Hours," "Millions of Strange
Shadows," and "The Venetian Vespers."

"Curriculum Vitae." Winston-Salem, North Carolina:
Palaemon Press, 1984. Broadside, signed by the author.
Limitation not stated.

The Hard Hours: Poems. Illustrated by Leonard Baskin. New
York: Atheneum, 1967. Dust jacket. Published at $5.00.

"Humoresque." N.p.: Privately printed for the poet, 1983.
Broadside. One of 40 copies signed by Hecht.

Jiggery-Pokery: A Compendium of Double Dactyls, ed.
Anthony Hecht and John Hollander. Drawings by
Milton Glaser. New York: Atheneum, 1967. Dust jacket.
Published at $3.95.

A Love for Four Voices: Homage to Franz Joseph Haydn.
Illustrated by Michael McCurdy. Great Barrington,
Massachusetts: Penmaen Press, 1983. Boards, issued
without dust jacket. One of 50 copies signed by the
author and the illustrator in a total limitation of 300.
This copy contains an extra illustration, number 33 of
75 signed by McCurdy, loosely inserted.

Millions of Strange Shadows. New York: Atheneum, 1977.
Dust jacket. Published at $7.95. With the author's
presentation inscription.

The Seven Deadly Sins: Poems. Wood engravings by Leonard
Baskin. Northampton, Massachusetts: Gehenna Press,

1958. Glassine dust jacket as issued. One of 300 copies signed by Hecht and Baskin. This copy bears the poet's presentation inscription on the front endpaper.

A Summoning of Stones. New York: Macmillan, 1954. Dust jacket. Published at $2.50. The author's first book.

The Transparent Man: Poems. New York: Alfred A. Knopf, 1990. Dust jacket. Published at $18.95.

The Venetian Vespers. Etchings by Dimitri Hadzi. Boston: David R. Godine, 1979. Tissue dust jacket. One of 150 copies signed by the author and the artist in a total limitation of 165. The trade edition was published by Atheneum.

The Venetian Vespers: Poems. New York: Atheneum, 1979. Dust jacket. Trade edition. Published at $10.00. Review slip and publisher's publicity material loosely inserted.

Ȧ PROSE

The Hidden Law: The Poetry of W. H. Auden. Cambridge, Massachusetts: Harvard University Press, 1993. Dust jacket. Published at $35.00.

Obbligati: Essays in Criticism. New York: Atheneum, 1986. Dust jacket. Published at $18.95.

Paper on constraints prepared by Anthony Hecht for "Seminar on the Creative Process," 28 January 1966. N.p.: Wenner-Gren Foundation for Anthropological Research, 1966. Wrappers. A lecture delivered at Wayne State University. "Not for Publication." This copy is signed by Hecht.

Robert Lowell. Washington, D.C.: Library of Congress, 1983. Wrappers. A lecture.

⤳ TRANSLATION

Poem Upon the Lisbon Disaster, by François Marie Arouet de
Voltaire. Translated by Anthony Hecht. Wood
engravings by Lynd Ward. Introduction by Arthur
Wilson. Lincoln, Massachusetts: Penmaen Press, 1977.
Boards, in slipcase as issued. One of 200 copies signed
by Hecht, Ward, and Wilson in a total limitation of 500.
Publisher's flyer loosely inserted.

John Hollander

For John Hollander (b. 1929), poet, scholar, and theorist of literature at Yale University, traditional form is a way of exploring the mysteries of language—its music, its potential for seduction, its relation to truth. If language is an arbitrary sign system, he believes, then the personal or individual use of it is inevitably in dialogue with tradition. As Richard Poirier remarks of Hollander, "The changes that can be worked within form are made incumbent upon the discovery that any form is implicitly a substitute for or an interpretation of some other. Any form exists in the shadow of some other, and is on the verge of eliding into it."[1]

Hollander takes form quite literally in poems like "The Great Bear," a meditation on how meaning or interpretation requires a community with a shared frame of reference. A relation or connection is transposed to a new context, creating a constellation, a new way of getting one's bearings, and this is analogous to the way language works:

> *One solitary star would be quite useless,*
> *A frigid conjecture, true but trifling;*
> *And any single sign is meaningless*
> *If unnecessary . . .*[2]

Hollander has written critical studies on music, echo, and refrain in poetry, and in his own work is fascinated with repetition and reflection, with the power of rhyme and meter to soothe and woo. In the "In Time" sequence from *In Time and Place*, which narrates the solitary period just after a marital separation has occurred, rhymed verse provides a form for grief, a means of facing loss with dignity and wit, in a time when the absence of the beloved is a painful presence. The poet may wish "To rhyme you back to bed again,"[3] but also realizes that "rhymed lines know best when to stop":

> *Because there is too much to say*
> *I cast it into such a form*
> *As this, to keep your hearing warm*
> *On my love's silent, chilly day.*
>
> *Not that you need the hollow chime*
> *Of these old bells to make you hear,*
> *But lest each thought run on a year*
> *Or more, some measure must keep time.*[4]

Hollander shared the Bollingen Prize in Poetry with Anthony Hecht in 1983.

⁊ POETRY

"After an Old Text." Storrs: University of Connecticut Library, 1976. Broadside. One of 250 copies on the occasion of a reading by the poet. Inscribed "For Richard Ludwig and the Milberg Collection. John Hollander."

"A Beach Vision." Text by Hollander. Four drawings by Reginald Pollack. N.p., 1962. A series of five broadsides signed by the poet and the artist, this set is also inscribed by Pollack to Hollander. According to Hollander, only 23 sets were run off.

Blue Wine and Other Poems. Baltimore, Maryland: Johns Hopkins University Press, 1979. Dust jacket. Published at $8.95.

A Book of Various Owls. Illustrated by Tomi Ungerer. New York: W. W. Norton, 1963. Boards; not issued in dust jacket. A juvenile.

"Broken Column." Emory, Virginia: Iron Mountain Press, 1969. Broadside. One of 160 copies signed by the author. This copy is inscribed "To Richard Ludwig and the Milberg Collection."

"Coiled Alizarine." Emory, Virginia: Iron Mountain Press, 1971. Broadside. One of 200 copies.

An Entertainment for Elizabeth. Introduction by Irving Cummings. Storrs: University of Connecticut, 1972. Wrappers. "English Literary Renaissance Monographs, Number 1, volume 1." Costume designs by Anne Hollander.

Harp Lake: Poems. New York: Alfred A. Knopf, 1988. Dust jacket. Published at $16.95.

The Head of the Bed. With a commentary by Harold Bloom. Boston: David R. Godine, 1974. Boards; not issued in dust jacket. Published at $2.50. Number 3 in the "First Godine Poetry Chapbook Series."

In Place: A Sequence. Omaha: Abbatoir Editions, University of Nebraska, 1978. Boards. One of 247 copies in a total limitation of 271.

In Time and Place. Baltimore, Maryland: Johns Hopkins University Press, 1986. Dust jacket.

Jiggery-Pokery: A Compendium of Double Dactyls, ed. Anthony Hecht and John Hollander. Drawings by Milton Glaser. New York: Atheneum, 1967. Dust jacket. Published at $3.95.

Kinneret. New Haven, Connecticut: Eighty Seven Press, 1986. Boards. Not issued in dust jacket. Copy O–2 of an edition of 180 copies, signed by the poet, the designer Jayne Hertko, and the binder.

Looking Ahead. New York: Nadja, 1982. Boards. One of 100 copies signed by the author in a total limitation of 126. The flyer for the book is loosely inserted.

"Looking East in Winter." New York: Nadja, 1990. Wrappers. "Printed in 1990 for the friends of Nadja. Best wishes from Carol Sturm & Douglas Wolf."

"The Night Mirror." State University College at Brockport, New York, 1969. Wrappers. Invitation to a poetry reading. Signed by the author.

The Night Mirror: Poems. New York: Atheneum, 1971. Paperback. Not issued in cloth.

"Night Observations." New Haven, Connecticut: Yale University, 1978. Broadside, "printed on the Vandercook Press in the Sterling Memorial Library." A Bibliographical Press Broadside printed on the occasion of a reading by the poet on 2 March 1978. One of 70 copies signed by the author.

"169." Winston-Salem, North Carolina: Palaemon Press, 1984. Broadside, signed by the author. Limitation not stated.

"Ontology is a Matter of Midnight." Winston-Salem, North Carolina: Palaemon Press, 1980. Broadside. One of 75 copies signed by the author, the total limitation.

Philomel. London: Turret Books, 1968. Wrappers. One of 100 signed copies.

Poems of Our Moment, ed. John Hollander. New York: Pegasus, 1968. Dust jacket. Published at $7.50. An anthology of recent poetry in English with contributions by John Ashbery, James Dickey, Allen

Ginsberg, Anthony Hecht, John Hollander, Kenneth Koch, and others.

Powers of Thirteen: Poems. New York: Atheneum, 1983. Dust jacket. Published at $13.95.

The Quest of the Gole. Drawings by Reginald Pollack. New York: Atheneum, 1966. Dust jacket. Published at $3.95.

Reflections On Espionage: The Question of Cupcake. New York: Atheneum, 1976. Dust jacket. Published at $8.95.

Selected Poems. London: Secker & Warburg, 1972. Dust jacket. Published at £1.50. No comparable American edition.

Selected Poetry. New York: Alfred A. Knopf, 1993. Dust jacket. Published at $27.50.

Some Fugitives Take Cover. New York: Sea Cliff Press / Jordan Davies, 1986. Wrappers. One of 100 signed copies in a total limitation of 115.

"Sparklers." Emory, Virginia: Iron Mountain Press, 1983. Broadside. One of 200 copies. Inscribed "For Richard Ludwig and the Milberg Collection."

Spectral Emanations: New and Selected Poems. New York: Atheneum, 1978. Dust jacket. Published at $12.50.

"Summer Questions." Winston-Salem, North Carolina: Palaemon Press, 1983. Broadside. Total limitation is 76 copies, this being one of 26 lettered and signed copies. Inscribed "For Richard Ludwig and the Milberg Collection." Accompanied by one of 50 signed copies.

"Swan and Shadow." N.p., 1969[?]. Broadside. A shaped poem beginning "Dusk above the water . . ." Artist's proof, titled in the author's hand and inscribed by him to Richard Ludwig and the Milberg Collection.

Tales Told of the Fathers: Poems. New York: Atheneum, 1975. Dust jacket. Published at $7.95

Tesserae and Other Poems. New York: Alfred A. Knopf, 1993. Dust jacket. Published at $20.00.

Town & Country Matters: Erotica & Satirica. Boston: David R. Godine, 1972. Dust jacket. One of 3,850 copies in a total limitation of 4,000. Illustrator not identified.

Types of Shape: Poems. New York: Atheneum, 1969. Wrappers. Published at $2.95. Also published in cloth.

Types of Shape. New Expanded Edition. New Haven, Connecticut: Yale University Press, 1991. Dust jacket.

Visions from the Ramble. New York: Atheneum, 1965. Dust jacket. Published at $4.50.

"White Noise." Illustrated by Virgil Burnett. N.p., n.d. Broadside. Artist's proof signed by the artist. Limitation not stated.

❧ PROSE

Dal Vero: Portraits by Saul Steinberg. Text by John Hollander. New York: Whitney Museum of American Art, 1983. Boards, in cloth box as issued. One of 140 copies signed by the author. The intaglio prints are signed by the artist.

The Figure of Echo: A Mode of Allusion in Milton and After. Berkeley: University of California Press, 1981. Dust jacket.

Images of Voice: Music and Sound in Romantic Poetry. Cambridge, England: W. Heffer & Sons, 1970. Wrappers. Published at 7s. "Churchill College Overseas Fellowship Lectures number 5."

The Immense Parade on Supererogation Day and What Happened to It. Pictures by Norman MacDonald. New York: Atheneum, 1972. Dust jacket. Published at $5.50. Printed dos-à-dos.

Larry Day: Paintings and Drawings. Philadelphia: Gross McCleaf Gallery, 1983. Wrappers. Illustrated exhibition catalogue with an introduction by Hollander.

A Lost Lady, by Willa Cather. Illustrated by William Bailey. Introduction by John Hollander. New York: Limited Editions Club, 1983. Cloth boards, leather spine. In slipcase as published. One of 1,500 copies signed by William Bailey.

"The Poem as Silhouette: A Conversation with John Hollander," ed. Philip L. Gerber and Robert J. Gemmett. Ann Arbor: Michigan Quarterly Review, 1970. Wrappers. Offprint from *Michigan Quarterly Review* 9, no. 4 (Fall 1970). Signed by Hollander and Gemmett.

"The Poetry of Everyday Life." New Brunswick, New Jersey, 1981. Wrappers. Offprint from *Raritan: A Quarterly Review*, Fall 1981. Signed by Hollander.

"A Poetry of Restitution." New Haven, Connecticut, 1981. Wrappers. Offprint from *The Yale Review*, Winter 1981. Signed by Hollander.

Rhyme's Reason: A Guide to English Verse. New Haven, Connecticut: Yale University Press, 1981. Dust jacket.

Rhyme's Reason: A Guide to English Verse. New enlarged edition. New Haven, Connecticut: Yale University Press, 1989. Dust jacket.

The Untuning of the Sky: Ideas of Music in English Poetry, 1500–1700. Princeton: Princeton University Press, 1961. Dust jacket. Published at $8.50. Publisher's compliments slip loosely inserted.

Vision and Resonance: Two Senses of Poetic Form. New York: Oxford University Press, 1975. Dust jacket. Published at $12.50.

William Bailey. Foreword by Giuliano Briganti. Illustrated with plates. New York: Rizzoli, 1991. Dust jacket.

William Bailey: Recent Paintings. New York: Robert Schoelkopf Gallery, 1982. Wrappers. Catalogue for an exhibition, 3 April–4 May 1982, with an introduction by John Hollander. Illustrated.

Andrew Hudgins

Andrew Hudgins (b. 1951) is a Southern poet of "extravagant morbidity," as Robert Shaw has said.[1] Hudgins's work contains powerful, sometimes shocking images of guilt, violence, and sacrifice. Obsessively concerned with decay and mortality and with the overlap between religious fervor and madness, Hudgins writes often ironic, always compassionate dramatic monologues in a colloquial blank verse. Associated with fiction writers like Flannery O'Connor and William Faulkner, and often called a Southern Gothic poet, Hudgins is dubious about the characterization: "It just seems like things I've seen all my life."[2] Hudgins sees and makes us see. As Henri Coulette says, "There is a quality that good witnesses and great liars share—particularly of detail—and Hudgins possesses this in the extreme, whether describing the horrors of war, the fevers of illness or a dog covered with porcupine quills."[3]

Born in Texas, Hudgins spent his adolescence in Montgomery, Alabama, where he attended Sidney Lanier High School, named after the nineteenth-century Southern poet who became the narrator of his second volume, *After the Lost War*. His first volume, *Saints and Strangers*, explores religious fundamentalism in poems like "Awaiting Winter Visitors: Jonathan Edwards, 1749," and the eight-part title poem narrated by an itinerant preacher's daughter. *After the Lost War* is a series of poems spoken by Sidney Lanier, ranging from his traumatic Civil War experiences to his attempts to face his own impending early death:

> *It's strange*
> *how everything I say becomes*
> *a symbol of mortality . . .*

he muses in "A Christian on the Marsh."[4] In "After the Lost War," vultures set on fire by sailors become an image for the post-bellum South, the generation for whom "pretty much / the whole of life has been not dying." These birds, a grotesque image of hope, burn brightly, then

> *. . . fall, like burnt-out stars,*
> *into the Alabama River.*
> *One night, preoccupied with work,*
> *I think I made a wish on one.*[5]

Hudgins's quiet sensitivity is highly developed in *The Never-Ending*, in which personal experience and public tragedy are often linked. His narrators express their pain, loss, and tenderness simply and with humor, as in "Praying Drunk":

> *Our Father who art in heaven, I am drunk.*
> *Again. Red wine. For which I offer thanks.*
> *I ought to start with praise, but praise*
> *comes hard to me. I stutter. Did I tell you*
> *about the woman whom I taught, in bed,*
> *this prayer? It starts with praise; the simple form*
> *keeps things in order. I hear from her sometimes.*
> *Do you? And after love, when I was hungry,*
> *I said,* Make me something to eat. *She yelled,*
> Poof! You're a casserole!—*and laughed so hard*
> *she fell out of bed. Take care of her.*[6]

⇗ POETRY

After the Lost War: A Narrative. Boston: Houghton Mifflin, 1988. Dust jacket. Published at $12.50.

The Never-Ending: New Poems. Boston: Houghton Mifflin, 1991. Dust jacket. Published at $17.95.

Praying Drunk. New York: Dim Gray Bar Press, 1991. Wrappers. One of 150 copies signed by the author.

Saints and Strangers. Introduction by John Frederick Nims. Boston: Houghton Mifflin, 1985. Dust jacket. Published at $13.95. The author's first book, the thirteenth selection in the Houghton Mifflin New Poetry Series.

David Ignatow

David Ignatow (b. 1914) does what, in a 1969 review, he describes James Wright as doing: he makes "an organic graft of the surrealist technique upon the body of hard reality, one enhancing and reinforcing the other so that we have a mode as evocative as a dream and as effective as a newspaper account."[1] For Ignatow, the real is surreal, and the surreal is real. Dreams and absurdities are told in absolutely plain language, as if there were nothing remarkable about them. The capitalist system, the Vietnam War, random acts of violence in the city: all have a logic with an absurdity at its core, which is exposed by Ignatow's "consciously skeletal aesthetic."[2] In an interview with William Spanos, Ignatow compares his writing process to a walk in his native Brooklyn; both have that "touch of paranoia" necessary to survival. "My avocation is to stay alive; my vocation is to write about it."[3]

Ignatow's early work exposes the implicit assumption in capitalism that all value can be measured monetarily:

> There is no money in breathing . . .
> besides keeping me alive
> breathing doesn't give enough
> of a return.[4]

His war poems examine the idea of righteous violence, as in "All Quiet," dedicated to Robert Bly and written during one of the pauses in our bombing of North Vietnam:

How come nobody is being bombed today?
I want to know, being a citizen
of this country and a family man.

There should have been a "news leak, at which I could have voiced a protest, / running my whole family off a cliff."[5] Ignatow writes powerfully of our despair and sense of power-lessness in the systems we have created or agreed to accept. In "Nice Guy," he notes, "I had a friend and he died. Me." But he can't take time to mourn,

getting an offer of a job
I answered politely, saying yes,
his death unfortunate at midday
during business. I apologized
but had no one to apologize to,
buried without me at work . . .
. . . he had lost his teeth
and had to swallow whole.
He died of too much.[6]

In his work from the mid-1970s to the present, Ignatow more frequently identifies with natural forces, finding in their transformations the sources of his despair and also the way out.

The sky makes no sense to me.
What is it saying? Blue? That blue is enough?
The blue of emptiness?[7]

This is not the static emptiness of idea, but the emptiness of drifting cloud, or of continual change.

Ignatow won the Bollingen Prize in Poetry in 1977.

❧ POETRY

The Animal in the Bush: Poems on Poetry, ed. Patrick Carey. Pittsburgh: Slow Loris Press, 1977. Wrappers. One of 50 signed copies in a total limitation of 1,000.

Despite the Plainness of the Day: Love Poems. Pittsburgh: Mill Hunk Books, 1991. Dust jacket. One of 26 copies signed by the author.

Earth Hard. London: Rapp & Whiting, 1968. Dust jacket. Published at 21s. "Poetry USA Series 5."

Facing the Tree: New Poems. Boston: Little, Brown, 1975. Dust jacket. Published at $6.95. Signed by the author on the title page.

Figures of the Human. Middletown, Connecticut: Wesleyan University Press, 1964. Dust jacket. Published at $4.00.

"The Form Falls In On Itself . . ." Illustration by Wang Hsü. N.p., 1971. Broadside. Signed by the author and the artist. Limitation not stated.

The Gentle Weight Lifter. New York: Morris Gallery, 1955. Dust jacket. Published at $3.00. Review slip loosely inserted. Five hundred copies were printed but not all of them were bound.

Leaving the Door Open: Poems. New York: Sheep Meadow Press, 1984. Dust jacket. Published at $13.95. With the author's presentation inscription on the half-title page.

The Notebooks. Edited with an introduction by Ralph J. Mills, Jr. Chicago: Swallow Press, 1973. Dust jacket. Published at $9.95.

On Equal Terms: Poems by Charles Bernstein, David Ignatow, Denise Levertov, Louis Simpson, Gerald Stern, ed. Hank Lazer. Tuscaloosa, Alabama: Symposium Press, 1984. Wrappers. One of 275 copies. The Ignatow poems are "What" and "If We Knew." Poems by participants in

"The Eleventh Alabama Symposium on English and American Literature: What Is a Poet?"

Poems, 1934–1969. Middletown, Connecticut: Wesleyan University Press, 1970. Dust jacket. Published at $7.95.

"Rescue the Dead." Emory, Virginia: Iron Mountain Press, n.d. Broadside. One of 200 copies.

Rescue the Dead: Poems. Middletown, Connecticut: Wesleyan University Press, 1968. Dust jacket. Published at $4.00.

Say Pardon. Middletown, Connecticut: Wesleyan University Press, 1961. Dust jacket. Published at $4.00.

Selected Poems. Chosen, with introductory notes and an afterword, by Robert Bly. Middletown, Connecticut: Wesleyan University Press, 1975. Dust jacket. Published at $7.50. This copy is inscribed by Ignatow to Gerard Malanga.

Shadowing the Ground. Middletown, Connecticut: Wesleyan University Press, 1991. Dust jacket.

Sunlight: A Sequence for My Daughter. Drawings by Rose Graubart. Brockport, New York: BOA Editions, 1979. Boards, glassine dust jacket. One of 25 copies signed by the author and the artist, and containing a holograph poem by Ignatow, in a total limitation of 500.

Ten Poems. Illustrated by Patricia Apatovsky. New York: Silver Hands Press, 1981. Wrappers, silver foil endpapers. One of 129 copies signed by the author in a total limitation of 155. This copy is inscribed by Ignatow.

Tread the Dark: New Poems. Boston: Little, Brown, 1978. Dust jacket. Published at $7.95. Review slip loosely inserted.

Whisper to the Earth: New Poems. Boston: Little, Brown, 1981. Dust jacket. Published at $10.95. With the author's presentation inscription on the half-title page.

☙ PROSE

Conversations. New York: Survivors' Manual Books, 1980. Wrappers. Published at $3.50. Signed by Ignatow on the title page.

The One in the Many: A Poet's Memoirs. Middletown, Connecticut: Wesleyan University Press, 1988. Dust jacket. Published at $19.95.

Talking Together: Letters of David Ignatow, 1946 to 1990. Selected, edited, and introduced by Gary Pacernick. Tuscaloosa: University of Alabama Press, 1992. Dust jacket. Contains a chronology and a checklist.

Randall Jarrell

Randall Jarrell (1914–1965) had a "great flair for the poetry of desperation," says John Crowe Ransom.[1] Shaped by his experiences as a young man in World War II, Jarrell's early poems express the dehumanizing force of war; his later dramatic monologues speak of the desire to regain worlds that have been lost, perhaps never known.

Jarrell came into his own as a poet with his two books of war poems, *Little Friend, Little Friend* and *Losses*.[2] "Under the shock of war," Hayden Carruth says, "his mannerisms fell away. He began to write with stark, compressed lucidity."[3] For the young soldiers who are the speakers and subjects of Jarrell's poems, war is a painful, confusing experience, surreal yet ordinary, from which it is impossible to draw a moral or an overarching meaning. His soldiers stumblingly attempt to remain human; they are wounded innocents implicated in the pain of others: "Men wash their hands, in blood, as best they can."[4]

According to Helen Vendler, the war poems see the emergence of "the pity that [is Jarrell's] tutelary emotion."[5] His later poems of ordinary life, inhabited by mythic creatures and lost children, yearn to recover a child's sense of direct experience. Here Jarrell's pity arises from a sense of shared loss. As imaginative acts, the poems themselves approach this lost experience, becoming an antidote to that "want of imagination, that inaccessibility to experience, of which each of us who dies a natural death will die."[6] Sometimes, in the later poetry, and in poetic books for children and adults such as *The Bat Poet* and *The Animal Family*,[7] the experience Jarrell seeks comes to him. A perfect example is "Well Water":

> *What a girl called "the dailiness of life"*
> *(Adding an errand to your errand. Saying,*
> *"Since you're up . . ." Making you a means to*
> *A means to a means to) is well water*
> *Pumped from an old well at the bottom of the world.*
> *The pump you pump the water from is rusty*
> *And hard to move and absurd . . . And yet sometimes*
> *The wheel turns of its own weight, the rusty*
> *Pump pumps over your sweating face the clear*
> *Water, cold, so cold! you cup your hands*
> *And gulp from them the dailiness of life.*[8]

Jarrell won the National Book Award in 1961 for *The Woman at the Washington Zoo.*

∽ POETRY

The Animal Family. Decorations by Maurice Sendak. New York: Pantheon, 1965. Dust jacket. Published at $3.50.

Blood for a Stranger. New York: Harcourt, Brace, 1942. Dust jacket. Published at $2.00. The poet's first book. Seventeen hundred copies were printed.

Five Young American Poets. Norfolk, Connecticut: New Directions, 1940. Dust jacket. Published at $2.50. Precedes Jarrell's first book by two years. The other poets included are George Marion O'Donnell, John Berryman, Mary Barnard, and W. R. Moses.

Fly By Night. Pictures by Maurice Sendak. New York: Farrar, Straus & Giroux, 1976. Dust jacket. Published at $5.95. A juvenile. There were 26,699 sets of sheets printed, of which 20,209 had been bound by 1986.

"Letters." Winston-Salem, North Carolina: Shadowy Waters Press, 1983. Broadside. One of only five copies, total limitation, printed for Mary Jarrell in late January and early February, 1983. None for sale.

"The Lost Children." Winston-Salem, North Carolina: Stuart Wright, 1980. Broadside. "Forty copies have been privately printed for distribution by Mary Jarrell and Stuart Wright." First separate edition, second printing. The first printing was suppressed because of errors in the text.

The Lost World. New York: Macmillan, 1965. Dust jacket. Published at $3.95. Four thousand copies printed.

Pictures from an Institution: A Comedy. New York: Alfred A. Knopf, 1954. Dust jacket. Published at $3.50. Six thousand copies printed.

Selected Poems. New York: Alfred A. Knopf, 1955. Dust jacket. Published at $4.00. This copy is in what Stuart Wright, Jarrell's bibliographer, describes as a trial binding.

Selected Poems, ed. William H. Pritchard. New York: Farrar, Straus & Giroux, 1990. Dust jacket. Published at $17.95.

"The Sign." Greensboro: University of North Carolina, 1966. Broadside. A keepsake for friends of the library. Illustrated by Bert Carpenter and printed at the Chapman Press. Approximately 100 copies were printed, none for sale.

The Woman at the Washington Zoo: Poems & Translations. New York: Atheneum, 1960. Dust jacket. Published at $3.75. Thirty-five hundred copies printed.

❧ PROSE

About Popular Culture. Winston-Salem, North Carolina: Palaemon Press, 1981. Wrappers. One of 100 copies in a total limitation of 150, despite the limitation notice which calls for 175 copies. There were also 13 overrun copies used for review.

Kipling, Auden & Co.: Essays and Reviews, 1935–1964. New York: Farrar, Straus & Giroux, 1980. Dust jacket. Published at $17.95. Fifty-five hundred copies printed.

Poetry and the Age. New York: Alfred A. Knopf, 1953. Dust jacket. Published at $4.00. Two thousand copies were printed. A collection of essays.

Randall Jarrell's Letters: An Autobiographical and Literary Selection, ed. Mary Jarrell assisted by Stuart Wright. Plates. Boston: Houghton Mifflin, 1985. Dust jacket. Published at $29.95.

A Sad Heart at the Supermarket: Essays & Fables. New York: Atheneum, 1962. Dust jacket. Published at $4.50. Four thousand five hundred copies printed.

❧ TRANSLATIONS

The Fisherman and His Wife: A Tale from the Brothers Grimm. Translated by Randall Jarrell. Pictures by Margot Zemach. New York: Farrar, Straus & Giroux, 1980. Dust jacket. Published at $10.95. There were 31,500 sets of sheets printed, of which 12,075 had been bound by 1986.

Goethe's Faust, Part I. . . . An English translation by Randall Jarrell. New York: Farrar, Straus & Giroux, 1976. Dust jacket. Published at $15.00. Six thousand seven hundred copies printed; 2,700 clothbound and 4,000 in wrappers.

The Golden Bird, and Other Fairy Tales of the Brothers Grimm.
Translated and introduced by Randall Jarrell. Illustrated
by Sandro Nardini. New York: Macmillan, 1962.
Boards. Not issued in dust jacket.

The Rabbit Catcher, and Other Fairy Tales of Ludwig Bechstein.
Translated and introduced by Randall Jarrell. Illustrated
by Ugo Fontana. New York: Macmillan, 1962. Boards.
Not issued in dust jacket. Published at $1.95.

*Snow-White and the Seven Dwarfs: A Tale from the Brothers
Grimm.* Translated by Randall Jarrell. Pictures by Nancy
Ekholm Burkert. New York: Farrar, Straus & Giroux,
1972. Dust jacket. Published at $5.95. A Caldecott
Honor Book.

Donald Justice

The poems of Donald Justice (b. 1925), formal, reserved, even genteel, evoke a quiet melancholy and tenderness that are very powerful. Influenced by Auden's formalism, understatement, and aesthetic distance, Justice's voice and vision are nevertheless clearly his own. He is certainly distant from his subjects—personal connections survive, he says, "only indirectly, which is, I believe, the way of art"[1]—but his distance is not one of judgment, control, or moralization; it bespeaks rather a thorough empathy with human isolation, "the ardent yearning of the self baffled in loneliness:"[2]

Lights are burning
In quiet rooms
Where lives go on
Resembling ours . . .

And lives go on
. . . like the lights
In quiet rooms
Left on for hours,
Burning, burning.[3]

The rhyme "ours" and "hours" in the same poem seems to reveal Justice's sense of the relation between human presence and absence. We are possessed of an isolated and insufficient self that is full only of empty time. "Taking our places we wait / We wait to be moved";[4] and "She waits surrounded by huge stills of herself";[5] and "Across the back of a chair / Skins of animals / Dried in the moon."[6] Even sexuality is empty:

> The captain, smiling,
> Unfolds his spyglass
> And offers to show you
>
> The obscene shapes
> Of certain islands
> Low in the offing.
>
> I sit by in silence.[7]

Here, with the near rhyme of "islands" and "silence," the suggestion of sexuality musically enters its original nullity.

Allusions to absent fathers are frequent throughout his work. "Sonatina in Yellow" has the "voice of your father, / Insisting you must listen," who

> rises
> In the familiar pattern of reproof,
> For some childish error, a nap disturbed,
> Or vase broken . . .

and later imagines the father "scrupulously clean / Unwrinkled."[6] In the hands of a Confessional poet, this could turn to whimpering self-pity. Justice's reserved and successful striving for artifice, even formal perfection, somehow meets and embodies that father, and leaves the pity to us.

Justice won the Pulitzer Prize in 1980 for *Selected Poems* and the Bollingen Prize in Poetry for 1991.

⚜ POETRY

The Death of Lincoln: A Documentary Opera, by Edwin London on an original libretto by Donald Justice.

Austin, Texas: W. Thomas Taylor, 1988. Dust jacket.
One of 125 specially bound copies signed by London
and Justice in a total limitation of 1,225.

Departures. Iowa City, Iowa: Penumbra Press, Stone Wall
Press, 1973. Boards; glassine dust jacket as issued. One
of 175 copies signed by Justice. Errata slip.

Departures. New York: Atheneum, 1973. Wrappers; not
issued in cloth. First trade edition. Review copy with
promotional material loosely inserted. Inscribed by the
author on the title page.

A Donald Justice Reader: Selected Poetry and Prose.
Middlebury, Vermont: College Press, 1991. Dust jacket.
"The Bread Loaf Series of Contemporary Writers."

From a Notebook. Iowa City, Iowa: Seamark Press, 1972.
Boards. One of 317 copies.

"In the Attic." N.p: Toothpaste Press, 1980. Broadside. One
of 150 signed copies. Printed for the fourth
Midwestern Writers' Festival and Book Fair, 25 April
1980.

Night Light. Middletown, Connecticut: Wesleyan University
Press, 1967. Dust jacket. Published at $4.00.

Night Light. Revised edition. Middletown, Connecticut:
Wesleyan University Press, 1981. Dust jacket.

Selected Poems. New York: Atheneum, 1979. Dust jacket.
Published at $10.95.

The Seven Last Days. Text by Donald Justice. Music by
Edward Miller. Boston: E. C. Schirmer Music
Company, 1971. Wrappers.

Sixteen Poems. Iowa City, Iowa: Stone Wall Press, 1970.
Wrappers. One of 250 copies.

The Summer Anniversaries. Middletown, Connecticut:
Wesleyan University Press, 1960. Dust jacket. Published
at $3.00. The 1959 Lamont Poetry Selection.

The Summer Anniversaries. Revised edition. Middletown, Connecticut: Wesleyan University Press, 1981. Dust jacket.

The Sunset Maker: Poems, Stories, A Memoir. New York: Atheneum, 1987. Dust jacket. Published at $16.00.

Tremayne: Four Poems. Cover drawing by Laurence Donovan. Iowa City, Iowa: Windhover Press, 1984. Wrappers. One of 210 copies.

✿ PROSE

Platonic Scripts. Ann Arbor: University of Michigan Press, 1984. Paperback. Not issued in cloth. "Poets on Poetry" series.

✿ TRANSLATION

The Man Closing Up, by Guillevic. Translation and an improvisation by Donald Justice. Iowa City, Iowa: Stone Wall Press, 1973. Wrappers. One of 150 copies, this one is inscribed "to Stuart Wright from Don Justice."

Robert Kelly

Robert Kelly (b. 1935) is concerned with "language [as] the intersection of consciousness with society," as he says in "Going With the Poem." "The mind of life speaks us in detail, and language is responsible to it."[1] The poet's work is to allow this speaking to arise:

> Finding the measure is finding the mantram,
> is finding the moon, as index of measure,
> is finding the moon's source;
>
>   if that source
> is Sun, finding the measure is finding
> the natural articulation of ideas.[2]

Kelly's work often seems hermetic, drawing on alchemy and religious mysteries. "Sentence" explains itself as "a simple poem cathected with complexities,"[3] yet, as Jed Rasula points out, "the substance of the difficulties [in reading Kelly] are maelstroms of psychic energy rather than hermetic lore."[4] At the center of Kelly's work is a heart, taking in and circulating, "because I am a lover, & that process never ends."[5]

Kelly's experiments with language and form are another way of finding the measure, finding a way out, for "Style is death." Since 1982 Kelly's Buddhist practice has led him to an awareness of "the root . . . beneath the tongue,"[6] the dancing of the earth that goes on below the playful, quirky language that expresses it.

> *it is rude*
> *to be so nude*
>
> *so take*
> *that paper off*
>
> *a word's*
> *a transparent thing*
>
> *a subterfuge*
>
> *and I alone of mortals*
> *prefer climbing*
> *to going down*
>
> *except on you*[7]

For this lover, language shows everything, yet teases, and its susceptibility to punning ambiguity leads beyond it to the lover's true object.

❧ POETRY

The Alchemist to Mercury. Collected and edited by Jed Rasula. Richmond, California: North Atlantic Books, 1981. Issued without dust jacket. Number 16 of an unspecified number of signed copies.

Alpha. Gambier, Ohio: Pot-Hanger, 1968. Wrappers. One of 26 lettered and signed copies in a total limitation of 326.

Ariadne. Rhinebeck, New York: St. Lazaire Press, 1991. Wrappers.

Armed Descent. New York: Hawk's Well Press, 1961. Wrappers. The author's first book.

"As he would contribute . . ." Photograph by Charles Stein. Storrs: University of Connecticut, 1974. Folded broadside. One of 250 copies on the occasion of a reading by the poet, 7 October 1974.

Axon Dendron Tree. Annandale-on-Hudson, New York: Salitter Books, 1967. Wrappers. Five hundred copies were printed.

The Book of Persephone. New Paltz, New York: Treacle Press, 1978. Dust jacket. One of 100 signed copies in a total limitation of 1,000.

A California Journal. London: Big Venus, 1969. Wrappers.

Cities. West Newbury, Massachusetts: Frontier Press, 1971. Wrappers. Published at $1.00.

The Common Shore, Books I–V: A Long Poem about America in Time. Los Angeles: Black Sparrow Press, 1969. Glassine dust jacket. One of 250 hardcover copies signed by the author in a total limitation of 1,276.

The Convections. Santa Barbara, California: Black Sparrow Press, 1978. Glassine dust jacket. One of 250 hardcover copies signed by the author in a total hardbound limitation of 300. There was also a trade issue in wrappers.

The Cruise of the Pnyx. Barrytown, New York: Station Hill, 1979. Wrappers. Published at $2.95. With the author's presentation inscription.

"Deasil & Widdershins." Amherst, Massachusetts: Poetry Signature V, Autumn 1969. Wrappers. An offprint from *Massachusetts Review,* Autumn 1969.

Devotions. Annandale-on-Hudson, New York: Salitter Books, 1967. Wrappers.

Finding the Measure. Los Angeles: Black Sparrow Press, 1968. Wrappers. One of 950 copies in a total limitation of 1,000.

Flesh Dream Book. Los Angeles: Black Sparrow Press, 1971. Glassine dust jacket. One of 200 hardbound copies signed by the author in a total limitation of 1,226.

In Time. West Newbury, Massachusetts: Frontier Press, 1971. Wrappers. Published at $3.00.

A Joining: A Sequence for H.D. Los Angeles: Black Sparrow Press, 1967. Wrappers. One of 115 signed copies in a total limitation of 125.

Kali Yuga. London: Cape Goliard Press, 1970. Dust jacket. One of 50 copies signed by the author. Accompanied by a copy of the trade edition in glassine jacket.

Kill the Messenger Who Brings Bad News. Santa Barbara, California: Black Sparrow Press, 1979. Glassine dust jacket. One of 250 hardbound copies signed by the author.

The Lady Of. Santa Barbara, California: Black Sparrow Press, 1977. Wrappers. "Sparrow 55." Twelve hundred copies were printed, this being one of a small number of untrimmed copies signed by the author.

Lectiones. Placitas, New Mexico: Duende Press, 1965. Wrappers. Limitation not stated.

The Loom. Los Angeles: Black Sparrow Press, 1975. Glassine dust jacket. One of 50 copies handbound in boards by Earle Gray, signed by the author and with a holograph poem, in a total hardbound limitation of 300.

Lunes. Drawings by Amy Mendelson. New York: Hawk's Well Press, 1964. Wrappers. Also contains Jerome Rothenberg's "Sightings."

The Mill of Particulars. Los Angeles: Black Sparrow Press, 1973. Glassine dust jacket. One of 200 hardcover copies signed by the author.

Not This Island Music. Santa Barbara, California: Black Sparrow Press, 1987. Glassine dust jacket. One of 150 copies signed by the author.

The Pastorals (Book Seven of The Common Shore). Los Angeles: Black Sparrow Press, 1972. Wrappers. "Sparrow I." Second printing.

Ralegh. Los Angeles: Black Sparrow Press, 1972. Wrappers. One of 220 copies signed by the author in a total limitation of 246.

Sentence. Barrytown, New York: Station Hill, 1980. Wrappers. One of 256 copies in a total limitation of 356. This copy is signed by the author.

Sixteen Odes. Santa Barbara, California: Black Sparrow Press, 1976. Wrappers. "Sparrow 41." One of a small number of untrimmed copies, this one is signed by the author.

Song XXIV. Cambridge, Massachusetts: Pym-Randall Press, 1967. Wrappers. One of 100 copies signed by the author in a total limitation of 126.

Songs I–XXX. Cambridge, Massachusetts: Pym-Randall Press, 1968. Dust jacket. One of 90 clothbound copies signed by the author in a a total hardbound limitation of 400. There were also 600 copies in wrappers.

Spiritual Exercises. Santa Barbara, California: Black Sparrow Press, 1981. Glassine dust jacket. One of 250 hardcover copies signed by the author.

Statement. Los Angeles: Black Sparrow Press, 1968. Wrappers. First issue, with the names of eight poets, in addition to Kelly's, on the cover. One of 1,000 copies of this issue.

A Strange Market. Santa Rosa, California: Black Sparrow Press, 1992. Glassine dust jacket. One of 125 hardbound copies signed by the author.

"Tabula." Lawrence, Kansas: Dialogue Press, 1964. Broadside, printed on both sides. Limitation not stated. "Broadside Poems 10."

Thor's Thrush. Oakland, California: Coincidence Press, First Season, 1984. Wrappers. One of 300 copies.

Twenty Poems. Annandale-on-Hudson, New York: Matter, 1967. Wrappers. Five hundred copies were printed.

Under Words. Santa Barbara, California: Black Sparrow Press, 1983. Glassine dust jacket. One of 50 copies handbound in boards by Earle Gray, each containing a unique holographic painting and a poem by the author, and signed by him.

The Well Wherein a Deer's Head Bleeds: A Play for Winter Solstice. Los Angeles: Black Sparrow Press, 1968. Wrappers. A Christmas greeting from the press with the overall title "A Play and Two Poems." Other contributors are Ron Loewinsohn and Diane Wakoski. One of 300 copies in a total limitation of 400.

Wheres. Santa Barbara, California: Black Sparrow Press, 1978. Wrappers. "Sparrow 68." One of a small number of untrimmed, signed copies.

The Wise Men DRAWN to Kneel in Wonder at the FACT So of ITSELF. Los Angeles: Black Sparrow Press, 1971. Kelly contributed "Yesod & Malkuth, that is, Advent & Christmas from 'Spheres'" to the booklet. Wrappers. Publisher's Christmas greeting. Also contains Diane Wakoski's "The Magi" and David Bromige's "The Nest."

ॐ PROSE

Cat Scratch Fever: Fictions. Kingston, New York: McPherson & Company, 1990. Glassine dust jacket.

Doctor of Silence: Fictions. Kingston, New York: McPherson & Company, 1988. Issued without dust jacket.

The Scorpions: A Novel. London: Calder and Boyars, 1969. Dust jacket. First British edition, published at 30s.

A Transparent Tree: Fictions. New Paltz, New York: McPherson & Company, 1985. Dust jacket. Published at $20.00.

X. J. Kennedy

X. J. Kennedy (b. 1929) says of his predilection for strict formal rhymed verse, "What I like is song and balladry, the freedom of not having to express myself, not being obliged to write what the top of my head thinks ought to be written."[1] In witty, precise, musical language, he gives us particular moments in history, humorous and sensitive love poems, and meditations on the foibles of human existence, which, at poetry readings, he often sings to his audience.

Kennedy's light verse and parody are among the best of the century; their accuracy and depth force us to re-evaluate the way we categorize poetry into "light" and "serious." His unfailing and merciless ear allows him to capture the styles of poets as diverse as Allen Ginsberg, T. S. Eliot, Robert Frost, and Emily Dickinson:

> *I called one day— on Eden's strand*
> *But did not find her— Home—*
> *Surfboarders triumphed in— in Waves—*
> *Archangels of the Foam—.*[2]

Kennedy helps us to see how the funny or the absurd is part of any serious situation. In "Hangover Mass," which draws on his Catholic childhood in Dover, New Jersey, he describes being dragged along to Irish pubs by his father, where, after church, lonely, bitter old men sit drinking themselves to death. The poem's wit focuses on the incongruousness of the two worlds, church and pub, and its light touch makes the pain it depicts more poignant even while it serves to maintain a distance from that pain:

> Quickly the priest would drive us forth to graze
> Where among churchyard flocks I'd get a taste
> Of chronic loneliness.[3]

Quirky word choices, slang, and bits of popular culture assert themselves in Kennedy's work, emphasizing his point that formal rhymed verse can allow words to be themselves. A poet writing in rhythm and rhyme, says Kennedy, "is a mere mouse in the lion's den of the language—but with any luck, at times he can get the lion to come out."[4] In "Epiphany," an odd posture yields a fresh view on life:

> Flat on my belly, sprawled at the head of the stairs,
> I shuffled junk mail on the kitchen floor.
> Bills, begs, and bull. . . .
> For days I'd gone on trudging, too far dulled
> To take mere things in. Floored now, freed from airs
> Of uprightness, I raise astounded eyes
> To how they joined—the legs and rungs of chairs.[5]

Kennedy is also a prolific editor of poetry textbooks and anthologies.

≯ POETRY

The Beasts of Bethlehem. Drawings by Michael McCurdy. New York: Margaret K. McElderry Books, 1992. Dust jacket. Published at $13.95. A juvenile.

Brats. Illustrations by James Watts. New York: Atheneum, A Margaret K. McElderry Book, 1986. Dust jacket. Published at $11.95. A juvenile.

Breaking and Entering. London: Oxford University Press, 1971. Paperback. Not published in cloth. Published at

£1.25. With the author's presentation inscription to Samuel French Morse.

Celebrations After the Death of John Brennan. Wood engravings by Michael McCurdy. Lincoln, Massachusetts: Penmaen Press, 1974. Dust jacket. One of 300 copies signed by the author and the illustrator in a total limitation of 326. Publisher's flyer loosely inserted.

Cross Ties: Selected Poems. Athens: University of Georgia Press, 1985. Dust jacket.

Dark Horses: New Poems. Baltimore, Maryland: Johns Hopkins University Press, 1992. Dust jacket. Published at $26.00.

Emily Dickinson in Southern California. Boston: David R. Godine, 1973. Issued without dust jacket. Number one in the first "Godine Poetry Chapbook Series."

"Flitting Flies." Palo Alto, California: Chimera Books, 1981. Broadside. Designed by Kathy Walkup. One of 100 copies in a total limitation of 150.

The Forgetful Wishing Well: Poems for Young People. Illustrations by Monica Incisa. New York: Atheneum, 1985. Dust jacket. Published at $9.95. A juvenile.

Fresh Brats. Illustrations by James Watts. New York: Margaret K. McElderry Books, 1990. Dust jacket. Published at $12.95. A juvenile.

Ghastlies, Goops & Pincushions: Nonsense Verse. Drawings by Ron Barrett. New York: Margaret K. McElderry Books, 1989. Dust jacket. Published at $12.95.

Growing into Love. Garden City, New York: Doubleday, 1969. Dust jacket. Published at $4.50.

Hangover Mass. Cleveland, Ohio: Bits Press, 1984. Boards. One of 33 signed copies in a total limitation of 333.

"Hickenthrift and Hickenloop." Illustrated by Margot Tomes. New York: Holiday House, 1978. Broadside. Limitation not stated.

The Kite that Braved Old Orchard Beach: Year-Round Poems for Young People. Illustrations by Marian Young. New York: Margaret K. McElderry Books, 1991. Dust jacket. Published at $12.95. A juvenile.

Nude Descending a Staircase. Garden City, New York: Doubleday, 1961. Dust jacket. Published at $2.50. The author's first book. This copy bears Kennedy's presentation inscription to John Malcolm Brinnin. The 1961 Lamont Poetry Selection label appears on the dust jacket.

One Winter Night in August, and Other Nonsense Jingles. Illustrated by David McPhail. New York: Atheneum, A Margaret K. McElderry Book, 1975. Dust jacket. Published at $5.95. A juvenile.

The Phantom Ice Cream Man: More Nonsense Verse. Illustrated by David McPhail. New York: Atheneum, A Margaret K. McElderry Book, 1979. Dust jacket. Published at $6.95. A juvenile.

Three Tenors, One Vehicle: A Book of Songs, by James Camp, X. J. Kennedy, & Keith Waldrop. Columbia, Missouri: Open Places Stephens College, 1975. Paperback; not issued in cloth.

❧ TRANSLATION

French Leave: Translations. Florence, Kentucky: Robert L. Barth, 1983. Wrappers. One of 175 copies signed by the author in a total limitation of 200.

Galway Kinnell

Galway Kinnell (b. 1927) writes in "On the Oregon Coast" that "as post-Darwinians it was up to us to anthropomorphize the world less and animalize, vegetablize, and mineralize ourselves more."[1] As with other poets associated with the Deep Image School — such as James Wright and W. S. Merwin, Kinnell's Princeton classmate — many of Kinnell's poems reach toward a condition of existence without thought, toward a consciousness whose basis is physical life. In "Poem of Night" he addresses his lover: "You lie here now in your physicalness, / This beautiful degree of reality," and says of himself that it is "as if the life in me / Were slowly remembering what it is."[2] Kinnell wants to allow animals and the natural world to be what they are, and also to transform himself into bear or flower, as a way of understanding who he is. Charles Molesworth calls him "a shamanist, not a historicist, of the imagination."[3]

His transformations often involve pain or death, as if the self is able to learn what it is only by dying into a new self. Death is close to birth, as in "Flower Herding on Mount Monadnock," where his deathlike face reflected in a pool and his face at birth are equally grotesque. Both have behind them

"The old, shimmering nothingness, the sky." This is a blessed nothingness, releasing him from the self-pity over "all I claim to have suffered" that begins the poem:

> I kneel at a pool,
> I look through my face
> At the bacteria I think
> I see crawling through the moss.
>
> My face sees me,
> The water stirs, the face,
> Looking preoccupied,
> Gets knocked from its bones.[4]

The line-break after "bacteria I think" removes thought from its position of supremacy and makes it just another form of life feeding.

For Kinnell, both inflicting and suffering pain are necessary parts of life that must be accepted. In poems like "The Bear," in which an Eskimo hunter reaches a state of identification with the bear he is tracking and the wounded animal's suffering becomes his own, Kinnell explores how to conduct oneself in the presence of life's pain and cruelty. When the hunter reaches the bear's carcass, he "hack[s] / a ravine in his thigh" and climbs inside to sleep and dream of being a wounded bear. When he awakes, he is changed:

> the rest of my days I spend
> wandering: wondering
> what, anyway,
> was that sticky infusion, that rank flavor of blood, that
>   poetry, by which I lived?[5]

In 1983 Kinnell won the Pulitzer Prize and the American Book Award for *Selected Poems*, and shared the National Book Award with Charles Wright.

🐟 POETRY

"After Making Love We Hear Footsteps." Port Townsend, Washington: Copper Canyon Press, 1980. Broadside.

First separate edition. Limitation not stated but there were 205 signed copies. "Centrum Poetry Symposium 1980."

Angling, A Day, and Other Poems. Concord, New Hampshire: William B. Ewert, 1980. Wrappers. One of 150 copies signed by the author in a total limitation of 176.

Apparitions: Poems by John Ashbery, Galway Kinnell, W. S. Merwin, L. M. Rosenberg, Dave Smith. Northridge, California: Lord John Press, 1981. Boards. One of 300 copies signed by each poet in a total limitation of 350.

The Auction. Woodcuts by Mary Azarian. Concord, New Hampshire: William B. Ewert, 1989. Loose sheets. One of ten advance copies in a special printed folder, in a total limitation of 90. Signed by the author and the artist.

"The Avenue Bearing the Initial of Christ into the New World." New York: Hudson Review, 1960. Unbound. Offprint from *The Hudson Review* 12, no. 4 (Winter 1960). Signed by the author.

"The Bear." Photograph by Edward S. Curtis. Santa Cruz, California: Bookshop Santa Cruz, 1975. Broadside. First separate edition. Limitation not stated.

"Blackberry Eating." Concord, New Hampshire: Rara Avis Press for William B. Ewert, 1980. Broadside. One of 100 signed copies in a total limitation of 126.

Body Rags. London: Rapp & Whiting, 1969. Dust jacket. First English edition. One of 100 copies signed by the author. "Poetry USA Series 7."

The Book of Nightmares. London: Omphalos Press / J-J Publications, 1978. Revised from the 1971 American edition. Paperback; not published in cloth. Published at £2.00. Signed by the author.

"Brother of My Heart: A Poem." Canberra / Toronto: Open Door Press, 1977. Two broadsides, consisting of the title page and the text page, laid into a printed folder. One of 20 numbered copies folded into Strathmore Artlaid boards, in a total limitation of 40. All copies are signed by the author.

"Daybreak." Napa, California: Privately printed, 1980. Broadside. Illustrated by Jill Hall. One of only twelve copies, but reportedly Kinnell ruined one by sitting on it.

"Divinity." Concord, New Hampshire: William B. Ewert, 1989. Broadside. One of 40 signed copies printed at the Firefly Press.

"Farm Picture." Concord, New Hampshire: William B. Ewert, 1985. Broadside. One of 100 copies signed by the author.

Fergus Falling. With a handcolored lithograph by Claire Van Vliet. Newark, Vermont: Janus Press, 1979. Boards. One of 120 copies signed by the author and the artist. Bound with Kizuki paper over museum boards by James Bicknell and printed on Toyama Kayazuki.

"The Ferry Stopping at McMahon's Point." San Francisco: Intersection, 1981. Broadside. One of 100 signed copies.

"First Song." Concord, New Hampshire: William B. Ewert, 1982. Broadside. First separate edition. One of 150 copies for private distribution, signed by the author.

"First Song." Illustrated by Gary Young. Carmel, California: Poet's Place, 1983. Broadside. One of 200 copies signed by the author, but this copy is numbered 32/130. First illustrated edition, published issue. Some copies were destroyed because of defects in the paper.

"First Song." Carmel, California: Greenhouse Review
  Press for Poet's Place, 1991. Broadside. One of 200
  copies illustrated with an original woodcut and signed
  by the author.

"Fisherman." Toronto: Massey Press, 1980. Three
  broadsides, consisting of title page, text page, and
  publication data page, laid into a green paper folder.
  One of only 60 copies signed by the author.

The Fundamental Project of Technology. Illustrated by Gillian
  Tyler. Concord, New Hampshire: William B. Ewert,
  1983. Wrappers. One of 100 copies signed by the
  author in a total limitation of 154. The Phi Beta Kappa
  poem presented 7 June 1983 at Harvard University.

"The Fundamental Project of Technology." Boston:
  Houghton Mifflin, 1984. Single sheet folded to make
  four pages. Revised edition, one of a small quantity
  printed for employees of the publisher. This copy is
  signed by the author.

"The Geese." West Burke, Vermont: Janus Press, 1985.
  Broadside. One of 100 copies signed by the author and
  by Claire Van Vliet, who made the paper.

"Getting the Mail." Illustrated by Bill Davison.
  Montpelier: Vermont Council on the Arts, 1974.
  Broadside. Twelve hundred copies were printed; this
  one is signed by the author.

"The Gray Heron." Calligraphy by R. P. Hale. Concord,
  New Hampshire: William B. Ewert, 1990. Broadside.
  One of 50 copies printed on special paper and signed
  by the author and the calligrapher in a total limitation
  of 150.

"The Hen Brooding." Illustrated by Joann Brady. Durham:
  University of New Hampshire Library, 1982. Broadside.
  One of 100 signed copies in a total limitation of 350.

Printed to accompany the Friends of the University of New Hampshire Library Notes, Winter 1982.

The Hen Flower. Frensham, Farnham, Surrey, United Kingdom: Sceptre Press, 1970. Wrappers. One of 74 copies in a total limitation of 100.

How the Alligator Missed Breakfast. Illustrated by Lynn Munsinger. Boston: Houghton Mifflin, 1982. Dust jacket. Published at $8.95. A juvenile.

"How Many Nights." Nyack, New York: The Fellowship of Reconciliation, ca. 1968. Greeting card format with a watercolor by S. C. Yuan.

"How Many Nights." Brockport, New York: State University of New York, 1969. Wrappers. Invitation to a reading by the poet on 22 October 1969.

The Last Hiding Places of Snow. Illustrated with wood engravings by Barry Moser. New York: Red Ozier Press, 1980. Boards. One of 150 copies signed by the author and the artist.

"Little Children's Prayer." Huntington, New York: A Poem A Month Club, 1978. Broadside, signed by the author. Limitation not stated.

"Looking at the Sea with Maud and Fergus." Concord, New Hampshire: William B. Ewert, 1987. Broadside. One of 70 copies signed by the author.

"The Milk Bottle." Santa Cruz, California: Two Pears Press, 1980. Broadside. One of 200 copies signed by the author, this one marked "for the author."

The Mind. Concord, New Hampshire: William B. Ewert, 1984. Wrappers. One of 36 copies signed by the author in a total limitation of 136. Accompanied by a copy of the unbound issue limited to 100 copies

Mortal Acts, Mortal Words. Boston: Houghton Mifflin, 1980. Dust jacket. Published at $8.95.

"Mount Fuji at Daybreak." Concord, New Hampshire: William B. Ewert, 1985. Greeting card, one of 36 signed copies in a total limitation of 136.

"The Music Box." Concord, New Hampshire: William B. Ewert, 1983. Single sheet folded twice; greeting card format, enclosed in the original unprinted envelope. One of 100 copies in a total limitation of 136.

"1984 Poetry Calendar." Napa, California: Lily of the Valley, 1983. A calendar, stapled, each month reproducing a Kinnell poem. Published at $2.95. This copy is signed by the poet.

Oatmeal: A Poem. Concord, New Hampshire: William B. Ewert, 1990. Wrappers. Illustrations reproduced from original wood engravings by Thomas Bewick. One of 65 copies signed by the author.

The Past. Boston: Houghton Mifflin, 1985. One of 200 copies signed by the author. In the publisher's slipcase as issued. Accompanied by a copy of the trade edition in dust jacket, published at $13.95.

Poems of Night. London: Rapp and Carroll, 1968. Dust jacket. Published at 21s. "Poetry USA Series."

"Prayer." Saratoga Springs, New York: Yaddo, 1988. Broadside laid into wrappers. One of 26 author's copies, this one signed, in a total limitation of 200.

"Saint Francis and the Sow." Silkscreen design by Darcie Sanders. Evanston, Illinois: Whole Earth Center, 1976. Broadside. One of 150 signed copies. "No Mountains Poetry Project: Broadside Number 9."

The Seekonk Woods. With three photographs by Lotte Jacobi. Concord, New Hampshire: William B. Ewert, 1985. Boards. Printed at the Janus Press. One of 155 copies signed by the author and the photographer in a total limitation of 170.

Selected Poems. Boston: Houghton Mifflin, 1982. One of 200 signed copies. In the publisher's slipcase as issued. Accompanied by a copy of the trade edition in dust jacket, published at $12.50.

The Snow Rabbit: Poems, by Patti Hill. Illustrated by Galway Kinnell. Boston: Houghton Mifflin, 1962. Dust jacket. Published at $3.00. Signed by Kinnell on the title page.

"Some Song." Brattleboro, Vermont: Brattleboro Museum, 1985. Broadside. Limitation not stated, but there were 400 signed copies.

Thoughts Occasioned by the Most Insignificant of All Human Events. Concord, New Hampshire: William B. Ewert, 1982. Wrappers. One of 150 signed copies in a total limitation of 186.

Three Poems. New York: Phoenix Book Shop, 1976. Wrappers. One of 100 signed copies in a total limitation of 126. Number 19 in the "Oblong Octavo Series."

"To Christ Our Lord." Wood engraving by John DePol. N.p.: Privately printed, 1983. A Christmas card, signed by Kinnell. "A Merry Christmas to everyone from Michael, Dianne, Brent, and Alysia Peich."

Two Poems. Offset lithographs by Claire Van Vliet. Newark, Vermont: Janus Press, 1979. Boards. One of 185 copies signed by the author and the artist.

Two Poems, by Galway Kinnell and Diane Wakoski. Wood engraving by Barry Moser. Madison, Wisconsin: Red Ozier Press, 1981. Wrappers. Publisher's New Year greeting, signed by Kinnell and Wakoski. Limitation not stated. Kinnell's poem is "Daybreak."

"The Vow." Concord, New Hampshire: William B. Ewert, 1989. Broadside. One of 40 signed copies printed at the Firefly Press.

When One Has Lived a Long Time Alone. New York: Alfred A. Knopf, 1990. Dust jacket. Published at $18.95.

"Woodsmen." Wood engraving by Gillian Tylor. Concord, New Hampshire: William B. Ewert, 1982. Single sheet folded to make a four-page greeting card. One of 150 copies printed by Christy Bertelson at the Rara Avis Press in Riverside, California.

❧ **PROSE**

Black Light: A Novel. San Francisco: North Point Press, 1980. Extensively revised from the Houghton Mifflin 1966 edition. Paperback, not issued in cloth. Published at $5.00.

"'Deeper Than Personality': A Conversation with Galway Kinnell," ed. Philip L. Gerber and Robert J. Gemmett. Iowa City: Iowa Review, 1970. Wrappers. Offprint from *The Iowa Review* 1, no. 2 (May 1970). Signed by Robert J. Gemmett.

Remarks on Accepting the American Book Award for Poetry, April 28th, 1983. Concord, New Hampshire: William B. Ewert, 1984. Wrappers. Designed by Claire Van Vliet. One of 100 signed copies in a total limitation of 115.

3 Self-Evaluations. Beloit, Wisconsin: Beloit Poetry Journal, 1953. Wrappers. "Chapbook No. 2, 1953." Published at $1.00. The other poets included are Anthony Ostroff and Winfield Townley Scott.

Walking Down the Stairs: Selections from Interviews. Ann Arbor: University of Michigan Press, 1978. Paperback; not published in cloth. "Poets on Poetry Series."

❧ TRANSLATIONS

Bitter Victory (Amère Victoire), by René Hardy. Translated by Galway Kinnell. Garden City, New York: Doubleday, 1956. Dust jacket. Published at $3.50. Kinnell's first book, preceding *What a Kingdom It Was* by four years.

On the Motion and Immobility of Douve, by Yves Bonnefoy. Translated by Galway Kinnell. Athens: Ohio University Press, 1968. Dust jacket. Published at $5.50.

The Poems of François Villon. A new translation with an introduction by Galway Kinnell. New York: New American Library, A Signet Classic, 1965. Paperback; not issued in cloth. French / English text.

Selected Poems, by Yvan Goll. Translated by Robert Bly, George Hitchcock, Galway Kinnell, and Paul Zweig. Drawings by Jean Varda. San Francisco: Kayak Books, 1968. Wrappers. Published at $2.00. Twelve hundred copies were printed.

Carolyn Kizer ❧

Carolyn Kizer (b. 1925) writes about feminine energy and sensibility in a restrained voice that conveys pain and passion as much by what it does not say as by what it does. Kizer's early work, traditional in form, has given way to a transparent style, influenced by Japanese and Chinese writers, that blends the lyric with various kinds of occasional prose: letters, family memoirs, and, most frequently, journal entries, as if to emphasize the poetic energy of the ordinary. Kizer explores not only her personal emotional relationships—to mother, father, lovers, children—but through them, the nature of Western female consciousness. Like Theodore Roethke, with whom she studied in the mid-1950s, Kizer uses gardens, rivers, and creatures to understand the human psyche.

Poems and sequences like "A Muse of Water,"[1] "Pro Femina,"[2] and "Fanny"[3] take an unflinching, sometimes angry look at women's traditional roles and how they shape or impede the role of the woman artist. In "A Muse of Water," women "must act as handmaidens / To our own goddess"; water is the metaphor of female creativity and generative power that male artists have tried to harness and run dry, and that female artists must find in fresh sources. "Fanny" is the journal in poetic form of Robert Louis Stevenson's wife, who enters into a frenzy of fruit and vegetable planting on Samoa while Stevenson falls ill and writes *Catronia*, published in America as *David Balfour*. The poem evokes the frustrated creative energy of a woman in the shadow of a male artist:

> Louis has called me a peasant. How I brooded!
> Confided it to you, diary, then crossed it out.
> Peasant because I delve in the earth, the earth I own.
> Confiding my seed and root—I too a creator?
> My heart melts over a bed of young peas. A blossom
> On the rose tree is like a poem by my son.
> My hurt healed by its cause. I go on planting.

Kizer writes about love and loss with a powerful containment, as in "A Widow in Wintertime," in which a widow faces loneliness and grief with what she calls

> These arbitrary disciplines of mine,
> Most of them trivial: like covering
> The children on my way to bed, and trying
> To live well enough alone, and not to dream
> Of grappling in the snow, claws plunged in fur,
>
> Or waken in a caterwaul of dying.[4]

And in the long sequence "A Month in Summer," which combines diary entries and haiku to chart the disintegration of a love affair, Kizer wonders why she has appropriated Japanese forms, and answers, "Perhaps because the only way to deal with sorrow is to find a form in which to contain it."[5]

Kizer was founder and editor of *Poetry Northwest* (1953–1965) and won the Pulitzer Prize in 1985 for *Yin: New Poems*.

🐟 POETRY

Knock Upon Silence. Garden City, New York: Doubleday, 1965. Dust jacket. Published at $2.95. The author's second book.

Mermaids in the Basement: Poems for Women. Port Townsend, Washington: Copper Canyon Press, 1984. Dust jacket. Published at $14.00.

Midnight Was My Cry: New and Selected Poems. Garden City, New York: Doubleday, 1971. Dust jacket. Published at $5.95.

The Nearness of You: Poems. Port Townsend, Washington: Copper Canyon Press, 1986. Dust jacket. Published at $15.00. Signed by the author on the title page.

"Tu Fu to Li Po." San Francisco: Small Press Distribution, 1985. Broadside. Printed to commemorate Kizer's receiving the 1985 Pulitzer Prize for Poetry.

Yin: New Poems. Brockport, New York: BOA Editions, 1984. Dust jacket.

PROSE

Hilda Morris: Recent Bronzes. Portland, Oregon: Art Museum, 1973. An illustrated exhibition catalogue.

TRANSLATION

Carrying Over: Poems from the Chinese, Urdu, Macedonian, Yiddish, and French African. Translated by Carolyn Kizer. Port Townsend, Washington: Copper Canyon Press, 1988. Dust jacket. Published at $15.00.

Kenneth Koch

In his breezy, playful poems, Kenneth Koch (b. 1925) moves fluidly between the ordinary and the surreal. Cascades of random thoughts and everyday details splatter on the page like paint on a Jackson Pollock canvas; breathless exclamations create a continual sense of surprise; "how-to" poems combine the authoritative objectivity of an instruction manual with impossible dream or fantasy images. Koch was one of the principal members of the anti-academic, abstract-expressionist-influenced New York School in the mid-1950s. David Lehman comments on the playfulness central to Koch's poetry: "[He] takes a great deal of delight in the sounds of words and his consciousness of them; he splashes them like paint on a page with enthusiastic puns, internal rhymes, titles of books, names of friends . . . and seems surprised as we are at the often witty outcome."[1]

Koch's favorite subjects are love and writing poetry. His 1962 conversation poem, "On the Great Atlantic Rainway," describes his philosophy of poetry:

> To, always in motion, lose nothing . . .
> Formulalessness, to go from the sun
> Into love's sweet disrepair.[2]

His long poem, "The Art of Poetry," discusses how to write and how not to write in a matter-of-fact, almost prosaic tone, exploring the paradoxes of poetic control: "The lyric adjusts to us like a butterfly, then epically eludes our grasp." The fortuitous recognition of the limits of control should be passed to the reader, whom the poet invites to

> *. . . put your work down puzzled,*
> *Distressed, and illuminated, ready to believe*
> *It is curious to be alive.[3]*

Koch is well known for his love poems, which convey a sense of mystery in desire, and for his satires of other poets. His "Variations on a Theme by William Carlos Williams" is a send-up of Williams's "This Is Just to Say":

> 1
>
> *I chopped down the house that you had been saving to live*
> *   in next summer.*
> *I am sorry, but it was morning, and I had nothing to do*
> *and its wooden beams were so inviting.*
>
> 2
>
> *We laughed at the hollyhocks together*
> *and then I sprayed them with lye.*
> *Forgive me. I simply do not know what I am doing. . . .[4]*

Koch has also worked on poetry with children and the elderly. *Wishes, Lies, and Dreams: Teaching Children to Write Poetry* portrays his experiences in New York's P.S. 61 and his techniques for making poetry fun for children. *I Never Told Anybody* is devoted to his work with aged people in nursing homes. He is also the author of a series of short verse plays.

❧ POETRY

The Art of Love: Poems. New York: Random House, 1975. Dust jacket. Published at $6.95.

The Burning Mystery of Anna in 1951. New York: Random House, 1979. Dust jacket. Published at $7.95.

Days and Nights. New York: Random House, 1982. Dust jacket. Published at $10.50.

The Duplications. New York: Random House, 1977. Dust jacket. Published at $6.95. This copy is signed by the author on the title page.

From the Air. With six paintings by Rory McEwen reproduced in color. London: Taranman, 1979. Boards. Limited to 500 copies of which 40 contain an original etching and are signed by the author and the artist. This copy is numbered H.C.II, contains the etching, and is signed by the artist.

Ko; or, A Season on Earth. New York: Grove Press, 1959. Dust jacket. Published at $3.50. The author's first published book. With Kay Boyle's signature on the front endpaper.

On the Edge: Poems. New York: Viking, Elisabeth Sifton Books, 1986. Dust jacket. Published at $18.95. The dust jacket is by Larry Rivers.

The Pleasures of Peace and Other Poems. New York: Grove Press, 1969. Dust jacket. Published at $3.95.

Poems from 1952 and 1953. Los Angeles: Black Sparrow Press, 1968. Wrappers. One of 250 copies signed by the author in a total limitation of 300.

The Red Robins. New York: Vintage Books, 1975. Paperback; not published in cloth. Published at $5.95.

Seasons on Earth. New York: Penguin Books, Elisabeth Sifton Books, 1987. Paperback; not issued in cloth. Published at $12.95. "The Penguin Poets" series.

Selected Poems, 1950–1982. New York: Random House, 1985. Dust jacket. Published at $17.95.

Thank You and Other Poems. New York: Grove Press, 1962. Paperback; not published in cloth. Published at $1.95.

When the Sun Tries to Go On. Illustrated by Larry Rivers. Los Angeles: Black Sparrow Press, 1969. Glassine dust jacket. One of 200 hardbound copies signed by the author and the artist. Loosely inserted is an invitation to the Gotham Book Mart publication party.

⇜ PROSE

Bertha, & Other Plays. New York: Grove Press, 1966. Paperback; not issued in cloth. Published at $1.95.

A Change of Hearts: Plays, Films, and Other Dramatic Works 1951–1971. New York: Random House, 1973. Dust jacket. Published at $6.95.

I Never Told Anybody: Teaching Poetry Writing in a Nursing Home. New York: Random House, 1977. Dust jacket. Published at $8.95. Author's compliments slip loosely inserted.

Interlocking Lives, by Alex Katz and Kenneth Koch. New York: Kulchur Press, 1970. Boards, not issued in dust jacket. Text by Koch, illustrations by Katz. This copy is signed by both the artist and the poet.

John Ashbery and Kenneth Koch (A Conversation). Tucson, Arizona: Interview Press, ca. 1965. Wrappers. Published at $1.00.

One Thousand Avant-Garde Plays. New York: Alfred A. Knopf, 1988. Dust jacket. Published at $16.95.

Talking to the Sun: An Illustrated Anthology of Poems for Young People. Selected and introduced by Kenneth Koch and Kate Farrell. New York: Metropolitan Museum of Art / Holt, Rinehart and Winston, 1985. Dust jacket. Published at $18.95.

Wishes, Lies, and Dreams: Teaching Children to Write Poetry. New York: Chelsea House, 1970. Dust jacket. Published at $7.95. Written in conjunction with the students of P.S. 61 in New York City. Kay Boyle's copy with her signature on the front endpaper.

Stanley Kunitz

Stanley Kunitz (b. 1905) is humble before the making of poetry and the accumulated experience of life; "I did not choose the way, the way chose me."[1] In his particular practice of organic form, Kunitz, "a fine and quiet singer,"[2] lets sound and image lead him toward the collective unconscious, or archetypal mind. For Kunitz, our experience makes us and unmakes us at the same time. "What do I really know except that I am living and dying at once? The taste of that knowledge on my tongue is that last secret I have to tell."[3]

Kunitz's work is informed by the traumatic shaping event of his life, his father's suicide in a public park before his birth. His mother's anger denies him any information or other link to this lost father. His poems, efforts at connection and understanding, are gentle, haunting and haunted, as in "The Portrait," one of several poems that deal directly with the trauma:

> She locked his name
> in her deepest cabinet
> and would not let him out,
> though I could hear him thumping[4]

or in "Father and Son," where he follows his father back
through time to before his own birth:

> Strode years; stretched into bird;
> Raced through the sleeping country where I was young,
> The silence unrolling before me as I came . . .

He pleads with his father to return:

> O teach me how to work and keep me kind.
>
> Among the turtles and the lilies he turned to me
> The white ignorant hollow of his face.[5]

Perhaps through the confrontation with the unknown, the
refusal of the dead to respond, Kunitz learns to value the
unknown for its own sake.

> We are not souls but systems, and we move
> In clouds of our unknowing
>
> > like great nebulae.[6]

and, in "An Old Cracked Tune," like an inverted nursery
rhyme:

> . . . my mother's breast was thorny,
> and father I had none.
>
> . . .
>
> I dance, for the joy of surviving,
> on the edge of the road.[7]

"The Mulch," about the closeness of growth and decay,
contains a powerful image of Kunitz as poet:

> A man with a leaf in his head
> watches an indefatigable gull
> dropping a piss-clam on the rocks
> to break it open.
> Repeat. Repeat.
> He is an inlander
> who loves the margins of the sea,
> and everywhere he goes he carries
> a bag of earth on his back.
>
> . . .

"Try! Try!" clicks the beetle in his wrist,
his heart is an educated swamp,
and he is mindful of his garden,
which prepares to die.[8]

Kunitz won the Pulitzer Prize in 1959 for *Selected Poems 1928–1958*, and the Bollingen Prize in Poetry in 1987.

❧ POETRY

The Coat Without a Seam: Sixty Poems, 1930–1972. Northampton, Massachusetts: Gehenna Press, 1974. Glassine dust jacket. One of 145 signed copies in a total limitation of 150. The portrait of the poet is by Leonard Baskin.

Intellectual Things. Garden City, New York: Doubleday, Doran, 1930. Dust jacket. Published at $2.00. The author's first book.

The Lincoln Relics: A Poem. Port Townsend, Washington: Graywolf Press, 1978. Wrappers. One of 26 signed copies in a total limitation of 326.

"The Long Boat." Winston-Salem, North Carolina: Palaemon Press, 1984. Broadside, signed by the author. Limitation not stated.

My Sisters. Charlottesville: University of Virginia, 1980. Nine sheets laid into printed folder. "A Poetry Festival Honoring Stanley Kunitz." Contains poems by Louise Glück, Daniel Halpern, Robert Hass, and others. One of 150 copies in a total limitation of 176.

"The New York State Walt Whitman Citation of Merit." State University of New York, Albany, 1987. Wrappers, containing three poem cards by Kunitz, "The Snakes of September," "Father and Son," and "The Quarrel." Kunitz's appointment as New York State Poet. This copy is signed by Kunitz.

Next-to-Last Things: New Poems and Essays. Boston: Atlantic Monthly Press, 1985. Dust jacket. Published at $17.95.

Passport to the War: A Selection of Poems. New York: Henry Holt, 1944. Dust jacket. Published at $2.00.

The Poems of Stanley Kunitz, 1928–1978. Boston: Little, Brown, 1979. Dust jacket. Published at $12.50. This copy is signed by the author.

Selected Poems 1928–1958. Boston: Little, Brown, 1958. Dust jacket. Published at $3.75.

The Terrible Threshold: Selected Poems 1940–1970. London: Secker & Warburg, 1974. Dust jacket. Published at £2.50. No comparable American edition.

The Testing-Tree: Poems. Boston: Atlantic Monthly Press, 1971. One of 150 copies signed by the author. Accompanied by a copy of the trade edition in dust jacket, published at $4.95.

The Wellfleet Whale and Companion Poems. Photograph by the poet. Riverdale-on-Hudson, New York: Sheep Meadow Press, 1983. Boards, glassine jacket.

✺ PROSE

From Feathers to Iron. Washington, D.C.: Library of Congress, 1976. Wrappers. A lecture.

Interviews and Encounters with Stanley Kunitz, ed. Stanley Moss. Riverdale-on-Hudson, New York: Sheep Meadow Press, 1993. Dust jacket. Published at $22.50.

A Kind of Order, A Kind of Folly: Essays and Conversations. Boston: Little, Brown / Atlantic Monthly Press, 1975. Dust jacket. Published at $10.00. Review slip loosely inserted.

Robert Lowell, Poet of Terribilità. New York: Pierpont Morgan Library, 1974. Wrappers.

❧ TRANSLATION

Story Under Full Sail, by Andrei Voznesensky. Translated by
    Stanley Kunitz with Vera Reck, Maureen Sager, and
    Catherine Leach. Garden City, New York: Doubleday,
    1974. Dust jacket. Published at $5.95.

Richmond Lattimore

Richmond Lattimore (1906–1984), born in China, taught at Bryn Mawr College for thirty-six years. He is best known for his translations of Homer, Pindar, and Aeschylus. These graceful, bold, exceptionally sensitive translations helped redefine what translation could be. As John Malcolm Brinnin says, "Lattimore jettisons much of the baggage of classical rhetoric. His renderings of the archaic show the bite and speed appropriate to the age of Pound."[1] Lattimore's own poetry goes hand in hand with his translations. His published volumes all include both original work and translations, and his approach to writing poetry is often that of reading—artifacts, experience, documents.

"Dry Light from Pylos," for example, is Lattimore's interpretation of the Mycenaean Linear B script on a clay tablet from Western Greece. In a simple style that approaches scientific notation, he evokes both the reading process and the subjects it imaginatively and sympathetically creates.

> Contents: sheer fact; inventory,
> lists, and accounts of work. You will not find
> heroic action, myths, or poetry . . .

Lattimore forges a living, poignant image out of this methodical reading:

> *Thirty-seven workers with their woman-sign*
> *and fatherless girls and boys on patient feet*
> *stand there forever waiting in a line*
> *for whatever they are to be given to eat.[2]*

And in sequences like his "Notes from the Odyssey," Lattimore takes his own translations one step further, reading between the lines of the epic to create complex portraits of the inner lives of its characters. He sensitively captures Penelope's ambivalence at Odysseus's return, and her grief at the violently shattered order of her life:

> *Cherish my heart recaptured. It must surge*
> *to love again, sweet unity, but how*
> *shall I forget these things which have been done:*
>
> *my faithless weeping maids with bucket and sponge*
> *mopping the mess, then hanged all in a line,*
> *my suitors stacked like cordwood by the wall?*
>
> *I sent my suitors chits and promises.*
> *I fed my tame geese milk and grains of corn:*
> *my snowy geese, who now lie wrecked and maimed.[3]*

➤ POETRY

Continuing Conclusions: New Poems and Translations. Baton Rouge: Louisiana State University Press, 1983. Dust jacket.

Hanover—Poems, by R. A. Lattimore and A. K. Laing. New York: Harold Vinal, 1927. Dust jacket. Published at $1.50. Lattimore's first book.

Poems. Ann Arbor: University of Michigan Press, 1957. Dust jacket. Published at $3.75.

Poems from Three Decades. New York: Charles Scribner's Sons, 1972. Dust jacket. Published at $7.95.

Sestina for a Far-Off Summer: Poems 1957–1962. Ann Arbor: University of Michigan Press, 1962. Dust jacket. Published at $3.75.

The Stride of Time: New Poems and Translations. Ann Arbor: University of Michigan Press, 1966. Dust jacket. Published at $4.00.

⪧ TRANSLATIONS

Greek Lyrics. Translated by Richmond Lattimore. Chicago: Phoenix Books, University of Chicago Press, 1969. Second edition, revised and enlarged. Paperback issue. A gift to the Milberg Collection from Edmund Keeley.

Hesiod. Translated by Richmond Lattimore. Illustrated by Richard Wilt. Ann Arbor: University of Michigan Press, 1959. Dust jacket. Published at $3.95. Contains "The Works and Days," "Theogony," and "The Shield of Herakles."

The Revelation of John. Translated by Richmond Lattimore. New York: Harcourt, Brace & World, 1962. Dust jacket. Published at $3.25.

Some Odes of Pindar in New English Versions. Translated by Richmond Lattimore. Norfolk, Connecticut: New Directions, Poet of the Month, 1942. Boards, dust jacket. Published at $1.00.

Denise Levertov

Denise Levertov (b. 1923) emigrated to the United States from England in 1948, learning the American idiom by steeping herself in the poetry of William Carlos Williams. In adopting an American voice, she found her own, and, as Kenneth Rexroth puts it, came into "a kind of animal grace of the word, a pulse like the footfalls of a cat or the wingbeats of a gull. It is the intense aliveness of an alert domestic love—the wedding of form and content."[1]

For Levertov, form and content, the material and the spiritual, are inseparable. In "A Testament and a Postscript," she explains her own version of projective verse. In the making of a poem, "content and form are in a state of dynamic interaction." They are not predetermined, but act on each other during the process. Structure comes from inside this process, rather than being imposed on it. "I believe every space and comma is a living part of the poem and has its function, just as every muscle and pore of the body has its function. And the way the lines are broken is a functioning part essential to the poem's life."[2]

Likewise, for Levertov, descendent of Hasidic and Welsh mystics, the source of the spiritual is the material world.

Religious vision emerges in the midst of the ordinary, itself an insistent, concrete presence: in "Caedmon," about the earliest English Christian poet, an illiterate cowherd, inspiration comes,

> but the cows as before
> were calm, and nothing was burning,
>   nothing but I, as that hand of fire
> touched my lips and scorched my tongue
> and pulled my voice
>   into the ring of the dance.[3]

Levertov is also a poet of social conscience. "The poem has a social *effect* of some kind whether or not the poet wills that it have. It has kinetic force, it sets in motion . . . elements in the reader that otherwise would be stagnant."[4] In the late 1960s and early 1970s, she was an outspoken opponent of American policy in Vietnam. Her antiwar poetry incorporates polemical speeches and mixes verse and prose, creating a disruption of poetic balance that expresses the deep anguish of the historical moment and the poet's passionate engagement with it.

2a POETRY

"April in Ohio." Austin, Texas: Cold Mountain Press, 1973. "Cold Mountain Press Poetry Post Card, Series I, Number 9." This copy is signed by the author.

"Blue Africa." Illustrated by Maurice Lapp. N.p.: Calliopea Press, 1986. Broadside. Limitation not stated. Signed by the author and the artist.

"The Blue Rim of Memory." Huntington, New York: A Poem A Month Club, 1978. Broadside, signed by the author. Limitation not stated.

Breathing the Water. New York: New Directions, 1987. Dust jacket. Published at $16.95.

"Caedmon." Concord, New Hampshire: William B. Ewert, 1984. Broadside. One of 100 copies signed by the author in a total limitation of 126.

"Candles in Babylon." Waldron Island, Washington: Brooding Heron Press, 1988. Broadside, one of 14 under the overall title "Transition." Limited to 55 sets for sale signed by each author, plus an unspecified number for the authors and friends of the Press. Enclosed in a cloth box with Japanese-style closures.

"City Psalm." Berkeley, California: Oyez, 1964. Broadside. "Oyez 7." Three hundred fifty copies were printed.

The Cold Spring & Other Poems. Norfolk, Connecticut: New Directions, 1968. Dust jacket. One of 100 copies signed by the author. Not actually published until February 1969.

A Door in the Hive. New York: New Directions, 1989. Dust jacket. Published at $16.95.

The Double Image. London: Cresset Press, 1946. Dust jacket. Published at 5s. The author's first book, spelling her name Levertoff.

The Double Image. Waldron Island, Washington: Brooding Heron Press, 1991. Boards. One of 26 copies signed by the author and the publisher and accompanied by a chapbook, in wrappers, containing a previously unpublished poem in facsimile holograph. The whole is contained in Japanese-style cloth wrap-around boards.

El Salvador: Requiem and Invocation. N.p., 1984. Wrappers. First revised edition. This copy is signed by the author.

Embracing the Multipede. Ink wash drawing by Thomas Ingmire. N.p.: Tangram, 1992. Wrappers. One of 93 copies signed by the author.

Embroideries. Los Angeles: Black Sparrow Press, 1969. Wrappers. One of 300 signed copies in a total limitation of 700.

"An English Field in the Nuclear Age." Illustrated by Katy Festinger. Palo Alto, California: Matrix Press, 1981. Folded broadside. One of 100 copies in a total limitation of 200. "Proceeds from this broadside are being donated to Physicians for Social Responsibility & the anti-nuclear movement."

Evening Train. New York: New Directions, 1992. Dust jacket. Published at $17.95.

Footprints. New York: New Directions, 1972. Dust jacket. Published at $5.00.

The Freeing of the Dust. New York: New Directions, 1975. Dust jacket. Published at $7.00.

Here and Now. San Francisco: City Lights Bookshop, 1957. Wrappers. Published at 75 cents. "The Pocket Poets Series Number Six." Five hundred copies were printed.

The Jacob's Ladder. New York: New Directions, 1961. Paperback; not published in cloth. Published at $1.55.

The Jacob's Ladder. London: Cape, 1965. Dust jacket. Published at 18s. First English and first hardbound edition.

Lake Mountain Moon. N.p.: Tangram, 1990. Wrappers. One of 270 unsigned copies in a total limitation of 300.

Life in the Forest. New York: New Directions, 1978. Dust jacket. Published at $8.00. Trade edition.

Light Up the Cave. New York: New Directions, 1981. Dust jacket. Published at $13.95.

"Mappemonde." Washington, D.C.: Folger Library, 1982. Broadside. "Folger Evening Poetry Series 1982–1983." This copy is signed by the author.

A Marigold from North Viet Nam. New York: Albondocani Press, 1968. Wrappers. One of 300 copies to be used as a holiday greeting by the author and the publisher. None for sale. Enclosed in the original unprinted envelope.

Mass for the Day of St. Thomas Didymus. Concord, New Hampshire: William B. Ewert, 1981. Boards. One of 26 lettered hardbound copies signed by the author in a total limitation of 136. Accompanied by one of 100 signed copies in wrappers.

The Menaced World. Concord, New Hampshire: William B. Ewert, 1985. Wrappers. One of 100 signed copies in a total limitation of 136.

A New Year's Garland for My Students / MIT 1969–1970. Mount Horeb, Wisconsin: Perishable Press, 1970. Wrappers. One of 225 copies, this one is inscribed by the author.

"A Note on the Dedication." Port Townsend, Washington: Copper Canyon Press, 1974. Broadside. One of 100 copies. Extracted from "Copperhead: A Giftbox for Kenneth Rexroth."

On Equal Terms. Poems by Charles Bernstein, David Ignatow, Denise Levertov, Louis Simpson, Gerald Stern, ed. Hank Lazer. Tuscaloosa, Alabama: Symposium Press, 1984. Wrappers. One of 275 copies. The Levertov poems are "St. Peter and the Angel" and "Grey Sweaters." Poems by participants in "The Eleventh Alabama Symposium on English and American Literature: What Is a Poet?"

Overland to the Islands. Highlands, North Carolina: Jonathan Williams, 1958. Wrappers. One of 450 copies in a total limitation of 500. "Jargon 19."

Pig Dreams: Scenes from the Life of Sylvia. Pastels by Liebe Coolidge. Woodstock, Vermont: Countryman Press, 1981. Dust jacket and box as issued. One of 150 copies signed by the author and the artist in a total limitation of 176. Accompanied by a copy of the trade edition in dust jacket, published at $12.95.

Poems 1960–1967. New York: New Directions, 1983. Dust jacket. Published at $14.50.

Poems 1968–1972. New York: New Directions, 1987. Dust jacket. Published at $19.95.

"Psalm Concerning the Castle." Madison, Wisconsin: W. S. Hamady, 1966. Broadside. One of 70 copies.

Relearning the Alphabet. New York: New Directions, 1970. Dust jacket. Published at $4.75. This copy is signed on the front endpaper by the author.

Summer Poems, 1969. Berkeley, California: Oyez, 1970. One of 50 hardcover copies signed by the author in a total limitation of 350. Accompanied by one of 300 copies in wrappers.

"Talk in the Dark." N.p.: Square Zero Editions, 1980. Broadside. One of 26 signed copies in a total limitation of 126.

"The Task." Oakland, California: Red Star Black Rose Press, 1982. Broadside. One of 274 copies in a total limitation of 300.

Three Poems. Mount Horeb, Wisconsin: Perishable Press, 1968. Wrappers. One of 250 copies.

To Stay Alive. New York: New Directions, 1971. Dust jacket. Published at $6.50.

A Tree Telling of Orpheus. Drawings by the the author. Los Angeles: Black Sparrow Press, 1968. Wrappers. One of 250 signed copies in a total limitaton of 329.

Two Poems. Wood engraving by Gillian Taylor. Concord, New Hampshire: William B. Ewert, 1983. Wrappers. One of 175 copies signed by the author and the artist in a total limitation of 225.

"Voyage." Port Townsend, Washington: Copper Canyon Press, 1974. Broadside. One of 100 copies. Extracted from "Copperhead: A Giftbox for Kenneth Rexroth."

Wanderer's Daysong. Port Townsend, Washington: Copper Canyon Press, 1981. Boards, glassine dust jacket. One of approximately 240 copies signed by the author.

⪢ PROSE

Denise Levertov, In Her Own Province. Edited with an introduction by Linda Welshimer Wagner. New York: New Directions, 1979. Paperback, not issued in cloth. Published at $4.95. "Insights II Working Papers in Contemporary Criticism." Contains two interviews and eleven essays by Levertov. Errata slip.

New & Selected Essays. New York: New Directions, 1992. Dust jacket. Published at $21.95.

"U.S. Buried Iraqi Soldiers Alive in Gulf War." Philo, California: Am Here Books, 1992. Two stapled sheets, issued gratis in January 1992. The first sheet reproduces a letter from Levertov to Richard Emmett Aaron.

⪢ TRANSLATIONS

In Praise of Krishna: Songs from the Bengali. Translations by Edward C. Dimock, Jr., and Denise Levertov. With an introduction and notes by Edward C. Dimock, Jr. Illustrations by Anju Chaudhuri. Garden City, New York: Doubleday, Anchor Books, 1967. Paperback; not issued in cloth. Published at $1.25.

Oblique Prayers, by Jean Joubert. Translated by Denise Levertov. New York: New Directions, 1984. Dust jacket. Published at $12.00.

Selected Poems, by Guillevic. Translated by Denise Levertov. New York: New Directions, 1969. Dust jacket. Published at $5.95. The paperback issue preceded the cloth by about a month.

Selected Writings, by Jules Supervielle. Translated by Denise Levertov and others. New York: New Directions, 1967. Dust jacket.

White Owl and Blue Mouse, by Jean Joubert. Translated by Denise Levertov. Illustrations by Michel Gay. Cambridge, Massachusetts: Zoland Books, 1990. Dust jacket. Published at $13.95.

Philip Levine

Philip Levine (b. 1928), perhaps more than any poet, writes from American working-class experience. Unlike Gary Snyder's work poems, which are a Buddhist's entrance into the grace and rhythm of actual labor, and unlike the immense compassion of James Wright for a class he is glad, through art and scholarship, to have escaped, Levine writes *from* a people, from his identification with our baffled weariness and bitterness. Born and raised in Detroit, he counts the Latin American surrealists as well as Kenneth Rexroth and the San Francisco Beats among his influences. Since 1958 he has been teaching at California State University in Fresno.

For Levine, there is no escape from poverty and oppression, and the intimations of redemption the world offers are unsatisfactory, if not undesirable. In "Heaven," we meet the supposition that

> *If you were twenty-seven*
> *and had done time for beating*
> *your ex-wife . . .*
> > *you might*
> *lie on your bed and listen*
> *to a mad canary sing*

in a room that suggests a working man's Byzantium with its "network of golden ladders" and floor and ceiling painted the primary colors of earth and sky. But it

> would do no good
> to have been one of the few
> that climbed higher and higher . . .

> for now there would be the poor
> asking for their share,
> and hurt men in uniforms . . .[1]

Poetry is not a way out; even the angels (as in "Angel Butcher") ask to be slaughtered in order to understand what it is to be flesh.[2] With a workman's understanding of tools, Levine asks for a transparent language: "You look through them [words] into a vision of . . . the people, the place."[3]

Levine asks us to imagine ourselves in a person's life, usually a life that is tired of being relentlessly called to act for a reason that is never quite satisfactory. In "Something Has Fallen," an object found in the garbage turns out to be "only a shadow / that has darkened your fingers."[4] It is a memory that cannot be cauterized.

Through Levine's second-person narratives, we arrive at "a vision of people," one that asks us to be broad enough and brave enough to participate in working-class America as it looks to those of us who are in it, and without the refracted gaze of pity, or help. Because implicit in any idea of redemption is always the unworthiness of that which needs to be redeemed, this absence of pity dignifies us and our pain.

In 1979, Levine won the National Book Critics Circle Award for two books, *Ashes* and *7 Years from Somewhere*. He won the National Book Award twice, for *Ashes* in 1980 and for *What Work Is* in 1991.

🐾 POETRY

Ashes: Poems New & Old. Port Townsend, Washington: Graywolf Press, 1979. Boards. One of 220 copies signed by the author.

Ashes: Poems New and Old. New York: Atheneum, 1979. Wrappers; not issued in cloth. Trade edition.

Blue. West Chester, Pennsylvania: Aralia Press, 1989. Wrappers. One of 175 copies. Title page drawing by Nadya Brown.

5 Detroits. Santa Barbara, California: Unicorn Press, 1970. One of 450 clothbound copies in a total limitation of 1,500.

The Names of the Lost. Iowa City, Iowa: Windhover Press, 1976. Cloth boards. One of 200 copies signed by the author.

The Names of the Lost: Poems. New York: Atheneum, 1976. Paperback, not issued in cloth. Trade edition, published at $3.95. The author's presentation inscription appears on the title page.

New Season. Port Townsend, Washington: Graywolf Press, 1975. Wrappers. One of 165 copies in a total limitation of 225. "Graywolf Pamphlet Series I."

New Selected Poems. New York: Alfred A. Knopf, 1991. Dust jacket. Published at $24.00.

1933: Poems. New York: Atheneum, 1974. Wrappers; only about a dozen copies were issued in cloth for the use of the author and the publisher.

Not This Pig: Poems. Middletown, Connecticut: Wesleyan University Press, 1968. Dust jacket. Published at $4.00

On the Edge & Over: Poems, Old, Lost & New. Oakland, California: Cloud Marauder Press, 1976. Wrappers. Published at $2.50.

One for the Rose: Poems. New York: Atheneum, 1981. Dust jacket. Published at $10.95. Review slip and promotional material loosely inserted.

Pili's Wall. Santa Barbara, California: Unicorn Press, 1971. One of 200 copies bound in boards in a total limitation of 750. This copy is signed by the author.

Pili's Wall. Greensboro, North Carolina: Unicorn Press, 1979. Boards. Reissue. One of 500 copies.

Selected Poems. New York: Atheneum, 1984. Dust jacket. Published at $18.95.

7 Years from Somewhere: Poems. New York: Atheneum, 1979. Wrappers. Not published in cloth. Published at $4.95.

"Sources." Berkeley, California: Moe's Books, 1981. Single sheet folded twice and used as a New Year's greeting.

Sweet Will: Poems. New York: Atheneum, 1985. Dust jacket. Published at $10.95.

They Feed They Lion: Poems. New York: Atheneum, 1972. Wrappers. Only about a dozen copies were bound in cloth with a dust jacket. Published at $3.95.

Thistles. London: Turret Books, 1970. Wrappers. One of 100 copies signed by the author, but this copy is unsigned.

A Walk with Tom Jefferson: Poems. New York: Alfred A. Knopf, 1988. Dust jacket. Published at $16.95.

What Work Is: Poems. New York: Alfred A. Knopf, 1991. Dust jacket. Published at $19.00

☙ PROSE

Don't Ask. Ann Arbor: University of Michigan Press, 1981. Paperback. Not issued in cloth. "Poets on Poetry Series."

☙ TRANSLATION

Off the Map: Selected Poems, by Gloria Fuertes. Edited and translated by Philip Levine and Ada Long. Middletown, Connecticut: Wesleyan University Press, 1984. Dust jacket. Published at $17.00

J. D. McClatchy

J. D. McClatchy (b. 1945), poet, critic, and editor of *The Yale Review*, says of his own work, "I have wanted to write poems with shape and a rich sound, with ideas and a good deal of 'speech,' and with epigrammatic surfaces and resounding depths."[1] McClatchy's intricate, formal, musical poems create a dance between obfuscation and revelation, in which the search for truth and origin, the desire to show what is hidden, is tempered by a sense of inevitable loss, of a fallen condition that revels in the pain and pleasure of its own indirection. As McClatchy has said, "If I had to pick out a dominant theme in my own work, it would be estrangement, or what Frost once called 'an extravagance about grief.'"[2]

In "Blue Horses," the horses, energies of dream, of imagination, of love, are both outside and inside the "you" of the poem; both are startled by their meeting: "But the horses take fright / And burn back behind your eyes, cold and blue."

Or, you've woken on the far side of that dream . . .

You've been borne, like a spark, up a charred,
Sky-hung flue, lifted, lured, the whole time
Rising from fire to ash to the very air

Of an indrawn breath that startles the horses
Into images of the life you once intruded on,
Which had, it now seems, these lives of its own.[3]

Whether in brief lyrics like "Little Elegy," in veiled treatments
like "The Lesson in Prepositions," which is structured around
a series of Latin prepositions, those small words that tell us
how things or people are connected,[4] or in more directly
autobiographical sequences such as "First Steps," McClatchy
seeks forms to narrate love's approaches and retreats, its deep
personal feeling and its wearying predictability. Like Ashbery
and Merrill, McClatchy tries to find ways to conceptualize
homosexual relationships, and "First Steps" is a kind of
memoir, using forms of indirection and straightforwardness to
tell of antecedents and causes, personal, literary, historical, for
this form of love. In search of *original relations,*" he defines
democracy as an ideal community of "'Intense and loving
comradeship, the personal / And passionate attachment of
man to man,'" calling it "a sexual system, a secret / society, the
underground in each self. . . ."[5]

⤞ POETRY

The Rest of the Way: Poems. New York: Alfred A. Knopf,
1990. Dust jacket. Published at $18.95.

Scenes from Another Life: Poems. With a note by Richard
Howard. New York: George Braziller, 1981. Paperback,
published at $4.95. Not published in cloth. The author's
first book. Accompanied by a copy of the English
edition, published in 1983 in cloth and dust jacket at
£5.50. The English edition drops the Richard Howard
note.

Stars Principal: Poems. New York: Macmillan, 1986. Dust
jacket. Published at $16.95.

William Meredith

William Meredith (b. 1919) distills experience into stately design, so that his people, animals, trees, stars, seem to have an existential mass, and at times an almost unbearable heaviness of being. At the same time, the idea that these forms are momentary coalescences, that we are fragile subjects threatened by flux and our own psychological wounds, also surfaces in the poems. Meredith's formalism is a way of expressing sympathy for our sense of isolation, comfort for our desire to be whole and inviolable.

Meredith's practice falls somewhere between the distance and mastery Richard Wilbur strives for and the abandonment to primal forces that James Dickey courts; he is unwilling to trust either pole. In "The Wreck of the Thresher," about a submarine lost at sea, the weight of the water crushing the sailors is perhaps the burden of our constructions to aid movement and safety, to withstand the elements, or of poetic design and control, as they become inadequate and give out.

> *I met a monstrous self trapped in the black deep:*
> All these years, *he smiled,* I've drilled at sea,
> For this crush of water. *Then he saved only me.*[1]

While James Dickey in his poem "Falling" leaves the steward-
ess who is swept suddenly out an airplane's emergency door to
the mercy of her fall and final crash, Meredith gives us Hazard,
who is painting a parachutist, and who himself enacts the
parachutist's drop repeatedly, "falling safely," closing the dis-
tance with the landscape below.[2] What is important is the
continual movement from danger to safety, from distance to
closeness—the movement between control and abandonment.

In "Roots," old Mrs. Leamington, who is thinking about
dying, imagines her body embraced by the roots of a tree like
a tree-house in branches, as if she would enter a comforting,
static, parallel world, where ". . . a tree repeats its structure,
up and down, / The roots mirroring the branches . . ." and
where "I meet my own image sleeping."[3] This mirror image
suggests an immortal, unchanging, discrete self, and its tone
of wishfulness or fancy seems at the same time to deny this
possibility. In "Walter Jenks' Bath," the same forces that hold
the self together also break it apart; between our constituent
parts is empty space:

> Outside the air it is all black.
> The far apart stars run and shine, no one has to tell them
> Stars, run and shine, or the same who tells my atoms
> Run and knock so Walter Jenks, me, will stay hard and
>   real.
> And when I stop the atoms go on knocking,
> Even if I died the parts would go on spinning,
> Alone, like the far stars, not knowing it,
> Not knowing they are far apart, or running,
> Or minding the black distances between.
> This is me knowing, this is what I know.[4]

Ultimately, the comfort and curse of the self is to be aware of
its own porous and aggregate nature.

Meredith won the Pulitzer Prize in 1988 for *Partial Ac-
counts*.

❧ POETRY

"An Account of a Visit to Hawaii." N.p.: Published by the author, 1955. Single sheet folded to make four pages. New Year's greeting, signed by Meredith.

"Country Stars." N.p.: Published by the author, 1975. Single-page greeting card. Signed by Meredith and a gift from him to the Milberg Collection.

"Fables about Error." N.p., n.d. An unbound offprint, signed by the author.

"For Two Lovers in the Canadian Woods a Hundred Years from Now." Washington, D.C.: Folger Library, 1976. Broadside. For a reading on 6 December 1976. This copy is inscribed by the author.

"Freezing." Illustrated by Karyl Klopp. Cambridge, Massachusetts: Pomegranate Press, 1976. Broadside. One of 125 copies signed by the author and the artist in a total limitation of 172.

"Hazard, the Painter." N.p., 1972. Apparently an offprint, "Contents Copyright 1972 by Ironwood Press Inc." This copy is marked "#95" in ink and inscribed by the author to Robert Penn Warren. A single poem, preceding the book of the same name by three years.

"His Students." New London, Connecticut: Published by the author, 1971. Single sheet folded to make four pages. Christmas greeting, signed by Meredith.

"Homage to Paul Mellon, I. M. Pei, Their Gallery, and Washington City." N.p.: Published by the author, 1979. Single sheet; used as a holiday greeting. Inscribed by the author.

"In Loving Memory of the Late Author of the Dream Songs." Charlottesville, Virginia, 1973. Unbound. Offprint from the Winter 1973 issue of the *Virginia*

Quarterly Review. Inscribed "To Stuart" [Wright] by Meredith.

"Literary Uncle, Worldly Niece." N.p.: Published by the author, 1968. Card. A Christmas greeting. Signed by Meredith.

"Notes from Lake Como." New London, Connecticut: Published by the author, 1969. Single sheet folded to make four pages. A Christmas poem. Signed by the author.

"On Jenkins' Hill (The Old Name for Capitol Hill)." Washington, D.C.: Published by the author, 1980. Single sheet. Signed by Meredith and a gift from him to the Milberg Collection.

Partial Accounts: New and Selected Poems. New York: Alfred A. Knopf, 1987. Dust jacket. Published at $16.95.

Peter. Northampton, Massachusetts: Privately printed, 1972. Glassine dust jacket. Tributes to Peter Boynton by William Meredith, James Merrill, Richard Wilbur, and others. Printed at the Gehenna Press in an edition of 110 copies.

Poems Are Hard to Read. Ann Arbor: University of Michigan Press, 1991. Issued without dust jacket.

"Squire Hazard Walks." New London: Connecticut College, n.d. Single sheet folded to make four pages. Signed by Meredith and a gift from him to the Milberg Collection.

"Three Observations (Phrenological, Philosophical, Tactical) Submitted in Partial Fulfillment of the Requirements of Christmas." N.p.: Published by the author, 1954. Single sheet folded to make four pages. Christmas greeting, signed by Meredith.

"2 Pages from a Colorado River Journal." New London, Connecticut: Published by the author, 1967. Single sheet folded to make four pages. A Christmas poem, signed by the author.

"Whorls." New London, Connecticut: Published by the author, 1966. Poem on a card, enclosed in the original unprinted envelope. A Christmas poem. This copy is signed by the author.

"Winter on the River" and "Midnight." N.p.: Published by the author, 1978. Single sheet folded to make four pages. Two New Year's poems. This copy is signed by the author.

"Winter Verse." New London, Connecticut: Published by the author, 1964. Single sheet folded to make four pages. A Christmas poem. This copy is signed by the author.

"Year End Accounts." New London, Connecticut: Published by the author, 1965. Single sheet folded to make four pages. Christmas greeting. Signed by Meredith.

❧ PROSE

"A New Role for the College." New London: Connecticut College, n.d.. Offprint from *Connecticut College Alumnae News*.

Reasons for Poetry & The Reason for Criticism. Washington, D.C.: Library of Congress, 1982. Wrappers. Three thousand copies printed. Two lectures delivered at the Library of Congress on 7 May 1979 and 5 May 1980.

❧ TRANSLATIONS

"Three Translations from Guillaume Apollinaire." N.p.: Published by the author, 1963. Single sheet folded to make four pages. Christmas greeting, signed by the

translator. The three poems are "Mountebanks,"
"Annie," and "Autumn."

Window on the Black Sea: Bulgarian Poetry in Translation, ed.
Richard Harteis in collaboration with William
Meredith. Pittsburgh, Pennsylvania: Carnegie Mellon
University Press, 1992. Paperback. Not published in
cloth. Gift of Meredith and Harteis to the Milberg
Collection and inscribed by them.

James Merrill

James Merrill (b. 1926) began as a poet of strict formal elegance and wit. His technical virtuosity has deepened as he has moved toward a longer, more open form that can accommodate the exuberant leaps of his metaphysical imagination. His three-part epic, *The Changing Light at Sandover*,[1] begun in the mid-1970s and published in full in 1982, is a spiritual work whose mystical provenance questions the nature and limitations of authorial control. It is

> The Book of a Thousand and One Evenings Spent
> With David Jackson at the Ouija Board
> In Touch with Ephraim Our Familiar Spirit,[2]

as well as with angels and with bats that "speak from within the atom."

But Merrill has always "heard poems inhabited by voices."[3] In the *New York Times Book Review*, Merrill comments on an early diary entry from a vacation in Silver Springs, Florida, which took place not long after his parents' divorce when he was twelve: " 'Heavenly colors and swell fish.' What is that phrase but an attempt to bring my parents together, to remarry on the page their characteristic inflections—the lady-like gush and the regular-guy terseness?"[4] The search to echo these

voices involves "the search for magical places real or invented."
Merrill's spiritual questing, his efforts to find effective means
of homosexual expression, and his lively conversation and
delight in gossip are part of the same movement—to create or
discover a universe one can feel at home in.

Thus in "F" from "The Book of Ephraim" (which is
divided into 26 sections for the letters of the alphabet on the
Ouija board), Merrill ranges from a meeting with Miranda, a
chimpanzee who has been taught sign language, to a transmi-
gration of souls that proceeds by word of mouth:

> D has had
> Word from an ex-roommate, name of Thad,
> Whose wife Gin—that will be Virginia—West,
> A skier and Phi Bete, is on the nest.

Miranda's unexpected kiss is a

> Moment that in me made the 'happy' sign
> Like nothing I—like nothing but that whole
> Fantastic monkey business of the soul
> Between lives . . .[5]

Evolution, gossip, and rebirth are all part of a sharing, a
communication of something from one form to another, or
from one realm to another:

> . . . Still waking echoes of that give-and-take
>
> . . . Between one floating realm unseen powers rule
> (Rod upon mild silver rod, like meter
> Broken in fleet cahoots with subject matter)
> And one we feel is ours, and call the real,
>
> The flat distinction of Miranda's kiss
> Floods both. No longer, as in bad old pre-
> Ephraim days, do I naively pray
> For the remission of their synthesis.[6]

Merrill won the National Book Award in 1967 for *Nights
and Days* and again in 1979 for *Mirabell: Books of Number*. He
was awarded the Bollingen Prize in Poetry in 1973 and the
Pulitzer Prize in 1977 for *Divine Comedies*. In 1983, he won the

National Book Critics Circle Award for *The Changing Light at Sandover.*

⤳ POETRY

"Angel." Stonington, Connecticut: Privately printed for the author, 1959. Small broadside printed on pink paper loosely inserted in a greeting card. One of 180 copies. Inscribed by the author to Kimon Friar.

The Black Swan, and Other Poems. Athens, Greece: Icaros, 1946. Wrappers, with original tissue jacket. The author's second book. One of 100 copies. Cover design by Ghika.

Bronze. New York: Nadja, 1984. Boards. One of 150 copies signed by the author in a total limitation of 176. The fifteenth publication of the press, celebrating their sixth year.

The Changing Light at Sandover. New York: Alfred A. Knopf, 1992. Reissue of the 1982 edition as a companion volume to Merrill's *Selected Poems, 1946–1985.* Dust jacket. Published at $30.00.

"Crocheted Curtain." Illustrated by Virgil Burnett. N.p., 1971. Broadside. Limitation not stated but 200 copies were printed. This copy is an artist's proof, signed by the artist.

"Dear friends, it's medically known. . . ." N.p.: Privately printed for the author, n.d.. Poem card published anonymously. Written for his sister, Doris Magowan, after an operation, and for distribution to friends. A gift from the author to the Milberg Collection.

Divine Comedies: Poems. New York: Atheneum, 1976. Dust jacket. Published at $8.95.

"Eight Bits." Key West, Florida: Privately printed for the author, 1986. Wrappers. Issued as a party favor. Inscribed to Kimon Friar and enclosed in the original stamped and addressed envelope.

The Fire Screen. London: Chatto & Windus / Hogarth Press, 1970. Dust jacket. The first British, and the first hardbound, edition. The American edition was issued as a paperback. This edition drops the long final poem, "The Summer People," which appeared in the American edition.

First Poems. New York: Alfred A. Knopf, 1951. Dust jacket. Published at $3.00. One of 990 numbered copies. The author's first commercially published book.

"Five Inscriptions." Cambridge, Massachusetts: Pomegranate Press, 1974. Broadside. One of 100 signed copies in a total limitation of 180.

From the Cutting-room Floor. Omaha, Nebraska: Abbatoir Editions, University of Nebraska, 1983. Wrappers. One of 290 copies. The cover title reads "James Merrill with the shades of William Carlos Williams, Marianne Moore, Elvis Presley, Gertrude Stein, Mirabell, Maria Mitsotaki, Robert Morse, Wallace Stevens, and the angel Michael."

"From *McKane's Falls.*" Illustrated by Robert Perkins. New York: Glenn Horowitz, 1983. Broadside. One of 40 copies signed by the author and the artist.

"From *Mirabell.*" Charlottesville: Alderman Press, University of Virginia, 1978. Broadside. One of 100 copies.

"From a Notebook." N.p.: Privately printed for the author, 1961. Small broadside, "120 copies for the New Year." Inscribed by the author and enclosed in the original mailing envelope addressed to Kimon Friar.

"Hellen Plummer's brush with fame . . ." N.p.: Privately printed for the author, 1977. Poem card, published anonymously. One of approximately 100 copies reproducing the author's holograph and used by his mother as a thank-you for those who wrote to her on Merrill's receipt of the Pulitzer Prize for Poetry. A gift from Merrill to the Milberg Collection.

Ideas, Etc. Brooklyn, New York: Jordan Davies, 1980. Wrappers. One of 200 copies signed by Merrill.

The Inner Room. New York: Alfred A. Knopf, 1988. Dust jacket. Published at $16.95.

Late Settings: Poems. New York: Atheneum, 1985. Dust jacket. Published at $12.95.

Marbled Paper. Salem, Oregon: Rara Avis Press for Charles Seluzicki, 1982. Wrappers. One of 200 copies signed by the author. The illustrations were taken from photographs of funeral masks unearthed by Heinrich Schliemann at Mycenae.

Metamorphosis of 741. Pawlet, Vermont: Banyan Press, 1977. Wrappers. One of 440 copies.

Mirabell: Books of Number. New York: Atheneum, 1978. Dust jacket. Published at $10.95.

"More or Less." New York: DIA Center for the Arts, 1991. Folder, with a poem card laid in, announcing a reading by Merrill.

"1939. An American Woman Explores the Estate of Friends Who Have Fled France." Illustrated by Laurence Scott. Cambridge, Massachusetts: Lowell-Adams House Printers, 1965. Broadside. One of 50 copies signed by the artist.

"Orfeo." Winston-Salem, North Carolina: Palaemon Press, 1982. Broadside, signed by the author. Limitation not stated.

Overdue Pilgrimage to Nova Scotia. New York: Nadja, 1990. Wrappers, in printed dust jacket. One of 100 signed copies in a total limitation of 126.

Peter. Northampton, Massachusetts: Privately printed, 1972. Glassine dust jacket. Tributes to Peter Boynton by James Merrill, Richard Wilbur, William Meredith and others. Printed at the Gehenna Press in an edition of 110 copies.

Peter. Illustrations by Timothy Engelland. Old Deerfield, Massachusetts: Deerfield Press, 1982. Dust jacket. One of 300 copies signed by the author and hand colored by the illustrator.

"Pledge." London: Turret Bookshop, 1992. Broadside. Published by Bernard Stone and Raymond Danowski, July 1992. Reprinted from *Pequod* (New York, 1990). Not for sale.

Santorini: Stopping the Leak. Worcester, Massachusetts: Metacom Press, 1982. Wrappers. One of 300 copies signed by the author in a total limitation of 326.

Scripts for the Pageant. New York: Atheneum, 1980. Dust jacket. Published at $12.95.

"A Séance with W. H. Auden, from a Work in Progress." Illustrated by Marion Brody. N.p.: Lovell & Whyte, 1978. Broadside. One of 75 copies signed by the author.

Selected Poems. London: Chatto & Windus / Hogarth Press, 1961. Dust jacket. Published at 10s 6d. No comparable American edition.

Selected Poems, 1946–1985. New York: Alfred A. Knopf, 1992. Dust jacket. Published at $25.00.

"16. IX. 65." Illustrated by Laurence Scott. Boston: Impressions Workshop, 1968. Broadside. Limited to 100 copies, this one being an out-of-series artist's proof signed by the author and the artist.

"Snapshot of Adam." Illustrated by Laurence Scott. Cambridge, Massachusetts: Laurence Scott, 1984. Broadside. One of 60 copies signed by the author and the artist.

Souvenirs. New York: Nadja, 1984. Wrappers. One of 200 copies signed by the author in a total limitation of 226.

"Think Tank." Amherst, Massachusetts: Friends of Amherst College Library, 1983. Single sheet folded twice to make a greeting card. One of 450 copies. Signed by the author. In the original printed envelope, as issued.

Three Poems. Hod House, Child Okeford, Dorset, England: Words Press, 1988. Wrappers. One of 75 signed copies in a total limitation of 200. "Mir Poets Eleven."

To Remember J.J.J. Fourteen drawings by Jean Jones Jackson. With a poem by James Merrill and a note by John Bernard Myers. New York: Sea Cliff Press, 1985. Loose sheets contained in a cloth box as issued. One of 60 copies in a total limitation of 120.

"Trees Listening to Bach." Illustrated by Laurence Scott. Cambridge, Massachusetts: Laurence Scott, 1984. Broadside. One of 60 copies signed by the author and the artist.

Two Poems from The Cupola and The Summer People. London, Chatto and Windus / Hogarth Press, 1972. Dust jacket. No comparable American edition.

Violent Pastoral. Cambridge, Massachusetts, 1965. Wrappers. One of 100 copies "set and printed by hand by The Adams House & Lowell House Printers. . . ." Signed by the author. The photograph is by W. Krupsaw.

Voices from Sandover. N.p.: Privately printed for the author, 1989. Wrappers. Limitation not stated.

"Vol. XLIV, No. 3." New York: Sea Cliff Press, 1991. Poem card printed for the subscribers and friends of Sea Cliff Press, December 1991. In the original envelope.

Yannina. New York: Phoenix Book Shop, 1973. Wrappers. One of 100 signed copies in a total limitation of 126. "Phoenix Book Shop Oblong Octavo Series, No. 17."

The Yellow Pages: 59 Poems. Cambridge, Massachusetts: Temple Bar Bookshop, 1974. Boards; glassine dust jacket. One of 50 hardbound copies signed by the author in a total limitation of 800. Inscribed by the publisher.

↷ PROSE

Barbara Kassel: New Paintings. Introduction by James Merrill. New York: Maxwell Davidson Gallery, 1987. Wrappers. Illustrated in color. Catalogue for an exhibition of Kassel's paintings, 28 April – 30 May 1987.

The (Diblos) Notebook. New York: Atheneum, 1965. Dust jacket. Published at $4.50.

The Image Maker: A Play in One Act. New York: Sea Cliff Press, 1986. Boards. One of 220 copies signed by the author. The etching on the cover reproduces "The Image of the Miraculous St. Anthony," by José Guadalupe Posada.

"The Immortal Husband." In *Playbook: Five Plays for a New Theatre*. New York: New Directions, 1956. Dust jacket. Published at $3.75. The other authors are Lionel Abel, Robert Hivnor, Junjo Kinoshita, and I. A. Richards.

Japan: Prose of Departure. New York: Nadja, 1987. Wrappers. One of 74 copies signed by the author in a total limitation of 100 copies.

"National Book Award Acceptance Speech." New York, 1967. Two-page photocopy of the typescript. "Not Exact — 1967."

The Seraglio. New York: Alfred A. Knopf, 1957. Dust jacket. Published at $3.95. A novel.

The Seraglio. New York: Atheneum, 1987. Dust jacket. Published at $19.95. Reissue, with a new preface. Review copy with promotional material inserted.

Short Stories. Pawlet, Vermont: Banyan Press, 1954. Wrappers. Limited to 210 copies, 60 for sale and 150 for friends of the poet and the printer, Claude Fredericks. Inscribed by the author to Irma Brandeis, author of a book on Dante and the dedicatee of Merrill's poem "The 1002nd Night."

⤳ TRANSLATION

Three Poems, by C. P. Cavafy. Translated by James Merrill. West Chester, Pennsylvania: Aralia Press, 1987. Wrappers. One of 225 copies.

W. S. Merwin ∼

W. S. Merwin (b. 1927) ranges from a surrealist mode
reminiscent of André Breton, where images are drained
of substance and set free to flit rapidly on the courses of
the liminal—

> *Evening has brought its*
> *Mouse and let it out on the floor,*
> *On the wall, . . .*
>
> *You and your brothers*
> *Raise your knives to see by[1]*

—to a mode of descriptive ease perhaps equalled only by
Kenneth Rexroth and the poets of Sung China in which
language partakes of and verifies the immanent calm of falling
water and standing stone, about which nothing else need be
said:

> *in the stone frame high above the river*
> *looking out across the tops of plum trees*
> *tangle on the steep slope branches furred*
> *with green moss grey lichens the plums falling*
> *through them and beyond them the ancient*

> *walnut trees standing each alone on its*
> *own shadow²*

At these extremes of his voice, Merwin challenges conscious-
ness to bypass interpretation and become an open witness.

Merwin has also experimented with speakers whose voic-
es so uncannily become his that he seems at times to speak
from archetypal, rather than personal, experience. He is by
turns the young woman of "Departure's Girl-friend," carry-
ing a wreath to a ship of which she has been dispossessed,

> *. . . and the same fat chances roll*
> *Their many eyes; and I step once more*
> *Through a hoop of tears and walk on, holding this*
> *Buoy of flowers in front of my beauty,³*

and the shaman of "The Last One,"⁴ and the early explorer
and botanist David Douglas of "After Douglas":

> *. . . but not as a name unless*
> *perhaps as my*
>
> *name speaks of trees and trees do not know it.⁵*

These voices, as this last quotation says tellingly and
characteristically of Merwin, live out language's failure to
narrate. It is this quality, finally, that haunts us and calls us to
compassion, as in "Lives of the Artists," in which a youth who
was part of the 1877 Cheyenne escape from Fort Robinson
speaks about his drawings and their attempt to give domicile
to a dispossessed nation. Merwin shows us the open pages with
a bullet hole through them, in a museum, and against that
attempt to articulate a lost world,

> *. . . strangers*
> *pass and some of them pause there*
> *with all they know.⁶*

Merwin won the Pulitzer Prize in 1971 for *The Carrier of
Ladders*, and the Bollingen Prize in Poetry in 1979.

❧ POETRY

Apparitions: Poems by John Ashbery, Galway Kinnell, W. S. Merwin, L. M. Rosenberg, Dave Smith. Northridge, California: Lord John Press, 1981. Boards. One of 300 copies signed by each poet in a total limitation of 350.

Feathers from the Hill. Frontispiece by Kim Merker. Iowa City, Iowa: Windhover Press, 1978. Boards, glassine dust jacket. One of 270 copies signed by the author.

Finding the Islands. San Francisco: North Point Press, 1982. Dust jacket. Published at $11.00. Accompanied by a copy of the paperback issue in dust jacket, published at $6.00.

"For a Coming Extinction." Illustrated by Charles M. Scammon. Santa Cruz, California: Bookshop Santa Cruz, 1974. Broadside. Limitation not stated. Issued to celebrate "the migration of the California Gray Whale . . . Winter / Spring 1974 / 1975."

"Half the night sky deep cloud . . ." Anaheim, California: Toothpaste Press, 1982. Broadside. Limitation not stated. Printed as part of the Bookslinger exhibition at the 1982 A.B.A. convention.

"High Water." N.p.: Square Zero Editions, 1978. Broadside. One of 100 copies signed by the author.

KOA. New York: Nadja, 1988. Wrappers, in dust jacket. One of 74 copies signed by Merwin in a total limitation of 100 copies.

"Late Spring." Winston-Salem, North Carolina: Palaemon Press, 1984. Broadside, signed by the author. Limitation not stated.

The Lice: Poems. London: Rupert Hart-Davis, 1969. Dust jacket. Published at 25s.

Mary. New York: Nadja for Jordan Davies, 1976. Boards. One of 175 copies signed by the author.

One Story. New York: Nadja, 1989. Wrappers. "Printed in 1989 for the friends of Nadja. Best wishes from Carol Sturm & Douglas Wolf." No limitation stated.

"One Story." Berkeley, California: Black Oak Books, 1989. Broadside. Published as a gift on the occasion of a reading by Merwin.

Opening the Hand: Poems. New York: Atheneum, 1983. Dust jacket. Published at $13.95.

"Questions to Tourists Stopped by a Pineapple Field." N.p.: WBG / Headlands Press, 1989. Broadside. Limitation not stated but about 500 copies printed. "A Mokupuni Broadside."

The Rain in the Trees: Poems. New York: Alfred A. Knopf, 1988. Dust jacket. Published at $16.95.

The Second Four Books of Poems. Port Townsend, Washington: Copper Canyon Press, 1993. Paperback; not issued in cloth. Published at $14.00. First collected edition of *The Moving Target, The Lice, The Carrier of Ladders,* and *Writings to an Unfinished Accompaniment.*

Selected Poems. New York: Atheneum, 1988. Dust jacket. Published at $22.95.

"Strawberries." N.p.: Toothpaste Press for Bookslinger, 1981. Broadside. One of 90 signed copies printed for a reading at the Walker Art Center, 16 October 1981.

"Sun and Rain." N.p.: Square Zero Editions, 1979. Broadside. One of 100 copies in a total limitation of 126.

"Three Poems." Original linocuts by Steve Shrader. Honolulu: Petronium Press, 1975. Five loose sheets laid into paper wrappers. One of 75 signed copies.

"Tidal Lagoon." N.p.: Square Zero Editions, n.d. Broadside. One of 74 copies in a total limitation of 100.

"To Dana For Her Birthday." Illustrated by Andrew Rush. San Francisco: Intersection, 1981. Broadside. Limited to 100 copies signed by the author.

Travels: Poems. New York: Alfred A. Knopf, 1993. Dust jacket. Published at $20.00.

"Two Poems." N.p.: Solo Press Publishers, 1971. Broadside. One of 270 copies in a total limitation of 300. Printed at the Unicorn Press by Alan Brilliant.

"West Wall." N.p.: Square Zero Editions, 1983. Broadside. One of 100 copies signed by the author.

☞ PROSE

The Essential Wyatt. Selected and with an introduction by W. S. Merwin. New York: Ecco Press, 1989. Paperback; not issued in cloth. Published at $6.00. "The Essential Poets" series.

The Lost Upland. New York: Alfred A. Knopf, 1992. Dust jacket. Published at $22.00. Stories of Southwest France.

"On Receipt of P.E.N. Translation Award." New York: American Center of P.E.N., 1969. Wrappers. Contained in *The American Pen* 1, no. 1 (Summer 1969).

Regions of Memory: Uncollected Prose, 1949–82. Edited and with an introduction by Ed Folsom and Cary Nelson. Urbana: University of Illinois Press, 1987. Dust jacket.

Unframed Originals: Recollections. New York: Atheneum, 1982. Dust jacket. Published at $14.95.

⮞ TRANSLATIONS

Chinese Figures (Second Series). Mount Horeb, Wisconsin: Perishable Press, 1971. Wrappers. One of 75 copies in a total limitation of 120. "Printed on Shadwell papers made in the basement."

Four French Plays. Translations by W. S. Merwin. New York: Atheneum, 1985. Paperback, not issued in cloth. Published at $10.95.

From the Spanish Morning. Translations by W. S. Merwin. New York: Atheneum, 1985. Paperback, not issued in cloth. Published at $10.95.

Iphigeneia at Aulis, by Euripides. Translated by W. S. Merwin and George E. Dimock, Jr. Foreword by William Arrowsmith. New York: Oxford University Press, 1978. Dust jacket. Published at $8.50.

"Japanese Figures." Santa Barbara, California: Unicorn Press, 1971. "Poetry Post Card Series III, number 3." This copy has a signed autograph message from Merwin to C. K. Williams.

Japanese Figures. Santa Barbara, California: Unicorn Press, 1971. Wrappers. One of 250 copies signed by the author in a total limitation of 375.

The Life of Lazarillo de Tormes: His Fortunes and Adversities. Translated by W. S. Merwin. Introduction by Leonardo C. de Morelos. Garden City, New York: Doubleday, Anchor Books, 1962. Paperback; not published in cloth. Published at 95 cents.

The Peacock's Egg: Love Poems from Ancient India. Translated by W. S. Merwin and J. Moussaieff Masson. Introduction by J. Moussaieff Masson. San Francisco: North Point Press, 1981. Paperback, in dust jacket. Not issued in cloth. Published at $8.50.

The Poem of the Cid (El Poema del Mio Cid). A Verse Translation by W. S. Merwin. London: Dent, 1959. Dust jacket. No comparable American edition.

Products of the Perfected Civilization: Selected Writings of Chamfort. Translated with an introduction by W. S. Merwin. Foreword by Louis Kronenberger. New York: Macmillan, 1969. Dust jacket. Published at $7.50.

Robert the Devil. Translated by W. S. Merwin from an anonymous French play of the XIVth century. Wood engravings by Roxanne Sexauer. Iowa City, Iowa: Windhover Press, 1981. Boards. One of 275 copies in a total limitation of 310. Erratum slip loosely inserted.

The Satires of Persius. Translated by W. S. Merwin. Introduction and notes by William S. Anderson. Bloomington: Indiana University Press, 1961. Dust jacket.

Selected Poems of Osip Mandelstam. Translated by Clarence Brown and W. S. Merwin. Introduction by Clarence Brown. New York: Atheneum, 1974. Dust jacket. Published at $6.25.

Selected Translations, 1948–1968. New York: Atheneum, 1968. Dust jacket. Published at $5.95.

Selected Translations, 1968–1978. New York: Atheneum, 1979. Paperback. Not issued in cloth. Published at $6.95.

Sun at Midnight: 23 Poems, by Muso Soseki. Translated by W. S. Merwin with Soiku Shigematsu. Woodcuts by Antonio Frasconi. New York: Nadja, 1985. Wrappers. One of 200 copies signed by Merwin and Frasconi in a total limitation of 226.

Transparence of the World, by Jean Follain. Selected and translated by W. S. Merwin. New York: Atheneum, 1969. Dust jacket. Published at $6.95.

Twenty Love Poems and a Song of Despair, by Pablo Neruda. Translated by W. S. Merwin. London: Jonathan Cape, 1969. Wrappers in dust jacket. First British edition.

Vertical Poems, by Roberto Juarroz. Translated by W. S. Merwin. With drawings by Susana Wald. Santa Cruz, California: Kayak Books, 1977. Wrappers. One of 1,000 copies.

Voices, by Antonio Porchia. Translated by W. S. Merwin. Chicago: Big Table, 1969. Dust jacket. Published at $3.95.

Voices, by Antonio Porchia. Translated from the Spanish by W. S. Merwin. With drawings by Patrick Burke. Consigny, France: Embers Handpress, 1978. Wrappers in dust jacket. One of 26 copies signed by the author in a total limitation of 226. Accompanied by a copy of the trade edition, one of 200 copies.

Frederick Morgan

Frederick Morgan (b. 1922), founder and editor of *The Hudson Review*, published his first book of poetry, *A Book of Changes*, in 1972 at the age of fifty. The tremendous energy of this late flowering produced five volumes within a decade. Morgan's poems often blend fable or fairy tale with contemporary urban life, revealing that our daily existence still holds mysteries—glimmers of divinity or unconscious urges. What seems to have vanished, or to have ceased to exist, has a way of returning. A mermaid appears over Manhattan; uncouth centaurs behave outrageously at parties. Or, as in "When it rained and rained . . . ," the seemingly most ordinary childhood memory, his father's nightly return, expands hauntingly to include the adult poet as well as the little boy, running eagerly down the stairs of his subsequent life and back to this moment of union and shared language:

> *. . . and my father's voice*
> *rhythmic, searching*
> *rose up the stairwell*
> *calling a name,*
> *the name that was mine—*

> *and I cried out too*
> *naming him back*
> *in our secret tongue*
> *and ran down the deep*
> *stairway to find him:*
> *we met at the heart*
> *of the darkening house*
>
> *as evening set in . . . Soon*
> *the lights would go on.*[1]

For Morgan, poetry is both an act of faith and an act of communication. As Guy Davenport says, Morgan writes "with the age-old belief that poetry is a social bond, like language itself, and that poetry is the more meaningful for being public, transparent, and eloquent." Morgan's poetry is powerful because of "its brave anachronisms—grief sustained with religious conviction, love, loyalty, death, and all in the poet's own naked voice."[2] In fact, for Morgan the act of communication is an act of belief, a seeking out of the heart's understanding:

> *The saying changes what you have to say*
> *so that it all must be begun again*
> *in newer reconcilings of the heart.*[3]

❧ POETRY

Death Mother and Other Poems. Urbana: University of Illinois Press, 1979. Wrappers; published at $3.95. Also published in cloth.

Eleven Poems. New York: Nadja, 1983. Boards. One of 100 copies signed by the author in a total limitation of 126.

The Fountain & Other Fables. Cumberland, Iowa: Pterodactyl Press, 1984. Tissue dust jacket. One of 200 casebound copies in a total limitation of 1,000. Errata slip.

Northbook: Poems. Urbana: University of Illinois Press, 1982. Dust jacket. Published at $11.95.

Poems of the Two Worlds. Urbana: University of Illinois Press, 1977. Dust jacket. Published at $7.95.

Refractions. Omaha: Abbatoir Editions, University of Nebraska, 1981. Boards. One of 290 copies. Published at $25.00.

"Villanelle: The Christmas Tree." West Chester, Pennsylvania: Aralia Press, 1984. Christmas card, printed for Alysia, Brent, Dianne, and Michael Peich.

"The Walk." Illustrated by William Lint. Derry, Pennsylvania: Rook Press, 1976. Broadside. "Rook Folios 12." One of 250 copies signed by the author.

Howard Nemerov

Howard Nemerov (1920–1991) has a mordant wit, un-erringly lighting on the element in a scene that destroys our comfortable romantic illusions, forcing us to question our place in the world. In "The Goose Fish," for example, a romantic beach idyll is interrupted when the two lovers notice they are standing on the dead goose fish, who grins up at them, as if he has discovered their clandestine activity. Their attempts to make the fish into a readable symbol that they can incorporate into their romantic narrative are only half-successful:

> But never did explain the joke
> That so amused him, lying there
> While the moon went down to disappear
> Along the still and tilted track
> That bears the zodiac.[1]

Nemerov's serious joke is the difficulty, perhaps impossibility, of interpreting the natural world we are in relation with. Perhaps part of this difficulty comes from Nemerov's own tension between opposing impulses, which Willard Spiegelman has called "philosophical skepticism . . . and social satire on one side, and, on the other, an open-eyed, child-like appreciation of the world's miracles."[2] Thus the goose-fish does not merely prick the romantic balloon of the lovers; he also opens the possibility of a cosmic mystery.

Nemerov, who lived in Vermont for many years, saw himself as a medium for nature, expressing "an unknowably large part of a material world whose independent existence might be likened to that of the human unconscious, a sleep of causes, a chaos of the possible-impossible."[3] Or as he puts it in "A Spell before Winter":

> And I speak to you now with the land's voice,
> It is the cold, wild land that says to you
> A knowledge glimmers in the sleep of things . . .[4]

Nemerov emphasizes that our speech and writing are not sacred but, in fact, somewhat inglorious or embarrassing; yet they are at the same time our means of survival. In the quasi-biological "Life Cycle of the Common Man," the common man consumes energy mainly to talk, a fact that demonstrates both his absurdity and his bravery:

> Consider the courage in all that, and behold the man
> Walking into deep silence, with the ectoplastic
> Cartoon's balloon of speech proceeding
> Steadily out of the front of his face, the words
> Borne along on the breath which is his spirit
> Telling the numberless tale of his untold Word
> Which makes the world his apple, and forces him to eat.[5]

And in "Walking the Dog," Nemerov suggests first the disparity between human and other forms of life, then, comically, the similarity:

> Two universes mosey down the street
> Connected by love and a leash and nothing else.

But they share an "interest in shit . . . We move along the street inspecting it." After taking care of the dog's needs, "we both with dignity walk home / And just to show who's master I write the poem."[6]

In 1978 Nemerov won the National Book Award and the

Pulitzer Prize for *Collected Poems*. In 1981 he shared the Bollingen Prize in Poetry with May Swenson.

⪼ POETRY

"The Air Force Museum at Dayton." Winston-Salem, North Carolina: Palaemon Press, 1983. Broadside. Signed by the author. Limitation not stated.

The Blue Swallows: Poems. Chicago: University of Chicago Press, 1967. Dust jacket. Published at $4.50. Signed by the author on the title page.

By Al Lebowitz's Pool. New York: Nadja, 1979. Wrappers. One of 26 lettered and signed copies in a total limitation of 226.

Gnomes & Occasions: Poems. Chicago: University of Chicago Press, 1973. Dust jacket. Published at $5.95.

Gnomic Variations for Kenneth Burke: A Poem. Chapel Hill, North Carolina: Tinker Press, 1982. Wrappers. One of 40 copies signed by the author.

Guide to the Ruins: Poems. New York: Random House, 1950. Dust jacket. Published at $2.50. The author's presentation inscription appears on the title page.

The Image and the Law. New York: Henry Holt, 1947. Dust jacket. Published at $2.00. The author's first book.

Inside the Onion. Chicago: University of Chicago Press, 1984. Dust jacket.

"The Makers." Winston-Salem, North Carolina: Palaemon Press, 1980. Broadside. Signed by the author. Limitation not stated.

Mirrors & Windows: Poems. Chicago: University of Chicago Press, 1958. Dust jacket. Published at $2.75. The author's signature appears on the title page.

New & Selected Poems. Chicago: University of Chicago Press, 1960. Dust jacket. Published at $3.50. With the author's presentation inscription "To John" [Pauker].

The Next Room of the Dream: Poems and Two Plays. Chicago: University of Chicago Press, 1962. Dust jacket. Published at $5.00.

The Painter Dreaming in the Scholar's House. New York: Phoenix Book Shop, 1968. Wrappers. One of 26 lettered copies signed by the author in a total limitation of 126. Accompanied by one of 100 numbered and signed copies.

"Remembering the Way." St. Louis, Missouri: Washington University Libraries, 1985. Single sheet folded to make four pages. One of 50 signed copies in a total limitation of 300. "Published September 22, 1985 . . . on the occasion of the Howard Nemerov program for the Bookmark Society."

The Salt Garden: Poems. Boston: Little, Brown, 1955. Dust jacket. Published at $3.00. With the author's presentation inscription "To John and Gini" [Pauker].

Sentences. Chicago: University of Chicago Press, 1980. Dust jacket. Published at $8.95.

A Sequence of Seven. With a drawing by Ron Slaughter. Hollins College, Virginia: Tinker Press, 1967. Wrappers. One of 100 numbered copies.

"Small Moment." San Francisco: Poems in Folio, 1957. Broadside. One of 150 signed copies in a total limitation of 1,150. Accompanied by a copy of the prospectus.

"Small Moment." N.p.: Ward Ritchie Press, 1957. Broadside. One of 150 copies signed by the author.

A Spell Before Winter. With an illustration by Mary Moss Escalante. Madison, Wisconsin: Landlocked Press, 1981. Wrappers. One of 180 copies.

Trying Conclusions: New and Selected Poems, 1961–1991. Chicago: University of Chicago Press, 1991. Dust jacket. Published at $16.95.

War Stories: Poems about Long Ago and Now. Chicago: University of Chicago Press, 1987. Dust jacket. Published at $10.95.

The Western Approaches: Poems 1973–75. Chicago: University of Chicago Press, 1975. Dust jacket. Published at $7.95.

The Winter Lightning: Selected Poems. London: Rapp & Whiting, 1968. Dust jacket. Published at 21s. "Poetry USA, Series 2." Not published in the United States. Signed by the author on the title page.

❧ PROSE

A Commodity of Dreams & Other Stories. New York: Simon and Schuster, 1959. Dust jacket. Published at $3.75. Review slip inserted. Signed by the author on the title page.

Endor, Drama in One Act. New York: Abingdon Press, 1961. Wrappers. This copy is signed by the author.

Federigo; or, The Power of Love. Boston: Little, Brown, 1954. Dust jacket. Published at $3.75. Signed by the author on the title page.

Figures of Thought: Speculations on the Meaning of Poetry & Other Essays. Boston: David R. Godine, 1978. Dust jacket. Published at $15.00.

The Homecoming Game: A Novel. New York: Simon and Schuster, 1957. Dust jacket. Published at $3.50. Signed by the author on the title page.

A Howard Nemerov Reader. Columbia: University of Missouri Press, 1991. Dust jacket. Published at $24.95.

Journal of the Fictive Life. New Brunswick, New Jersey: Rutgers University Press, 1965. Dust jacket.

"Like Warp and Woof: Composition and Fate in the Short Novel." Unbound. Offprint from *The Graduate Journal* 5, no. 2 (Winter 1963).

The Melodramatists. New York: Random House, 1949. Dust jacket. Published at $3.00. Signed by the author on the title page.

New & Selected Essays. Introduction by Kenneth Burke. Carbondale: Southern Illinois University Press, 1985. Dust jacket.

The Oak in the Acorn: On Remembrance of Things Past, *and on Teaching Proust, Who Will Never Learn*. Baton Rouge: Louisiana State University Press, 1987. Dust jacket. Published at $16.95.

Poetry & Fiction: Essays. New Brunswick, New Jersey: Rutgers University Press, 1963. Dust jacket. Published at $7.50. Signed by the author on the title page.

Poets on Poetry, ed. Howard Nemerov. New York: Basic Books, 1966. Dust jacket. Published at $4.95.

Reflexions on Poetry & Poetics. New Brunswick, New Jersey: Rutgers University Press, 1972. Dust jacket. Published at $10.00

Stories, Fables & Other Diversions. Boston: David R. Godine, 1971. Dust jacket. Published at $7.50. Three thousand copies were printed.

"The Swaying Form: A Problem in Poetry." Wrappers. Offprint from *Michigan Alumnus Quarterly Review* 66, no. 10 (5 December 1959). Signed by Nemerov.

Frank O'Hara

Frank O'Hara (1926–1966), prolific art critic as well as poet, took from abstract expressionists like Jackson Pollock and Willem de Kooning a sense of art as process. He often composed quickly, jotting poems in his rare spare moments or during his lunch hour as a curator at the Museum of Modern Art. As John Ashbery comments in his introduction to *The Collected Poems of Frank O'Hara*, "His career stands as an unrevised work in progress."[1] In "Personism: A Manifesto," O'Hara rejects the notion of poetry as a fixed, highly crafted object placed on a pedestal, and restores it to its place in daily life—an activity neither more nor less important than eating lunch, loving, or going to the movies. He says of writing a particular poem, "I was realizing that if I wanted to I could use the telephone instead of writing the poem."[2]

This attitude freed O'Hara from the academic poetic climate of the late 1940s and early 1950s, which he and other members of the New York School found stultifying, and allowed him to create a new vernacular incorporating many influences, from Apollinaire's artless tone to John Cage's use of chance combination as a model for composition. O'Hara's inclusiveness extends to his concept of identity; in "In Memory of My Feelings" he asks for

> *Grace*
> *to be born and live as variously as possible. The conception*
> *of the masque barely suggests the sordid identifications.*
> *I am a Hittite in love with a horse. I don't know what*
> *blood's*
> *in me I feel like an African prince I am a girl walking*
> *downstairs*
> *in a red pleated dress with heels I am a champion taking a*
> *fall*
> *I am a jockey with a sprained ass-hole I am the light mist*
> *in which a face appears*[3]

O'Hara's "I do this I do that" poems, as he calls them in "Getting Up Ahead of Someone (Sun),"[4] recount in detail the sequence of his daily life, and include a variety of "unpoetic" materials such as newspaper headlines, trivia from the lives of movie stars, train schedules, and the contents of his pockets.

His poetry of experience chronicles a mixture of familiarity and estrangement, as in the end of "Music":

> *As they're putting up the Christmas trees on Park Avenue*
> *I shall see my daydreams walking by with dogs in blankets,*
> *put to some use before all those colored lights come on!*
> *But no more fountains and no more rain,*
> *and the stores stay open terribly late.*[5]

O'Hara died at the age of forty after being hit by a dune buggy on Fire Island. *The Collected Poems of Frank O'Hara* won the National Book Award in 1972.

ᐳ POETRY

Belgrade, November 19, 1963. New York: Adventures in Poetry, ca. 1973. Wrappers. One of 500 copies.

The Collected Poems of Frank O'Hara, ed. Donald Allen with an introduction by John Ashbery. New York: Alfred A.

Knopf, 1971. With the suppressed first issue dust jacket featuring Larry Rivers's portrait of the nude O'Hara. Published at $17.50.

"Down at the Box-Office . . ." Bolinas, California: Yanagi IV, 1977. Broadside. Limitation not stated but approximately 300 copies were printed.

The End of the Far West: 11 Poems. Preface by Ted Berrigan. Wivenhoe, England: Ted Berrigan, 1974. Wrappers. The first edition of these poems; they were not included in *The Selected Poems, 1974*.

Four Dialogues for Two Voices and Two Pianos. Music by Ned Rorem. New York: Boosey & Hawkes, 1969. Wrappers. Covers by Joe Brainard.

"Hotel particulier." Pleasant Valley, New York: Kriya Press of Sri Ram Ashram, 1967. Broadside. One of 100 copies.

Hymns of St. Bridget, by Bill Berkson and Frank O'Hara. Cover by Larry Rivers. New York: Adventures in Poetry, 1974. Wrappers.

In Memory Of My Feelings: A Selection of Poems, ed. Bill Berkson. New York: Museum of Modern Art, 1967. Loose signatures in slipcase as issued. One of 2,500 copies. Original decorations by Jasper Johns, Roy Lichtenstein, Robert Motherwell and others.

Lament and Chastisement: A Travelogue of War and Personality. New York: Simon Schuchat, 1977. Wrappers. Complete issue of *The 4 3 2 Review*. Carl Rakosi's copy with his signature.

Love Poems (Tentative Title). New York: Tibor de Nagy Editions, 1965. Wrappers. One of 500 copies.

Lunch Poems. San Francisco: City Lights Books, 1964. Wrappers. Published at $1.25. "The Pocket Poets Series Number Nineteen." Five hundred copies were printed.

"Macaroni," together with Patsy Southgate's "In
   Memoriam." Calais, Vermont: Z Press, 1974. Broadside.
   Limitation not stated.

Meditations in an Emergency. New York: Grove Press, 1957.
   Wrappers. Published at $1.00. There was also a
   hardbound numbered edition.

Odes. New York: Poets Press, 1969. Wrappers.

Poems Retrieved. Bolinas, California: Grey Fox Press, 1977.
   Not issued in dust jacket. One of only 201 copies
   bound in boards.

Second Avenue. New York: Totem Press, 1960. Wrappers.
   Published at 95 cents. First issue, with the cover
   printed in red and black and with the publisher's name
   at the bottom of the copyright page.

The Selected Poems, ed. Donald Allen. New York: Random
   House, 1974. Dust jacket.

Two Pieces. London: Long Hair Books, 1969. Wrappers.

❧ PROSE

Art Chronicles, 1954–1966. New York: George Braziller,
   1975. Dust jacket. Published at $12.50. Illustrated.

Art with the Touch of a Poet: Frank O'Hara. Storrs,
   Connecticut: University of Connecticut, 1983.
   "Exhibition Companion" for this exhibition,
   containing a number of loose sheets and pamphlets by
   or about O'Hara. Contained in a printed envelope.

Awake in Spain. New York: American Theatre for Poets,
   1960. Mimeographed sheets, stapled.

Early Writing, ed. Donald Allen. Bolinas, California: Grey
   Fox Press, 1977. Not issued in dust jacket. One of only
   201 copies bound in boards.

Nakian. New York: Museum of Modern Art, 1966. Dust jacket. Published at $4.95.

New Spanish Painting and Sculpture. New York: Museum of Modern Art, 1960. Wrappers. Illustrated.

Oranges. Cover by George Schneeman. New York: Angel Hair Books, n.d. Wrappers. One of 200 copies. Second edition, after the rare first edition of approximately 20 copies issued in conjunction with an exhibition at the Tibor de Nagy Gallery in 1953.

Robert Motherwell, with Selections from the Artist's Writings. New York: Museum of Modern Art, 1965. Dust jacket. Illustrated.

Selected Plays. New York: Full Court Press, 1978. Dust jacket. Published at $9.95.

Robert Pinsky

Robert Pinsky (b. 1940) is a discursive poet suspicious of our apparent certainties—our sense of our own benevolence, our denial of complicity in atrocities of taste or of human cruelty. Love, memory, even faith in the power of the intellect to control and understand, are all questioned. "In Pinsky," Barry Goldensohn writes, "apparent simplicity is the invitation to troubling complexity. It is an attractive movement of the mind: finding exceptions to simple rules, unexpected textures to smooth surfaces, division and ambivalence to simple feelings."[1] Pinsky seems to be searching for *how to feel*, once we question our myths of feeling. How constitutive are those myths? To what degree have they become our truth? He is an adept reader of popular culture, refraining from an attempt to explain what it means to us while drawing out the comedy and pathos of its emptiness and ours.

As a graduate student at Stanford, Pinsky worked with poet-critic Yvor Winters, and has absorbed his discursive mode while questioning his reach for moral certitude. In the long sequence "Essay on Psychiatrists," the psychiatrists are "the first citizens of contingency"; Winters himself is the old man who believes that

> Sometime in the middle
Of the Eighteenth Century . . .
> the logical
Foundations of Western thought decayed and fell apart.
When they fell apart, poets were left
>
> With emotions and experiences, and with no way
To examine them.[2]

Pinsky falls somewhere in the middle, finding ways "to examine them" that redefine truth.

An Explanation of America, for example, attempts not so much to analyze as to allow the presence of the dream-like images of consumer culture and the historical myths that define America to emerge. Addressing his eldest daughter, he muses about how we are part of a reality we have collectively made:

> A country is the things it wants to see.
If so, some part of me, though I do not,
Must want to see these things . . .
. . . I want to see the anthropomorphic
Animals drawn for children, as represented
By people in smiling masks and huge costumes.
I want to shake their hands . . .
I want our country like a common dream
To be between us in what we want to see—[3]

The only truths Pinsky relies on are a basic will to live and a leveling, impersonal force of change. "The Figured Wheel" is such a force:

> It is Jesus oblivious to hurt turning to give words to the
>> unrighteous,
> And it is also Gogol's feeding pig that without knowing it
>> eats a baby chick
>
> And goes on feeding . . .[4]

and in the title poem from *The Want Bone*, the dried mouth bones on the beach—all that remains of a shark—are the symbol of the unending desire to live. The flesh is gone, "Infinitesimal mouths bore it away"; but

The joined arcs made the shape of birth and craving
And the welded-open shape kept mouthing O.
. . . O I love you it sings, my little my country
My food my parent my child I want you my own
My flower my fin my life my lightness my O.[5]

⤳ POETRY

An Explanation of America. Princeton: Princeton University Press, 1979. Dust jacket. "Princeton Series of Contemporary Poets."

"The Garden." Berkeley, California: Black Oak Books, 1984. Broadside. No limitation stated. From *History of My Heart.*

"Ginza Samba." Columbus, Ohio: Logan Elm Press & Papermill, 1991. Broadside printed on the occasion of Pinsky's residency in the Creative Writing Program at Ohio State University, Fall 1991. One of 200 copies signed by the author.

History of My Heart. New York: Ecco Press, 1984. Dust jacket. Published at $12.50.

Sadness and Happiness: Poems. Princeton: Princeton University Press, 1975. Dust jacket.

The Want Bone. New York: Ecco Press, 1990. Dust jacket. Published at $17.95.

⤳ PROSE

Landor's Poetry. Chicago: University of Chicago Press, 1968. Dust jacket. The author's first book.

Poetry and the World. New York: Ecco Press, 1988. Dust jacket. Published at $19.95.

The Situation of Poetry: Contemporary Poetry and Its Traditions.
Princeton: Princeton University Press, 1978. First
paperback edition. A gift from the author.

ᴤ TRANSLATIONS

"Incantation," by Czeslaw Milosz. Translated by the author
and Robert Pinsky. Berkeley, California: Black Oak
Books, 1983. Broadside. New Year's gift from the
publisher. Limitation not stated.

The Separate Notebooks, by Czeslaw Milosz. Translated by
Robert Hass and Robert Pinsky, with the author and
Renata Gorczynski. New York: Ecco Press, 1984. Dust
jacket. Published at $17.50.

Sylvia Plath ❧

Sylvia Plath (1932–1963), more than Robert Lowell, Anne Sexton, or John Berryman, turned an obsession with death into poetic material. *Ariel*, published two years after she committed suicide at the age of thirty, includes the work of her last months of intense output, when she often composed two or three poems a day. These are poems of explosive feelings under intense compression, which Lowell called "controlled hallucination, the autobiography of a fever,"[1] and of which Sexton said, "These last poems stun me. They eat time."[2] Poems like "Lady Lazarus" and "Daddy" derive much power from the almost vicious sarcasm with which they handle excruciating pain:

> *Dying*
> *Is an art, like everything else.*
> *I do it exceptionally well.*
>
> *I do it so it feels like hell.*
> *I do it so it feels real.*
> *I guess you could say I've a call.*[3]

Plath's late poems incorporate the playful virtuosity of her early work and the more onomatopoetic, earthy style, influenced by Ted Hughes, that she adopted in the mid to late 1950s. In the late work, every sound counts, whether it is a savage, obsessive repetition of the same rhyme, as in the passage quoted above, or in "Daddy," or a complex and subtle music that becomes a language of emotion hovering on the verge of sense, as in "Sheep in Fog":

> O slow
> Horse the color of rust,
>
> Hooves, dolorous bells—
> All morning the
> Morning has been blackening,
>
> A flower left out.
> My bones hold a stillness, the far
> Fields melt my heart.[4]

While Plath unquestionably fed creatively on her own darkest emotions, it is important not to portray her as a doomed soul whose artistic consummation also represented her own undoing. As Marjorie Perloff has recently written, this myth has been aided by Ted Hughes's construction of *Ariel*, which changed Plath's intended order and created a sense of gradual and inevitable progression toward suicide.[5] In her last autumn she was also capable of hope, as she wrote alone in her London flat after separating from Hughes; in "Wintering," part of her Bee Sequence, she observes a group of female bees sleepily waiting out the winter in a small, dark space, in "a time of hanging on," and asks,

> Will the hive survive, will the gladiolas
> Succeed in banking their fires
> To enter another year?
> What will they taste of, the Christmas roses?
> The bees are flying. They taste the spring.[6]

Plath won the Pulitzer Prize posthumously in 1982 for *The Collected Poems*.

﹋ POETRY

Above the Oxbow: Selected Writings. Original wood engravings by Barry Moser. Northampton, Massachusetts: Catawba Press, 1985. Boards. One of 325 copies signed by the artist.

The Bed Book. Illustrations by Quentin Blake. London: Faber and Faber, 1976. Dust jacket. Published at £1.50. Precedes the American edition, which has different illustrations.

Collected Poems. Edited, and with an introduction, by Ted Hughes. London: Faber and Faber, 1981. Dust jacket. Published at £10.00.

The Colossus: Poems. London: Heinemann, 1960. Dust jacket. Published at 15s. The author's first commercially published book. The dust jacket reads "The Colossus and Other Poems."

Crossing the Water: Transitional Poems. New York: Harper & Row, 1971. Dust jacket. Published at $5.95. Differs from the English edition.

Dialogue Over a Ouija Board: A Verse Dialogue. With a drawing by Leonard Baskin. Cambridge, England: Rainbow Press, 1981. Wrappers. One of 100 copies in a total limitation of 140. Printed at the Rampant Lions Press. In slipcase as issued.

The Green Rock. Ely, England: Embers Handpress, 1982. Wrappers. One of 160 copies. Accompanied by one of six copies in a special envelope.

Lyonnesse: Poems. London: Rainbow Press, 1971. Boards, leather spine, in slipcase as published. One of 300 copies in a total limitation of 400. Printed by Will and Sebastian Carter at the Rampant Lions Press, Cambridge. Accompanied by a copy of the prospectus, a single sheet printed on both sides.

"Mirror." Loanhead, Midlothian, England: Tragara Press, 1966. Single leaf, printed on both sides. Accompanied by a holograph note on the letterhead of the Tragara Press: "Mirror by Sylvia Plath. This leaflet was set and printed by me on 1 January 1966. Some ten copies only were produced, and given to friends. Alan Anderson."

Stings: Original Drafts of the Poem in Facsimile. With an essay by Susan R. Van Dyne. Northampton, Massachusetts: Smith College Library, 1982. Wrappers. One of 5,000 copies.

Three Women. N.p., n.d. Wrappers. The pirated American edition.

Two Uncollected Poems. London: Anvil Press, 1980. Wrappers. One of 450 copies printed for subscribers.

Winter Trees. London: Faber and Faber, 1971. Dust jacket. Published at £1.00. First English edition, preceding the American publication. With a note by Ted Hughes. The contents of the English and American editions differ considerably.

Winter Trees. New York: Harper & Row, 1972. Dust jacket. Published at $5.95. First American edition, preceded by the English edition. With a note by Ted Hughes. Differs from the English edition.

❧ PROSE

The Bell Jar, by Victoria Lucas. London: Heinemann, 1963. Dust jacket. Published at 18s. A novel published under the pseudonym "Victoria Lucas."

A Day in June: An Uncollected Short Story. Ely, England: Embers Handpress, 1981. Wrappers. One of 82 copies on Hayle in a total limitation of 160.

Johnny Panic and the Bible of Dreams, and Other Prose Writings. Introduction by Ted Hughes. London: Faber and Faber, 1977. Dust jacket. Published at £4.95. Both the contents and Hughes's introduction differ from the American edition of 1979.

Johnny Panic and the Bible of Dreams: Short Stories, Prose and Diary Excerpts. Introduction by Ted Hughes. New York: Harper & Row, 1979. Dust jacket. Published at $10.95.

The Magic Mirror: A Study of the Double in Two of Dostoevsky's Novels. Rhiwargor, Llanwddyn, Powys, Wales: Embers Handpress, 1989. One of 50 specially bound copies in a total limitation of 226. In slipcase as issued. *The Magic Mirror* was submitted in partial fulfillment of the requirements of Special Honors in English at Smith College, Northampton, Massachusetts, in 1955.

Adrienne Rich 🖋

For more than twenty-five years, Adrienne Rich (b. 1929) has been exploring the ways in which political commitment, personal emotional truth, and poetic language are inseparable. Language is a tool that enables women, or any oppressed group, to recover authentic experience:

> *I came to explore the wreck.*
> *The words are purposes.*
> *The words are maps.*[1]

Beginning as a formal poet who looked to male literary tradition in *A Change of World* and *The Diamond Cutters*, Rich moved in the late 1950s and 1960s toward writing directly out of her own experience as a woman. The social ferment of the 1960s coincided with Rich's personal upheaval and transformation as woman and poet, and the two are linked in poems such as "The Burning of Paper Instead of Children," in which personal and political change are chaotic, potentially destructive but necessary forces. Something needs to be destroyed in the language so that it is no longer only "the oppressor's language": "Some of the suffering are: it is hard to tell the truth; this is America; I cannot touch you now. . . . I know it hurts to burn. The typewriter is overheated, my mouth is burning, I cannot touch you and this is the oppressor's language."² Intentionally stretching syntax, including prose, stripping and simplifying her imagery, Rich gives her language an urgency that is sometimes raw, sometimes supple.

In 1970 Rich identified herself as a radical feminist and lesbian, and began to explore the complexities of sexual identity in her work. In "Diving into the Wreck," the diver becomes both male and female, in uncharted waters where myth and identity can be redefined, made plural, made multivalent:

> We are, I am, you are
> by cowardice or courage
> the one who find our way
> back to this scene
> carrying a knife, a camera
> a book of myths
> in which
> our names do not appear.³

Rich's *Twenty-One Love Poems*, a loose sonnet sequence, charts the progress, and eventual end, of a lesbian love affair. This is no idealized, static love, but one which accepts the passing of time, the importance of history (personal and otherwise) in a relationship, the difficulty of being with another person:

> If I could let you know—
> two women together is a work
> nothing in civilization has made simple,
> two people together is a work
> heroic in its ordinariness,
> the slow-picked, halting traverse of a pitch
> where the fiercest attention becomes routine
> —look at the faces of those who have chosen it.⁴

In 1974 Rich won the National Book Award for *Diving into the Wreck: Poems 1971–1972*.

☙ POETRY

Adrienne Cecile Rich. Swinford, Eynsham, Oxon, England: Fantasy Press, 1952. Wrappers. "The Fantasy Poets Number Twelve."

Adrienne Rich's Poetry: Texts of the Poems, the Poet on Her Work, Reviews and Criticism, ed. Barbara and Albert Gelpi. New York: W. W. Norton, 1975. Paperback; not issued in cloth. "A Norton Critical Edition."

"Amends." Etching by Mary Warshaw. Santa Cruz, California: Moving Parts Press, 1991. Broadside, designed by Felicia Rice. One of 250 copies, this being one of only 50 copies signed by the author, the artist, and the designer. The information on limitation was supplied by the publisher.

Ariadne: A Play in Three Acts, and Poems. N.p.: Privately printed, 1939. Wrappers. The author's first book with her presentation inscription "To Dr. Sabin from Adrienne, Xmas 1939." Loosely inserted is a two-page holograph letter from the author's father describing the private printing of the book.

An Atlas of the Difficult World: Poems 1988–1991. New York: W. W. Norton, 1991. Dust jacket. Published at $17.95.

"Aunt Jennifer's Tigers." London: Poems on the Underground, 1990. Broadside poster.

A Change of World. Foreword by W. H. Auden. New Haven, Connecticut: Yale University Press, 1951. Dust jacket. Published at $2.50. Volume 48 of the "Yale Series of Younger Poets." Only 551 copies were printed.

Collected Early Poems, 1950–1970. New York: W. W. Norton, 1993. Dust jacket. Published at $27.50.

The Diamond Cutters and Other Poems. New York: Harper & Brothers, 1955. Dust jacket. Published at $2.75.

Diving into the Wreck: Poems 1971–1972. New York: W. W. Norton, 1973. Dust jacket. Published at $5.95.

The Dream of a Common Language: Poems 1974–1977. New York: W. W. Norton, 1978. Dust jacket. Published at $9.95.

The Fact of a Doorframe: Poems Selected and New 1950–1984. New York: W. W. Norton, 1984. Dust jacket. Published at $18.95.

"For an Album." Berkeley, California: Black Oak Books, 1989. Broadside. One of 200 copies printed to benefit "A Safe Place: Shelter for Battered Women."

Leaflets: Poems 1965–1968. New York: W. W. Norton, 1969. Dust jacket. Published at $4.95.

Necessities of Life: Poems 1962–1965. New York: W. W. Norton, 1966. Dust jacket. Published at $4.50.

Not I, but Death: A Play in One Act. N.p.: Privately printed, J. H. Furst, 1941. Boards, not issued in dust jacket. Rich's second and rarest book, a play in verse published when she was twelve years old. Inscribed to "Dearest Miss Preston," and accompanied by a holograph poem on a separate sheet of paper.

Poems Selected and New 1950–1974. New York: W. W. Norton, 1975. Dust jacket.

Selected Poems. London: Chatto & Windus / Hogarth Press, 1967. Dust jacket. Published at 18s. "The Phoenix Living Poets Series." No comparable American edition.

Snapshots of a Daughter-in-Law: Poems 1954–1962. New York: Harper & Row, 1963. Dust jacket.

Snapshots of a Daughter-in-Law: Poems 1954–1962. Revised edition. New York: W. W. Norton, 1967. Dust jacket. This edition contains some revisions and one hitherto unpublished poem.

"Song." N.p.: Golemics #2, n.d. Broadside. Limitation not stated.

"Song." Drawing by Leslie Walsh. Claremont, California: Scripps College Press, 1983. Broadside. One of 200 copies, this one signed by the author.

Sources. Frontispiece by Carole Romans. Woodside, California: Heyeck Press, 1983. Boards. One of 300 copies signed by the author.

Time's Power: Poems 1985–1988. New York: W. W. Norton, 1989. Dust jacket. Published at $15.95.

Twenty-One Love Poems. Emeryville, California: Effie's Press, 1976. One of 26 lettered copies, clothbound and signed by the author. Accompanied by a copy of the trade edition, one of 1,000 copies bound in wrappers.

"Upcountry." Woodside, California: Heyeck Press, 1984. Broadside printed on marbled paper. One of 100 copies.

"White Night." Illustrated by Karyl Klopp. North Cambridge, Massachusetts: Pomegranate Press, 1975. Broadside. One of 80 copies in a total limitation of 180. This copy is signed by the illustrator.

A Wild Patience Has Taken Me This Far: Poems 1978–1981. New York: W. W. Norton, 1981. Dust jacket. Published at $12.95.

Your Native Land, Your Life: Poems. New York: W. W. Norton, 1986. Dust jacket. Published at $14.95.

⌘ **PROSE**

Blood, Bread, and Poetry: Selected Prose 1979–1985. New York: W. W. Norton, 1986. Dust jacket. Published at $15.95.

Compulsory Heterosexuality and Lesbian Existence. Denver, Colorado: Antelope Publications, 1982. Wrappers. Published at $3.00.

The Meaning of Our Love for Women Is What We Have Constantly to Expand. Brooklyn, New York: Out & Out Books, 1977. Wrappers. Published at $1.00. "New York Lesbian Pride Rally June 26, 1977."

Of Woman Born: Motherhood as Experience and Institution. New York: W. W. Norton, 1976. Dust jacket. Published at $8.95.

On Lies, Secrets, and Silence: Selected Prose 1966–1978. New York: W. W. Norton, 1979. Dust jacket. Published at $13.95.

Women and Honor: Some Notes on Lying. Pittsburgh: Motheroot Publications, 1977. Wrappers. Published at $1.25.

❧ TRANSLATION

Poems, by Ghalib. Translated by Aijaz Ahmad with William Stafford and Adrienne Rich. Forenote by Aijaz Ahmad. New York: Hudson Review, 1969. Wrappers. Published at 50 cents.

James Richardson

James Richardson (b. 1950) is a professor of English who has also directed the Creative Writing Program at Princeton University. He appears to have incorporated the intensely felt natural image of the Deep Image poets and the surrealist nihilism of Charles Simic and Mark Strand into his own metaphysical style, at once vivid and discursive. Amy Clampitt calls his *As If* an homage to Wallace Stevens, "but also a dialogue with this great exemplar on what is to become of the lyric impulse in a time so unmistakably Post-Romantic."[1] Richardson draws on deep feeling and a deep connection to the natural world, but these provide no certainty, no fixed perspective. "Post-Romantic" plays on the two meanings of romantic, casting his relationship to nature as a failed love affair:

> Now that it's over
> between me and Nature
> I like her better.
> We've given up
> senseless fear,
> useless hope.
> She's got herself together.

In place of exaggerated emotion and a desperate desire for unity there is

> . . . the old courtesy
> of life for life,
> when sometimes, often,
> out for nothing,
> I stop for a minute
> to hear our songs
> high up, crossing.[2]

In the "To Autumn" section of *As If*, Richardson works through the pain and uncertainty of lost love at an oblique angle in the precise examination of natural phenomena, as in "Anyway," where he watches how things do and undo themselves, "The way an acre of starlings towers and pours / rapidly through itself, a slipping knot. . . ."[3] In these poems being itself is uncertain, threatened by changes in perspective, shifts in perception, as in "Blue Heron, Winter Thunder," where he sees "those hours-long clouds" as "great fish" in an ocean he is at the bottom of. They

> cruised over, soundless, or larger than hearing,
> or in the astonishment of congratulation,
> and I breathed thickly, safe at my depth.[4]

His diction ("larger than hearing") seems at once dislocated and accurate.

A letting-go in the face of these shifts is an important part of Richardson's approach. In "Cat Among Stones," as in some poems of James Wright, the self surrenders to nature and is consumed into a brightly burning core:

> . . . If it stepped across your back
> you would deepen, limbless as a pond,
> and go dark, all your thought
> a match flame at the end of a hall,
> wavering, stretched, righting itself.[5]

"The Will" is about the play between asserting the will and surrendering it, about the contingency of possession.

I,
being of sound,
do hereby take this time to tell you
what is left of the dead.
All my worldly possessions I leave
to themselves.[6]

☙ POETRY

As If. New York: Persea Books, 1992. Paperback; published at $9.95. Not published in cloth. "The National Poetry Series, Selected by Amy Clampitt."

Reservations: Poems. Princeton: Princeton University Press, 1977. Dust jacket. "Princeton Series of Contemporary Poets." The author's first book.

Second Guesses: Poems. Middletown, Connecticut: Wesleyan University Press, 1984. Dust jacket. Published at $17.00.

Theodore Roethke

Theodore Roethke (1908–1963), whose father owned the largest greenhouses in Michigan, felt an intimate connection to natural processes and objects: "I could say hello to things."[1] His poetry is an evolving exchange between nature and the human soul, in which human consciousness is articulated and transformed by remaining open to its environment. Playfully alluding to T. S. Eliot's celebrated essay, "The Metaphysical Poets," Roethke quotes a line from one of his own poems to describe the physical nature of this process: "'We think by feeling. What is there to know?' This . . . is a description of the metaphysical poet who thinks with his body: an idea for him can be as real as the smell of a flower or a blow on the head."[2] Or, more humorously, in his notebooks: "Look, I'm not neurotic: or making things up or inducing these symbols. These things happen to a human body."[3] Thus in "Cuttings," from his ground-breaking second volume, *The Lost Son*, Roethke presents the growth process of plant cuttings; and then in "Cuttings (*later*)" describes the human body and soul as cuttings:

> *I can hear, underground, that sucking and sobbing,*
> *In my veins, in my bones I feel it,—*

> *The small waters seeping upward,*
> *The tight grains parting at last.*
> *When sprouts break out,*
> *Slippery as fish,*
> *I quail, lean to beginnings, sheath-wet.*[4]

In *The Lost Son*, Roethke makes the greenhouses of his youth a psychic realm, "both heaven and hell," in which to explore psychological pain and spiritual growth. Roethke, who suffered from periodic mental breakdowns for most of his adult life, said of *Praise to the End!* and its sequence of interior monologues, ". . . [each poem] is a stage in a kind of struggle out of the slime; part of a slow spiritual progress; an effort to be born, and later, to become something more."[5]

David Wagoner, who studied with Roethke at the Pennsylvania State University, remembers his saying, "Motion is equal to emotion."[6] In Roethke's last volume, *The Far Field* (published posthumously), consciousness moves fluidly, and often hopefully, between the physical and the metaphysical:

> *The river turns on itself,*
> *The tree retreats into its own shadow,*
> *I feel a weightless change, a moving forward,*
> *As of water quickening before a narrowing channel*
> *When banks converge, and the wide river whitens . . .*[7]

Here a limpid description of moving water is at the same time a description of a life and a mind. "My mind moves in more than one place, / in a country that is half-land, half-water." And, in these last published lines of poetry:

> *And everything comes to One,*
> *As we dance on, dance on, dance on.*[8]

Roethke won the Pulitzer Prize in 1954 for *The Waking* and the Bollingen Prize in Poetry in 1959. He won the National Book Award in 1959 for *Words for the Wind* and in 1965 for *The Far Field*.

❧ POETRY

The Collected Poems. Garden City, New York: Doubleday, 1966. Dust jacket. Published at $5.95. Probable first issue with blue endpapers (sometimes found with white endpapers). Eighty-five hundred copies were printed.

"The Exorcism." Illustrated by Mallette Dean. San Francisco: Poems in Folio, 1957. Broadside. Limitation not stated but 1,150 copies were printed.

The Far Field. Garden City, New York: Doubleday, 1964. Dust jacket. Published at $3.50. Twenty-five hundred copies were printed.

Open House. New York: Alfred A. Knopf, 1941. Dust jacket. Published at $2.00. The author's first book. This copy bears Roethke's presentation inscription on the title page. One thousand copies were printed.

Praise to the End! Garden City, New York: Doubleday, 1951. Dust jacket. Published at $3.00. Seven hundred fifty copies were printed.

"The Right Thing." San Francisco: Marianne Hinckle, 1988. Broadside. A greeting for the Spring of 1988. Limitation not stated.

Words for the Wind. London: Secker & Warburg, 1957. Dust jacket. Published at 15s. Precedes the American edition, which was not published until 1958. "Poetry Book Society Christmas Choice."

❧ PROSE

On the Poet and His Craft: Selected Prose. Edited with an introduction by Ralph J. Mills, Jr. Seattle: University of Washington Press, 1965. Dust jacket. Published at $3.95. Six thousand copies were printed.

Selected Letters. Edited with an introduction by Ralph J. Mills, Jr. Seattle: University of Washington Press, 1968. Dust jacket. Published at $6.95. Five thousand copies were printed.

Straw for the Fire: From the Notebooks of Theodore Roethke, 1943–63. Selected and arranged by David Wagoner. Garden City, New York: Doubleday, 1972. One of 250 numbered copies. Issued without dust jacket. In slipcase and cardboard mailing box as published. Accompanied by a copy of the trade edition in dust jacket, published at $7.95.

James Schuyler

James Schuyler (1923–1991), poet, novelist, and play-
wright, links the natural world with urban images and
subtle emotional states through a string of breathtaking
associative jumps that assert themselves as the natural structure
of perception:

> the clouds
> hang in a traffic jam: summer
> heads home.[1]

Like Frank O'Hara, Schuyler worked at the Museum of
Modern Art and wrote criticism for *Art News*; but his models
in painting are more realist than abstract expressionist, and he
counts Elizabeth Bishop and Marianne Moore as poetic influ-
ences in their devotion to natural detail for its own sake.
Schuyler says, "To me, much of poetry is as concerned with
looking at things and trying to transcribe them as painting is."[2]
His transcribing is meticulous but never dull, and it derives
accuracy from the freedom of movement in its element, like
the fishes in his "Closed Gentian Distances": "Little fish
stream / by, a river in water."[3]

At the end of the title poem of *The Crystal Lithium*, which
is structured by a continual shifting of images, Schuyler

suggests, in a great ocean swell of language and image, that we can only know—each other, the natural world—by staying open to the shifting, the "unchanging change":

> . . . *and we stare at or*
> *into each*
> *Other's eyes in hope the other reads there what he reads:*
> *snow, wind*
> *Lifted; black water, slashed with white; and that which is,*
> *which is beyond*
> *Happiness or love or mixed with them or more than they or*
> *less, unchanging change,*
> *"Look," the ocean said (it was tumbled, like our sheets),*
> *"look into my eyes."*

A good example of his technique, "in which the scattered nature of experience is given, a catalogue of disparate phenomena, held in place like an assembly of restless lions by the trainer's commanding eye,"[4] is "Blizzard." The act of writing is a perpetual going forward, a kind of abandonment: "Tearing and tearing / ripped-up bits of paper, / no, it's not paper / it's snow."

> *"Mr. Park called. He*
> *can't come visiting*
> *today." Of course not,*
> *in this driving icy*
> *weather. How I wish*
> *I were out in it! A*
> *figure like an ex-*
> *clamation point seen*
> *through driving snow.*[5]

The poem itself is driven by associations flying thick and fast: from the driving Mr. Park cannot do, to the driving snow that is preventing him; from the exclamation itself, to the figure of exclamation, to a figure visible in snow. Schuyler's play with textual surfaces is grounded in perception of the physical world, and his associative movement is tight, producing poems with the intensity of a coiled spring.

Schuyler won the Pulitzer Prize in 1981 for *The Morning of the Poem*.

❧ **POETRY**

Alfred & Guinevere. New York: Harcourt, Brace, 1958. Dust jacket. Published at $3.75. Review slip loosely inserted. The author's first book, preceded by a mimeographed acting script, "Shopping and Waiting," 1953.

"Amy Lowell Thoughts." Winston-Salem, North Carolina: Palaemon Press, 1984. Broadside, signed by the author. Limitation not stated.

Early in '71. Berkeley, California: The Figures, 1982. Wrappers. One of ten copies signed by Schuyler in a total limitation of 500.

A Few Days: Poems. New York: Random House, 1985. Dust jacket. Published at $14.95.

Freely Espousing. New York: Sun Books, 1979. First paperback edition. Published at $4.00. The hardcover edition was published by Doubleday in 1969.

The Home Book: Prose and Poems, 1951–1970, ed. Trevor Winkfield. Calais, Vermont: Z Press, 1977. Wrappers. One of 1,000 copies in a total limitation of 1,026.

The Morning of the Poem. New York: Farrar, Straus & Giroux, 1980. Dust jacket. Published at $10.95.

Readings in Contemporary Poetry No. 9. New York: DIA Art Foundation, 1988. Wrappers, one of 500 copies. With the author's contemporary presentation inscription.

Selected Poems. New York: Farrar Straus Giroux, 1988. Dust jacket. Published at $25.00.

A Sun Cab. Illustrated by Fairfield Porter. New York: Adventures in Poetry, 1972. Wrappers. One of 26 lettered copies signed by the author and the artist in a total limitation of 300.

"Verge." San Francisco: Angel Hair Books, 1971. Broadside. Limitation not stated, but 300 copies were printed.

What's for Dinner? Santa Barbara, California: Black Sparrow Press, 1978. Glassine dust jacket. One of 26 lettered copies signed by the author. Accompanied by one of 500 hardcover trade copies.

❧ PROSE

A Nest of Ninnies, by John Ashbery and James Schuyler. New York: E. P. Dutton, 1969. Dust jacket. Published at $4.95. Six thousand copies were printed.

Delmore Schwartz

Delmore Schwartz (1913–1966) burst brilliantly onto the poetry scene at age twenty-four with his first collection, *In Dreams Begin Responsibilities*. Schwartz, who once said his main poetic theme was "the wound of consciousness,"[1] wrote in this early work about the deep divisions of our lives, our difficulties in knowing ourselves and in connecting with the world. Schwartz himself had painful difficulties in connecting; like his friends Robert Lowell and John Berryman, he suffered from bouts of mental illness. He was in and out of mental hospitals during the last twenty years of his life and died alone in a New York City hotel, having repudiated his friends a year before. It took three days to find someone to claim his body.

Drawing on Marx and Freud as well as on Socrates and Plato, Schwartz writes poems of philosophical questioning in a tone highly charged with emotion, using words in a reckless and unexpected way that prefigures Berryman, as evidenced in the titles, "Dogs Are Shakespearean, Children Are Strangers" and "A Dog Named Ego, the Snowflakes as Kisses."[2] For Schwartz, the quest for knowledge helps assuage the pain of living,

>   . . . O this
>   Consoles in the last illness all our pain:
>   Gazing upon the old life's vaudeville,
>   Viewing the motions of the struggling will,
>   Seeking the causes of each fresh event . . .[3]

But we are also caught in a state of unknowing,

>   For we are incomplete and know no future,
>   And we are howling or dancing out our souls
>   In beating syllables before the curtain:
>   We are Shakespearean, we are strangers.[4]

In the evocative "In the Naked Bed, in Plato's Cave," coming
to consciousness in the morning holds a wistful recognition
that we dwell in a nether world, unable to reach either the
transcendent or the phenomenal—yet at the same time our
waking each morning is an act of courage:

>   . . . So, so,
>   O son of man, the ignorant night, the travail
>   Of early morning, the mystery of beginning
>   Again and again,
>   while History is unforgiven.[5]

In his later work, Schwartz seeks a reconciling of division
in the ordinary natural world, the simple sensuous experience
of which is enough. He shifts stylistically to a freer, longer line
that often uses syntactical repetition and onomatopoesis. In
"Seurat's Sunday Afternoon along the Seine,"

>   The Sunday people are looking at hope itself.
>
>   They are looking at hope itself, under the sun, free from the
>   teething anxiety, the gnawing nervousness
>   Which wastes so many days and years of consciousness.[6]

Schwartz was awarded the Bollingen Prize in Poetry in
1960.

➳ POETRY

Last and Lost Poems, ed. Robert Phillips. New York:
  Vanguard Press, 1979. Dust jacket. Foreword by the
  editor.

Summer Knowledge: New and Selected Poems, 1938–1958. Garden City, New York: Doubleday, 1959. Dust jacket. Published at $4.95.

➢ PROSE

The Ego is Always at the Wheel: Bagatelles, ed. Robert Phillips. New York: New Directions, 1986. Dust jacket. Published at $14.95. A collection of nineteen humorous essays.

Delmore Schwartz and James Laughlin: Selected Letters, ed. Robert Phillips. New York: W. W. Norton, 1993. Dust jacket. Published at $19.95.

Letters of Delmore Schwartz. Selected and edited by Robert Phillips. Foreword by Karl Shapiro. Princeton: Ontario Review Press, 1984. Dust jacket. Published at $24.95.

Portrait of Delmore: Journals and Notes of Delmore Schwartz, 1939–1959. Edited and introduced by Elizabeth Pollet. New York: Farrar, Straus & Giroux, 1986. Dust jacket. Published at $35.00. Review slip and publicity notice laid in.

Successful Love and Other Stories. New York: Corinth Books, 1961. Dust jacket. Published at $4.50. Review slip loosely inserted.

The World is a Wedding. Norfolk, Connecticut: New Directions, 1948. Dust jacket. Published at $2.75.

➢ TRANSLATION

A Season in Hell, by Arthur Rimbaud. Translated by Delmore Schwartz. Norfolk, Connecticut: New Directions, 1939. Dust jacket. Published at $2.50. Seven hundred eighty copies were printed. English/French text; introduction by the translator.

Anne Sexton

Anne Sexton (1928–1974), who struggled with mental illness throughout her life and committed suicide at the age of forty-six, began to write poetry seriously in 1957 at the suggestion of her analyst. Deeply psychological, her poems explicitly treat her mental illness and bouts of institutionalization, her obsession with death and suicide, and her search for feminine identity, archetype, and deity. Sexton is usually considered a Confessional poet; like Sylvia Plath, she participated in Robert Lowell's poetry workshops at Boston University. She has said in numerous interviews that her first contact with the Confessional mode was W. D. Snodgrass' work, which validated the way she was already beginning to write.

Sexton has said of her poetry, "I think it should be a shock to the senses. It should almost hurt."[1] The poetry tries to shock us into awareness, into a recognition of being alive. In her early work, Sexton uses form as "a trick in order to get at the truth," a way to let "a lot of wild animals out in the arena, but enclosing them in a cage."[2] Form enables a controlled exploration of unconscious processes and conscious volatile emotions. In her later work, Sexton uses metaphor as a means of psychological exploration. Extended metaphors take on a life of their own, often functioning as psychological displacements and thus serving as keys to psychic processes. Or she accumulates details, "like piling stones one on top of the other,"[3] so that they take on emotional weight.

In "Flee on Your Donkey" she describes her sixth return to the mental hospital and her realization that she has learned what she can from it and needs to make the choice to leave. The donkey is a metaphor for the power of her dreams and metaphors, a power that can carry her out into survival and sanity:

> Anne, Anne,
> flee on your donkey,
> flee this sad hotel
> ride out on some hairy beast,
> gallop backward pressing
> your buttocks to his withers,
> sit to his clumsy gait somehow.
> Ride out
> any old way you please![4]

And in "The Fortress" the poet cannot prevent the passing of time, unexpected disease, or accident from affecting her young daughter, but she can offer metaphor and image as a source of connection through time, as a way to touch:

> I cannot promise very much.
> I give you the images I know.
> Lie still with me and watch.
> A pheasant moves
> by like a seal, pulled through the mulch
> by his thick white collar. He's on show
> like a clown. He drags a beige feather that he removed,
> one time, from an old lady's hat.
> We laugh and we touch.
> I promise you love. Time cannot take away that.[5]

Sexton won the Pulitzer Prize in 1967 for *Live or Die.*

❧ **POETRY**

The Awful Rowing Toward God. Boston: Houghton Mifflin, 1975. Dust jacket. Published at $5.95.

The Book of Folly. Boston: Houghton Mifflin, 1972. Tissue dust jacket; publisher's slipcase as issued. One of 500 copies signed by the author. Accompanied by a copy of the trade edition in dust jacket, published at $5.95.

Selected Poems. London: Oxford University Press, 1964. Dust jacket. Published at 21s. No comparable American edition.

Selected Poems. Edited with an introduction by Diane Wood Middlebrook and Diana Hume George. Boston: Houghton Mifflin, 1988. Dust jacket. Published at $21.95.

To Bedlam and Part Way Back. Boston: Houghton Mifflin, 1960. Dust jacket. Published at $3.00. The author's first book.

Transformations. Drawings by Barbara Swan. Boston: Houghton Mifflin, 1971. Tissue dust jacket, in publisher's slipcase as issued. One of 500 copies signed by the author. Accompanied by a copy of the trade edition in dust jacket, published at $5.00.

Words for Dr. Y.: Uncollected Poems with Three Stories, ed. Linda Gray Sexton. Boston: Houghton Mifflin, 1978. Dust jacket. Published at $8.95.

❧ **PROSE**

Anne Sexton: A Self-Portrait in Letters, ed. Linda Gray Sexton and Lois Ames. Boston: Houghton Mifflin, 1977. Dust jacket. Published at $15.00. Illustrated. This copy in three examples of the dust jacket plus an unpriced trial jacket.

Anne Sexton: A Self-Portrait in Letters, ed. Linda Gray Sexton and Lois Ames. Boston: Houghton Mifflin, 1991. Dust jacket. Published at $24.95. Illustrated with photographs. This edition contains a new foreword by Linda Gray Sexton.

45 Mercy Street, ed. Linda Gray Sexton. Boston: Houghton Mifflin, 1976. Dust jacket. Published at $6.95.

Joey and the Birthday Present, by Maxine Kumin and Anne Sexton. Illustrated by Evaline Ness. New York: McGraw-Hill, 1971. This copy in a library binding; not issued in dust jacket.

Karl Shapiro

Karl Shapiro (b. 1913) is an iconoclast whose long poetic career has been a search for identity, the poetry itself undergoing radical formal changes in the process. Shapiro achieved early recognition for his poems of social critique and war, winning the Pulitzer Prize in 1945 for *V-Letter and Other Poems*, written while he was stationed with the army in New Guinea. In the best of these war poems Shapiro balances an Auden-influenced ironic distance with an intimate, sometimes painful sense of empathy for his subject, as in "The Leg," about an amputee:

> For the leg is wondering where he is (all is not lost)
> And surely he has a duty to the leg;
> He is its injury, the leg is his orphan,
> He must cultivate the mind of the leg,
> Pray for the part that is missing, pray for peace
> In the image of man, pray, pray for its safety,
> And after a little it will die quietly.[1]

Shapiro's questioning of poetic form is a search for freedom, for an identity that is large enough to include disparate consciousnesses and registers of diction, for an aesthetic that can accept a manhole cover as an object of beauty. In *The*

Bourgeois Poet he takes the long-line, expansive free verse form of Walt Whitman and the Beats one step further into prose poetry, a form that has the flexibility and energy to encompass the new consciousness we are on the verge of, the "tremendous synthesis . . . between modern science, the ancient psychologies of the past, and what we call poetry or art."[2] Rather than distinguishing between poetry and prose, he says, we should distinguish between "greater or less heat."[3] Ideas of what poetry should be only separate us from it, when we could be participating in it:

> *Lower the standard: that's my motto. Somebody is always putting the food out of reach. We're tired of falling off ladders. Who says a child can't paint? A pro is somebody who does it for money. Lower the standards. Let's all play poetry.*[4]

In "Big Sonnet," the traditional love poem is allowed a larger, looser frame, which has its own suitability for expressing affection:

> *Fatlady, I love your face, sort of slapped together. And when you walk (white bathing suit, black) it's as if one hip, the right, for instance, were going out of joint, but to return, a throwing motion, throwing-away, a generosity.*[5]

This movement of throwing away and returning also describes the poetry itself.

Shapiro shared the Bollingen Prize in Poetry with John Berryman in 1969.

❧ POETRY

Adam & Eve. Etchings by Rosalyn Richards. Lewisburg, Pennsylvania: Press of Appletree Alley, Bucknell University, 1986. Cloth boards. Not issued in dust jacket. One of 125 copies signed by the author and the artist.

Adult Bookstore. New York: Random House, 1976. Dust jacket. Published at $6.00.

Auden (1907–1973): A New Poem. Davis, California: Putah Creek Press, 1974. Wrappers, in glassine dust jacket. One of 175 copies signed by the author.

Edsel. New York: Bernard Geis Associates, 1971. Dust jacket. Published at $6.95. With the author's presentation inscription on the title page.

Five Young American Poets: Second Series, 1941. Norfolk, Connecticut: New Directions, 1941. Dust jacket. Published at $2.50. The other poets are Clark Mills, Paul Goodman, David Schubert, and Jeanne McGahey.

Love & War, Art & God: The Poems. Winston-Salem, North Carolina: Stuart Wright, 1984. Boards; not issued in dust jacket. One of 50 copies signed by the author.

The Old Horsefly. Orono, Maine: Northern Lights, 1992. Dust jacket. Published at $12.95.

The Place of Love. Australia: Comment Publication, 1942. Wrappers. Inscribed on the title page "With the author's compliments." Published while Shapiro was in the armed forces in the Pacific during World War II.

"Poet in Residence—for Stuart Wright." Winston-Salem, North Carolina: Palaemon Press, 1984. Broadside, printed for private distribution. The total limitation was 20 copies signed by Shapiro.

A Room in Rome. New Rochelle, New York: James L. Weil, 1987. Wrappers. One of 50 copies designed by Martino Mardersteig and printed by Stamperia Valdonega, Verona. A gift to the Milberg Collection from Dale Roylance.

"The Sawdust Logs—for Bill Everson." Winston-Salem, North Carolina: Palaemon Press, 1983. Broadside, signed by the author. Limitation not stated.

Selected Poems. New York: Random House, 1968. Dust jacket. Published at $7.95.

The Tenor: Opera in One Act. Music by Hugo Weisgall. Libretto by Karl Shapiro and Ernst Lert. Bryn Mawr, Pennsylvania: Merion Music, 1957. Wrappers.

Trial of a Poet and Other Poems. New York: Reynal and Hitchcock, 1947. One of 250 specially printed and bound copies signed by the author. In slipcase, as issued.

White-Haired Lover. New York: Random House, 1968. Dust jacket. Published at $4.00.

☙ PROSE

In Defense of Ignorance. New York: Random House, 1960. Dust jacket. With the author's presentation inscription.

Poet: An Autobiography in Three Parts. Volume I: The Younger Son. Chapel Hill, North Carolina: Algonquin Books, 1988. Dust jacket. Published at $17.95. Illustrated with plates. To date, only this volume has been published.

The Poetry Wreck: Selected Essays, 1950–1970. New York: Random House, 1975. Dust jacket. Published at $10.00. With a foreword by the author.

Randall Jarrell. Washington, D.C.: Library of Congress, 1967. Wrappers. "The Gertrude Clarke Whittall Lecture."

To Abolish Children and Other Essays. Chicago: Quadrangle Books, 1968. Dust jacket. Published at $6.50.

The Writer's Experience, by Karl Shapiro and Ralph Ellison. Washington, D.C.: Library of Congress, 1964. Wrappers. "The Gertrude Clarke Whittall Lecture."

Charles Simic

Charles Simic (b. 1938), who emigrated to the United
States from Yugoslavia at the age of eleven, draws on
surrealism and European and American folklore (a kind
of ancestral form) to create his extraordinary everyday poetry.
His early volumes work with the nature of memory, with the
continuing presence of his experiences as a youth in war-torn
Belgrade: "I think every tragedy, every event, some place on
some scale continues."[1] The most humble objects of our daily
life—kitchen utensils, shirts, brooms, soup—pursue their own
life, independent of us, unsettling our sense of established
order, and challenging a desire for control. A malevolent
spoon jumps up and scratches "today's date / and your name
/ on the bare wall,"[2] like names scratched on walls in concen-
tration camps by those barely strong enough to hold an
implement. We are not safe from this presence of history,
which is inscribing us.

Writing these poems about common objects involved "an
act of faith" where a part of himself "had to become a knife
or an ax."[3] This process is not always ominous, as in "Shirt,"
where the efforts to submit to the shirt—or to the writing
process—lead to a kind of crazy joy:

> *To get into it*
> *As it lies*
> *Crumpled on the floor*
> *Without disturbing a single crease*
>
> *. . . Almost managing*
> *The impossible contortions*
> *Doubling back now*
> *Through a knotted sleeve*[4]

"In my poetry images think," says Simic. "My best images are smarter than I am."[5]

Simic's poetry often tries to approach silence, "what precedes language: the world and the sense of oneself existing."[6] His long poem *White*, written over a decade, contains a dialectic between the blank page and the writing that covers it,[7] and in "Invention of Nothing," the world disappears as the poet writes. Nothing remains "except my table and chair," and as the poem progresses, more disappearances occur:

> *Why am I so quiet then*
> *and so happy?*
>
> *I climb on the table*
> *(the chair is gone already)*
> *I sing through the throat*
> *of an empty beer bottle.*[8]

Simic accepts—laconically or ruefully—life's instability, as in "Windy Evening":

> *Better grab hold of that tree, Lucille.*
> *Its shape crazed, terror-stricken.*
> *I'll hold the barn.*
> *The chickens in it uneasy.*
> *Smart chickens, rickety world.*[9]

Simic won the Pulitzer Prize in 1990 for *The World Doesn't End*.

≈ POETRY

Austerities: Poems. New York: George Braziller, 1982. Dust jacket. Published at $7.95.

Biography and A Lament: Poems 1961–1967. Hartford, Connecticut: Bartholomew's Cobble, 1976. Wrappers. One of 200 copies in a total limitation of 250. This copy is signed by the author and has his holograph corrections on two pages.

The Book of Gods and Devils. New York: Harcourt Brace Jovanovich, 1990. Dust jacket. Published at $17.95. Signed by the author on the half-title page.

Charon's Cosmology. New York: George Braziller, 1977. Dust jacket. Published at $6.95.

The Chicken Without a Head: A New Version. Portland, Oregon: Trace Editions, 1983. Wrappers. One of 75 signed copies in a total limitation of 500. Accompanied by a copy of the trade edition, one of 425 copies.

Classic Ballroom Dances: Poems. New York: George Braziller, 1980. Dust jacket. Published at $6.95.

Dismantling the Silence: Poems. With a note by Richard Howard. New York: George Braziller, 1971. Wrappers; not published in cloth. Published at $3.95.

"Further Adventures of Charles Simic." Illustrated by William Lint. Derry, Pennsylvania: Rook Press, 1975. Broadside. One of 100 illustrated copies signed by the author in a total limitation of 300. "Rook Broadsides 3." Accompanied by another issue, one of 200 unillustrated copies.

Hotel Insomnia. New York: Harcourt Brace Jovanovich, 1992. Dust jacket. Published at $18.95.

"Interlude." Wood engraving by Sarah Chamberlain. Salem, Oregon: Charles Seluzicki, 1981. Broadside. One of 135 copies signed by the author and the printer.

"Knife." Lawrence, Kansas: Cottonwood Review, 1972. Broadside. Limitation not stated.

"The Message is Confined to the Species." New York: Nadja, 1970. Broadside. One of 100 copies. "Happy Holidays & Best Wishes for the New Year from Carol Sturm & Doug Wolf."

Nine Poems: A Childhood Story. Cambridge, Massachusetts: Exact Change, 1989. Wrappers. One of 25 copies signed by the author in a total limitation of 500.

"Poem." Stony Brook, New York: Stony Brook Poetics Foundation, 1968. Broadside. Issued as part of a portfolio produced for the benefit of the magazine *Stony Brook*.

Pyramids and Sphinxes. New York: Nadja, 1989. Wrappers. One of 25 *hors commerce* copies reserved for the poet, this one signed, in a total limitation of 125.

Return to a Place Lit by a Glass of Milk: Poems. New York: George Braziller, 1974. Dust jacket. Published at $5.95. "Compliments of the Author and Publisher" card loosely inserted.

School for Dark Thoughts. Baltimore, Maryland: Charles Seluzicki, 1978. Wrappers. One of 235 copies signed by the author. Printed at the Banyan Press.

Selected Poems, 1963–1983. New York: George Braziller, 1985. Dust jacket. Published at $14.95. This copy is signed by the author on the half-title page.

Shaving at Night: Poems. Woodcuts by Helen Siegl. San Francisco: Meadow Press, 1982. Boards. One of 200 copies signed by the author and the artist.

Somewhere Among Us a Stone Is Taking Notes. Prints by George Hitchcock. San Francisco: Kayak Books, 1969. Wrappers. Published at $1.50. One thousand copies were printed.

They Forage at Night. New York: Nadja, 1980. Wrappers. One of 74 copies signed by the author in a total limitation of 100.

"Three Poems." Santa Barbara, California: Unicorn Press, 1968. One sheet folded to make four pages. Issued as part of "Unicorn Folio II, #4." Three hundred fifty copies were printed.

Watch Repair. Illustrated by Michael Peterson. Seattle: M Kimberly Press, 1987. Boards. "Each book was individually hand watercolored, embellished, and bound by the artist." One of only 25 copies signed by the author and the artist. Enclosed in a cloth box as issued.

Weather Forecast for Utopia & Vicinity: Poems 1967–1982. Barrytown, New York: Station Hill, 1983. Glassine dust jacket. One of 43 copies signed by the author. Accompanied by a copy of the trade edition which was not issued in dust jacket.

What the Grass Says: Poems. With twelve prints by Joan Abelson. Santa Cruz, California: Kayak Books, 1967. Wrappers. One of 1,000 copies. The author's first book. Accompanied by a signed copy of the second printing, 1968.

White. Illustrated by the author. New York: New Rivers Press, 1972. Dust jacket. Published at $5.00. One of 300 clothbound copies in a total limitation of 1,300.

White: A New Version. Durango, Colorado: Logbridge-Rhodes, 1980. First revised edition. One of 22 copies bound in boards, signed by the author, and with a section of the poem in his holograph, in a total limitation of 722 copies.

The World Doesn't End: Prose Poems. New York: Harcourt Brace Jovanovich, 1989. Dust jacket. Published at $17.95.

ॐ PROSE

Dime-Store Alchemy: The Art of Joseph Cornell. Hopewell, New Jersey: Ecco Press, 1992. Dust jacket. Published at $19.95.

"In the Beginning . . ." Detroit, Michigan: Gale Research, 1986. Nine sheets loose in printed envelope, as issued. "Contemporary Authors Autobiography Series." This copy is signed by Simic on the envelope.

Wonderful Words, Silent Truth: Essays on Poetry, and a Memoir. Ann Arbor: University of Michigan Press, 1990. Not issued in dust jacket.

ॐ TRANSLATIONS

Atlantis: Selected Poems 1953–1982, by Slavko Mihalic. Translated by Charles Simic and Peter Kastmiler. Greenfield Center, New York: Greenfield Review Press, 1983. Wrappers. Published at $5.00. With an introduction by Simic.

Faceless Men & Other Macedonian Stories, by Meto Jovanovski. Translated by Jeffrey Folks, Milne Holton, and Charles Simic. London and Boston: Forest Books, 1992. Paperback; not published in cloth. Published at £6.95.

Fire Gardens: Selected Poems 1956–1969, by Ivan V. Lalić. Translated by Charles Simic and C. W. Truesdale. Drawings by Zivojin Turinski. New York: New Rivers Press, 1970. Wrappers.

Four Yugoslav Poets: Ivan V. Lalić, Branko Miljkovic, Milorad Pavic, Ljubomir Simovic. Translated by Charles Simic. Northwood Narrows, New Hampshire: Lillabulero Press, 1970. Wrappers. Published at $1.00.

Give Me Back My Rags, by Vasko Popa. English translation by Charles Simic. Portland, Oregon: Trace Editions,

1985. Loose sheets in paper wrappers as issued. One of 26 lettered copies signed by the author and translator and with a holograph poem by Simic.

Homage to the Lame Wolf: Selected Poems 1956–1975, by Vasko Popa. Translated with an introduction by Charles Simic. Oberlin, Ohio: Field Translation Series 2, 1979. Dust jacket. Published at $8.95. Paperback copies preceded cloth copies by about a month.

The Horse Has Six Legs: An Anthology of Serbian Poetry. Edited and translated by Charles Simic. St. Paul, Minnesota: Graywolf Press, 1992. Paperback; not issued in cloth. Published at $12.00.

Key to Dreams According to Djordje: Poems, by Djordje Nikolic. Translated by Charles Simic. Chicago: Elpenor Books, 1978. Dust jacket. Published at $4.95.

The Little Box, by Vasko Popa. Introduction and translations from the Serbian by Charles Simic. Washington, D.C.: Charioteer Press, 1970. Dust jacket. Published at $3.75. One of 350 copies.

Night Mail: Selected Poems, by Novica Tadić. Translations and introduction by Charles Simic. Oberlin, Ohio: Oberlin College Press, 1992. Dust jacket. Published at $24.95. "Field Translation Series 19."

Roll Call of Mirrors: Selected Poems of Ivan V. Lalić. Translated and with an introduction by Charles Simic. Middletown, Connecticut: Wesleyan University Press, 1988. Dust jacket. Published at $18.50.

Louis Simpson

Louis Simpson (b. 1923) deals in his poetry with what seems his life's central paradox, how to reconcile imagination and passion with intelligibility and responsibility. In "Why Do You Write about Russia?" he has written of poetry,

> *whatever numbing horrors*
> *it may speak of, the voice itself*
> *tells of love and infinite wonder.*[1]

He is of too subtle a mind to develop these parallels within rigid dichotomies, however, and often writes of just that dilemma. Later in the same poem he writes:

> *. . . Letting my mind*
> *wander where it will, from the page*
> *to Malaya, or some street in Paris . . .*
> *Drifting smoke. The end will be as fatal*
> *as an opium eater's dream . . .*

but he cannot reject out of hand the random, ephemeral flickerings of the mind, because

> *the way we live*
> *with our cars and power mowers . . .*

> *a life that shuns emotion*
> *and the violence that goes with it,*
> *the object being to live quietly*
> seems to deny the human truth that
>> *"Two things*
>> *constantly cry out in creation,*
>> *the sea and man's soul."*

"My Father in the Night Commanding No" gets close to the family drama perhaps responsible for Simpson's long work on this blind spot, or, better, center of turbulence.[2] As in many of his poems concerning his childhood, the mother here is seen as a source of story and emotion, the remote father of control, judgment, and responsibility. He wonders if "Beyond his jurisdiction as I move / Do I not prove him wrong," but recognizes the ultimate futility of trying to surpass or escape the father by saying "The actors in that playhouse always sit" like Freudian templates of roles we are each condemned to question and enact. However, one always has the sense that he is speaking with the mother's warmth, related to his Jamaican birthplace, about the harshness of his father and the Russia of his paternal ancestors. It is a poetry that looks with compassion and deceptive simplicity at a hard world.

He is closest to reconciliation in poems like "Chocolates," where Chekhov's offering of chocolates to some fans turns a nervous occasion of attempting to get close to a vicar of power into "a happy communion . . . as they were talking about something they liked."[3] Here is an equalizing ease and simplicity in subject, diction, and construction, which is what Simpson ultimately strives for.

Simpson won the Pulitzer Prize in 1964 for *At the End of the Open Road*.

❧ POETRY

Adventures of the Letter I. New York: Harper & Row, 1971.
   Paperback. Published at $2.65.

Air with Armed Men. London: London Magazine Editions, 1972. Dust jacket. Published at £3.50. Precedes the American edition, which was published under the title *North of Jamaica.*

Armidale. Brockport, New York: BOA Editions, 1979. Boards. One of 25 copies signed by the author and with a holograph poem. "BOA Pamphlets, Series A, No. 5."

The Arrivistes: Poems, 1940–1949. Preface by Theodore Hoffman. New York: Fine Editions Press, 1949. Wrappers. The author's first book.

At the End of the Open Road: Poems. Middletown, Connecticut: Wesleyan University Press, 1963. Dust jacket. Published at $4.00.

The Best Hour of the Night: Poems. New Haven, Connecticut: Ticknor & Fields, 1983. Dust jacket. Published at $12.95.

Caviare at the Funeral: Poems. New York: Franklin Watts, 1980. Dust jacket. Published at $7.95. This copy is signed by the author.

Collected Poems. New York: Paragon House, 1988. Dust jacket. Published at $24.95.

"Crystal Morning." Emory, Virginia: Iron Mountain Press, 1982. Broadside. One of 200 copies signed by the author.

A Dream of Governors: Poems. Middletown, Connecticut: Wesleyan University Press, 1959. Dust jacket. Published at $3.00. The author's presentation inscription appears on the title page.

In the Room We Share. New York: Paragon House, 1990. Dust jacket. Published at $18.95.

The Invasion of Italy: A Poem. Wood engravings by Barry Moser. Northampton, Massachusetts: Main Street, 1976. Boards. One of 75 copies signed by the author.

"The Mexican Woman." Cambridge, Massachusetts: Pomegranate Press, 1973. Broadside. One of 250 copies.

North of Jamaica. New York: Harper & Row, 1972. Dust jacket. Published at $6.95. Previously published in England under the title *Air with Armed Men.*

On Equal Terms: Poems by Charles Bernstein, David Ignatow, Denise Levertov, Louis Simpson, Gerald Stern, ed. Hank Lazer. Tuscaloosa, Alabama: Symposium Press, 1984. Wrappers. One of 275 copies. The Simpson poems are "A Bramble Bush" and "Lifers." Poems by participants in "The Eleventh Alabama Symposium on English and American Literature: What Is a Poet?"

Out of Season. Illustrations by Timothy Engelland. Northampton, Massachusetts: Deerfield Press, 1979. Dust jacket. One of 300 copies signed by the author.

People Live Here: Selected Poems 1949–1983. Brockport, New York: BOA Editions, 1983. Dust jacket. Volume 9 in the "American Poets Continuum Series."

Searching for the Ox. New York: Morrow, 1976. Dust jacket. Published at $5.95. With the author's presentation inscription.

Selected Poems. New York: Harcourt, Brace & World, 1965. Dust jacket.

"Tondelayo." Amherst, New York: Slow Loris Press, 1971. Broadside. One of 275 copies in a total limitation of 300.

Wei Wei and Other Friends. Illustrated by Robert White. Francestown, New Hampshire: Typographeum, 1990. Wrappers. One of 200 copies signed by the author.

❧ PROSE

A Revolution in Taste: Studies of Dylan Thomas, Allen Ginsberg, Sylvia Plath, and Robert Lowell. New York: Macmillan, 1978. Dust jacket. Published at $12.95.

Riverside Drive: A Novel. New York: Atheneum, 1962. Dust jacket. Published at $5.00.

Selected Prose. New York: Paragon House, 1989. Dust jacket. Published at $24.95.

Three on the Tower: The Lives and Works of Ezra Pound, T. S. Eliot and William Carlos Williams. New York: Morrow, 1975. Dust jacket. Published at $12.50.

W. D. Snodgrass

W. D. Snodgrass (b. 1926) writes to discover the truth of the human psyche, its limitations and responsibilities. His work ranges from a confessional mode in which he explores personal failure and loss in his own relationships, to a more public, political mode, such as his dramatic monologues spoken by nine men and women who died in Hitler's bunker in the last days of World War II, in which he searches for the sources of human evil.

"I believe that the only reality that a man can ever surely know is that self he cannot help being," he said in 1959, the same year his first volume of poetry, *Heart's Needle*, was published.[1] Often considered one of the originators of Confessional poetry, although he dislikes the label, Snodgrass began by writing a dense, intensely personal verse. Stanley Moss says of this early poetry, "[Snodgrass] has identified himself with exquisite suffering and guilt and with all those who barely manage to exist on the edge of life."[2] The long "Heart's Needle" is about his relationship with his three-year-old daughter from a broken marriage. The title comes from an Irish folk saying that "An only daughter is the needle of the heart." In this bittersweet poem of comings and goings, the poet's guilt and sense of loss are subtly piercing:

> *Winter again and it is snowing;*
> *Although you are still three,*
> *You are already growing*
> *Strange to me.*[3]

With the publication of *The Führer Bunker*, Snodgrass was accused of moral ambiguity and of "humanizing" the Nazis. Snodgrass responded, "What is involved here is one of the real, basic, terrible paradoxes of being alive, that your enemy *is* human and not so different from you. . . . The aim of a work of art surely is to stretch the reader's psyche, to help him to identify with more people, with more life than he normally does."[4] Each dramatic monologue has a kind of verse form typical of the speaker's personality. Thus Magda Goebbels speaks in villanelles; her husband, the Nazi propagandist, in "waspish couplets." Here is Magda deciding to kill her own children before she commits suicide:

> *The children? They'll just have to come with me.*
> *At their age, how could they find their own way?*
> *We must preserve them from disloyalty.*[5]

Form is revealing of character; here, as elsewhere, it helps Snodgrass to "get through the conscious areas of beliefs and half-truths into the subrational areas where it may be possible to make a real discovery."[6]

Snodgrass won the Pulitzer Prize in 1960 for *Heart's Needle*.

☙ POETRY

After Experience: Poems and Translations. New York: Harper & Row, 1968. Dust jacket. Published at $4.95.

Autumn Variations. New York: Nadja, 1990. Wrappers. One of 100 signed copies in a total limitation of 126.

The Boy Made of Meat: A Poem. Wood engravings by Gillian Tyler. Concord, New Hampshire: William B. Ewert, 1983. Boards. One of 26 lettered copies signed by the author and the artist in a total limitation of 151. This copy also has a four-line signed holograph poem on the half-title page.

"Coming Down from the Acropolis." Derry, Pennsylvania: Rook Society, 1976. Broadside. One of 75 copies in a total limitation of 100, all signed by the author. "Rook Broadside 7."

D. D. Byrde Callyng Jennie Wrenn. Concord, New Hampshire: William B. Ewert, 1984. Boards. One of 36 specially bound and signed copies in a total limitation of 136.

"Dance Suite: Minuet in F$^{\#\#}$." Calligraphy by R. L. Hale. Concord, New Hampshire: William B. Ewert, 1989. Poem card. One of 150 copies in a total limitation of 186, printed for private distribution.

The Führer Bunker: A Cycle of Poems in Progress. Brockport, New York: BOA Editions, 1977. Dust jacket. Published at $8.95. One of 500 clothbound copies in a total limitation of 1,050.

"He Bare Him Up, He Bare Him Down: An English Carol." Concord, New Hampshire: William B. Ewert, 1991. Broadside. One of 36 copies on special paper, signed by the author. The remaining 250 copies were issued folded.

Heart's Needle. New York: Alfred A. Knopf, 1959. Dust jacket. Published at $3.75. The author's first book.

Heart's Needle. Hessle, Yorkshire, England: Marvell Press, 1960. Dust jacket. Published at 15s. Contains an addendum, "Finding a Poem," not in the American edition.

Heinrich Himmler: Platoons and Files. San Francisco / Cumberland, Iowa: Pterodactyl Press, 1982. One of 60 post-bound copies (with attached key) signed by the author in a total edition of 500 copies.

If Birds Build with Your Hair. New York: Nadja, 1979. Wrappers. Printed on brown paper. One of 26 lettered and signed copies in a total limitation of 226.

The Kinder Capers: Poems. Illustrated by DeLoss McGraw. New York: Nadja, 1986. Wrappers. One of 100 copies signed by the author and the artist in a total limitation of 126.

A Locked House. Concord, New Hampshire: William B. Ewert, 1986. Wrappers. Limited to 126 copies, this one marked *hors commerce.*

The Lovers Go Fly a Kite. Brockport, New York: State University of New York, 1968. Wrappers, glassine dust jacket. Invitation to a reading by Snodgrass on 23 October 1968. This copy is signed by the poet.

Lullaby: The Comforting of Cock Robin. New York: Nadja, 1988[?]. Wrappers. Limitation not stated. "Printed for Friends of Nadja. Best Wishes from Carol Sturm & Doug Wolf."

"Lullaby: The Comforting of Cock Robin." Illustrated by DeLoss McGraw. San Diego, California: Brighton Press, 1987. Broadside. One of 200 copies signed by the author and the artist.

Magda Goebbels. Winston-Salem, North Carolina: Palaemon Press, 1983. Wrappers. One of 100 copies signed by the author in a total limitation of 150. Loosely inserted is the four-page "A Note from the Poet."

"Old Jewelry." Winston-Salem, North Carolina: Palaemon Press, 1984. Broadside, signed by the author. Limitation not stated.

"Owls: A Poem." Madison, Wisconsin: Crepuscular Press for William B. Ewert, 1983. Broadside, signed by the author. One of 126 copies of which only 90 copies survived.

Remains: Poems, by S. S. Gardons. Mount Horeb, Wisconsin: Perishable Press, 1970. Boards. One of 200 copies. S. S. Gardons is an anagram of Snodgrass. Printed on gray paper.

Remains: A Sequence of Poems. Foreword by A. Poulin, Jr. Brockport, New York: BOA Editions, 1985. Wrappers. One of 500 copies in a total limitation of 600. This copy is inscribed by Snodgrass to Stuart Wright.

Selected Poems, 1957–1987. New York: Soho Press, 1987. Paperback issue. Published at $15.95.

Six Minnesinger Songs. Providence, Rhode Island: Burning Deck, 1983. Wrappers. One of 26 lettered copies signed by the author. Accompanied by a copy of the trade edition in wrappers, one of 1,000 copies published at $6.00.

Six Troubadour Songs. Providence, Rhode Island: Burning Deck, 1977. Wrappers. One of 26 lettered and signed copies in a total limitation of 526.

Snow Songs. New York: Nadja, 1992. Wrappers, in dust jacket. One of 75 signed copies in a total limitation of 100.

These Trees Stand. . . . With a portrait series of the poet by Robert Mahon. New York: Carol Joyce, 1981. Bound in full leather with a tree design and contained in a cloth folding box. The total edition is limited to ten copies plus two artist's proofs, each signed by the author and the artist. The portraits are original photographs.

"Three Versicles." Concord, New Hampshire: William B. Ewert, 1987. Broadside. One of 70 copies signed by the author.

To Shape a Song. Illustrated by DeLoss McGraw. New York: Nadja, 1988. Wrappers. One of 74 copies signed by the author and the artist in a total limitation of 100.

W. D.'s Midnight Carnival. Illustrated by Deloss McGraw. Encinitas, California: Artra Publishing, 1988. Dust jacket. Published at $40.00.

☞ PROSE

Analysis of Depths: The Inferno. Durham: University of New Hampshire Press, 1969. Wrappers. "Spaulding Distinguished Lectures, 1969." This copy is signed by the author.

In Radical Pursuit: Critical Essays and Lectures. New York: Harper & Row, 1975. Dust jacket. Published at $10.00.

" 'No Voices Talk to Me': A Conversation with W. D. Snodgrass," ed. Philip L. Gerber and Robert J. Gemmett. N.p., 1970. Wrappers. Offprint from *The Western Humanities Review* 24, no. 1 (Winter 1970). This copy is signed by Gemmett.

"W. D. Snodgrass and *The Führer Bunker*: An Interview," ed. Paul L. Gaston. Carbondale, Illinois, 1977. Wrappers. Offprint from *Papers on Language & Literature* 13, no. 4 (Fall 1977).

☞ TRANSLATIONS

The Four Seasons, by Antonio Vivaldi. Translated by W. D. Snodgrass. New York: Targ Editions, 1984. Boards; tissue dust jacket. One of 150 copies signed by Snodgrass. Snodgrass' introduction states that the four

Italian sonnets on which *The Four Seasons* was based were probably written by Vivaldi.

Gallows Songs, by Christian Morgenstern. Translated by W. D. Snodgrass and Lore Segal. Drawings by Paul Klee. Ann Arbor: University of Michigan Press, 1967. Dust jacket. Published at $7.95.

"Somnoroase Pasarele," by Mihai Eminescu. Translated by W. D. Snodgrass with Augustin Maissen. Concord, New Hampshire: William B. Ewert, 1985. Broadside. One of 15 copies on variant paper signed by the author in a total limitation of 136.

"Star," by Mihai Eminescu. Translated by W. D. Snodgrass. Salem, Oregon: Charles Seluzicki, 1982. Single sheet folded twice to make four pages. This copy is signed by Snodgrass. Loosely inserted is a sheet printing the original Romanian text.

Traditional Hungarian Songs. With decorations cut by Dorian McGowan. Newark, Vermont: Janus Press for Charles Seluzicki, 1978. Wrappers. One of 285 signed copies in a total limitation of 300.

"Winter, from Vivaldi's *The Four Seasons*." Concord, New Hampshire: William B. Ewert, 1992. Broadside. One of 36 signed copies on special paper in a total limitation of 436. The remaining 400 copies were folded.

Gary Snyder

Gary Snyder (b. 1930) began writing poetry as a way of expressing his relationship to the mountains of his native Pacific Northwest. His work proposes as an alternative to Western cultural tradition the vision of the earth as a living organism whose parts are interconnected and interdependent. A life-long involvement with Native American tradition and forty years of Zen Buddhist practice inform this vision. Snyder's poems may move toward unmediated experience, "to *anything* direct—rocks or bushes or people,"[1] or between the present moment and the dimension of myth and history. "As poet I hold the most archaic values on earth. They go back to the late Paleolithic: the fertility of the soil, the magic of animals, the power-vision in solitude, the terrifying initiation and re-birth, the love and ecstasy of the dance, the common work of the tribe."[2] In "Burning the Small Dead," the scale of time stretches from the immediate ritual to the life of the burning tree:

> Burning the small dead
> branches
> broke from beneath
> thick spreading
> whitebark pine.

> *a hundred summers*
> *snowmelt   rock   and air*
>
> *hiss in a twisted bough.*[3]

Snyder sees poetry as an energy process, or what Charles Olson calls "the kinetics of the thing."[4] Says Snyder, "Each poem grows from an energy-mind-field-dance, and has its own inner grain. To let it grow, to let it speak for itself, is a large part of the work of the poet."[5] Snyder's work also reflects the influence of Chinese and Japanese poetics, including verb constructions that indicate action without a subject, and juxtapositions of images to create meaning without a metaphoric link.

Snyder has been active in the ecology movement since his return from Japan in 1968, and his poetry of the 1970s and 1980s has become more overtly political. He won the Pulitzer Prize in 1975 for *Turtle Island* and the American Book Award in 1984 for *Axe Handles*.

☞ POETRY

All in the Family. Illustrated by Mimi Osborne. Davis: University of California Library, 1975. Wrappers. One of 200 copies signed by the author and the illustrator. "Fine Arts Series Number Two."

"Anasazi." Portland, Oregon: Yes! Press, 1971. Broadside. Limitation not stated, but 406 copies were printed, none for sale.

"August on Sourdough, A Visit from Dick Brewer." N.p.: Keith Abbott, 1987. Broadside, signed by the author. Limitation not stated.

"Axe Handles." N.p., n.d. Broadside. With the author's presentation inscription. Limitation not stated.

The Back Country. London: Fulcrum Press, 1967. Dust jacket. One of 100 copies on fawn paper signed by the author. Accompanied by a copy of the trade edition in dust jacket, published at 30s.

The Back Country. New York: New Directions, 1968. Dust jacket. Published at $4.00. First American edition, expanded from the Fulcrum Press edition of the previous year.

"Bison rumble-belly . . ." Illustrated by Bob Giorgio. North San Juan, California: Bob Giorgio, 1979. Broadside. One of 50 copies signed by the author and the artist.

"The Canyon Wren." Stanislaus River, California: For James and Carol Katz, April 40081 [*sic*]. Broadside. One of 200 copies signed by the author.

"A Curse on the Men in Washington, Pentagon." Santa Barbara, California: Unicorn Press, 1968. Broadside. First issue with "Buddah" on line 16. There were also 30 signed copies. "Unicorn Broadsheet One." Printed in 1968 but not released until 1970.

"The Earth's Wild Places." Sacramento, California: Ellen's Old Alchemical Press, 1976. Broadside. Issued as part of the journal *Hard Pressed*, no. 2.

"Energy Is Eternal Delight." Berkeley, California, 1972. Broadside. Reprint of a *New York Times* article of 12 January 1972. Limitation not stated, but "at least 100 copies printed."

"Everybody Lying on their Stomachs, Head toward the Candle, Reading, Sleeping, Drawing." San Francisco: Maya Broadside One, 1969. Broadside. One of 50 copies signed by the author in a total limitation of 300.

"The Fates of Rocks & Trees: Two Poems, Two Photographs," by Gary Snyder and Michael Mundy. San Francisco: James Linden, 1986. Loose sheets in cloth portfolio as issued. One of 100 copies, with each poem signed by the author and each photograph signed by the artist, in a total limitation of 120.

"Fire Rules." Adams, Massachusetts: Second Life Books, 1982. Broadside. One of 300 copies.

"For All." Port Townsend, Washington: Copper Canyon Press, 1980. Broadside. "This broadside is issued in a signed edition of 200 copies as a benefit for the people of San Juan Ridge in their effort to halt the resumption of gold mining in their local tertiary gravels."

"Front Lines." Illustrated by Tom Killion. Santa Cruz, California: Bookshop Santa Cruz, 1978. Broadside. Limitation not stated. Issued in an effort "to preserve Santa Cruz's vanishing 'greenbelt.'"

"Go Round." Santa Barbara, California: Unicorn Press, 1967. Broadside. One of 325 copies. "Writ out on 6:1:67 for Ken & Missy Maytag = their marriage =." "Unicorn Folio I, #1." Accompanied by a copy of the first issue poetry postcard, measuring 5 x 7¼ inches.

Good Wild Sacred. Madley, England: Five Seasons Press, 1984. Wrappers. Published at £1.95. An earlier version entitled "Wild Sacred Good Land" appeared in *Resurgence 98*, Bideford, Devon, England.

"Hanamatsuri 1969, from the Dhammapada." Santa Barbara, California: Painted Cave, 1969. Broadside. Limitation not stated. Hand printed by friends for Gary Snyder, his wife and child, Lew Welch, David Meltzer, Brother Antoninus, Bobby Hyde, and Jack Shoemaker, on 8 April 1969.

Left Out in the Rain: New Poems 1947–1985. San Francisco: North Point Press, 1986. Dust jacket. Published at $15.95. Promotional material loosely inserted.

"The lessons we learn from the wild . . ." Berkeley, California: Black Oak Books, 1990. Broadside.

Limitation not stated. Issued on the occasion of a reading by the author.

"Manzanita." Kent, Ohio: Kent State University Library, 1971. Single sheet folded to make four pages. Issued as a keepsake at the dedication of the Library on 9–10 April 1971. Differs from the Four Seasons Foundation publication of 1972.

Manzanita. Bolinas, California: Four Seasons Foundation, 1972. Wrappers. Published at $1.00. Two thousand copies printed. Differs from the Kent State University Library issue of 1971.

"A Mind Like Compost." North San Juan, California: Bob Giorgio, 1979. Illustrated poetry card.

Myths & Texts. New York: New Directions, 1978. Dust jacket. Published at $6.50. First New Directions edition, in a completely revised format and with a new introduction by the author.

"Nanao Knows." San Francisco: Four Seasons Foundation, 1964. Broadside. Limitation not stated but 300 copies were printed.

No Nature: New and Selected Poems. New York: Pantheon Books, 1992. Dust jacket. Published at $25.00.

"North Beach." San Francisco: Osborne and Stewart, 1975. Broadside. Published anonymously. Limitation not stated, but 1,000 copies were printed.

North Sea Road. San Francisco: Planet / Drum Foundation, 1974. Wrappers. Originally part of a folder, with other contributions, entitled *North Pacific Rim Alive*, which is "Planet / Drum 3." Twenty-eight hundred copies printed.

"O Mother Gaia." California, Pennsylvania: Unspeakable Visions of the Individual, 1978. Poetry postcard.

"O Mother Gaia." Hereford, England: Five Seasons Press, 1984. Broadside. Limitation not stated. Published after 1984.

"On the Planet, Earth, September, 1969." Detroit, Michigan: Alternative Press, 1969. Broadside. Limitation not stated.

"Prayer for the Great Family." Block print by Paul Kissinger. San Francisco: Hermes Free Press, 1971. Broadside. One of 200 copies in a total limitation of 226, all signed by the author. Printed as a benefit for the Committee of Concern for the Traditional Indian.

A Range of Poems. Cover drawings and section headings by the author; drawings of man, bird, and deer by Will Petersen. London: Fulcrum Press, 1966. Dust jacket. Published at 35s.

Regarding Wave. New York: New Directions, 1970. Dust jacket. Published at $4.75. Expanded edition. Two thousand copies printed.

"Right in the Trail." Wood engraving by Michael McCurdy. Richmond, Massachusetts: Mad River, 1990. Broadside. One of 200 copies signed by the author and the artist. "Mad River 11."

"Ripples on the Surface." Berkeley, California: Black Oak Books, 1992. Broadside. Limitation not stated.

Riprap. Ashland, Massachusetts: Origin Press, 1959. Wrappers. The author's first book. Five hundred copies were printed.

Riprap & Cold Mountain Poems. San Francisco: Four Seasons Foundation, 1965. Wrappers. First issue, with no price on the rear cover. Three thousand sets of sheets were printed but only 1,000 were bound initially.

Six Sections from Mountains and Rivers Without End. San Francisco: Four Seasons Foundation, 1965. Wrappers.

"Writing 9." Correct first edition, with the date on the title page. This copy is signed by the author.

Six Sections from Mountains and Rivers Without End. London: Fulcrum Press, 1967. Dust jacket. Published at 21s. First English and first hardcover edition.

"Smokey the Bear Sutra." N.p.: Adler Offset Printing, ca. 1969. Broadside, printed in two columns. No limitation stated. "(May be reproduced free forever)."

Songs for Gaia. Port Townsend, Washington: Copper Canyon Press, 1979. Wrappers. Second printing, after a printing of 300 copies for the Kah Tai Alliance. Accompanied by the broadside prospectus. This copy is signed by the author.

"Spel Against Demons." Berkeley, California: Moe's Books, 1970. Broadside, printed letterpress. Fifteen hundred copies were printed. There were several offset piracies.

"Spel Against Demons." Kalamazoo, Michigan[?], 1970[?]. Broadside. An offset piracy of the Moe's Books 1970 printing. This copy is signed by the author.

"Tree Song." San Francisco: James Linden, 1986. Wrappers, enclosed in a printed envelope. The poem appears on one sheet; an original photograph, "Dogwood, forest— Yosemite" by Michael Mundy, is on the second sheet. One of 50 copies signed by the author and photographer in a total limitation of 226 copies.

Turtle Island. New York: New Directions, 1974. Dust jacket. Published at $6.75. Two thousand copies printed.

"Two Logging Songs." Berkeley, California: Serendipity Books, 1973. Broadside. Published for the International Antiquarian Book Fair, Spring 1973. Limitation not stated, but 2,000 copies were printed. None for sale.

"When to Not." Illustrated by Lin Colson. Kendrick, Idaho: Two Magpie Press, 1981. Broadside, signed by

the author. Limitation not stated. Accompanied by
another copy on cheap green paper, apparently a trade
issue.

"Why Log Truck Drivers Rise Earlier Than Students of
Zen." Olympia, Washington: Lightfoot Press, 1973.
Broadside. Limitation not stated, but 200 copies were
printed. "Lightfoot 4."

☙ PROSE

*Earth House Hold: Technical Notes & Queries to Fellow
Dharma Revolutionaries.* New York: New Directions,
1969. Dust jacket. Published at $5.00. Twenty-five
hundred copies were printed.

"Four Changes." N.p.: Earth-Read Out, 1969. Single sheet
folded to make four pages. Published anonymously.
Revised edition.

The Old Ways: Six Essays. San Francisco: City Lights
Books, 1977. Wrappers. Published at $2.50. Ten
thousand copies printed.

A Passage Through India. San Francisco: Grey Fox Press,
1983. Issued without dust jacket. Illustrated with plates.

The Practice of the Wild: Essays. San Francisco: North Point
Press, 1990. Dust jacket. Published at $22.95.

The Real Work: Interviews & Talks, 1964–1979. Edited with an
introduction by William Scott McLean. New York:
New Directions, 1980. Dust jacket. Published at $10.95.

William Stafford

William Stafford (1914–1993) said of his poetry, "It is much like talk, with some enhancement."[1] His method was to rise early each morning and begin by writing whatever occured to him at the moment, following his impulses and associations. This process, like meditation, allows the poet "to find out what the world is trying to be"; it does not seek to control or impose.[2] As M. L. Rosenthal has said of the poems, "Nothing is forced. [They] shape themselves, discover their right images and perceptions."[3]

This unforced form is consonant with Stafford's deeply committed pacifism. He began to write according to this method while serving at conscientious objector camps in Arkansas and California during World War II. His poems thus contain an implied or overt critique of contemporary American culture, and suggest an alternative way of living in the natural world without needing to master it.

Stafford wrote to explore, "like Daniel Boone going into Kentucky. The thing is being there and finding it."[4] Writing is like fishing: one must be receptive and "willing to fail . . . I am following a process that leads so wildly and originally into new territory that no judgment can at the moment be made about values, significance, and so on."[5]

Stafford's territories included the Kansas of his childhood and the Oregon of his later years, where he taught English at Lewis and Clark College and was the state's Poet Laureate. For him, the land is the basis for our psychic topography, if we open ourselves, if we wait for it to come to us:

> *It is*
> *better that no one follow even the pattern*
> *I look onto the back of my hand, for many*
> *visions I haven't dared follow may*
> *gather and combine in a flash. Away off,*
> *in a space in the sky, I let the sky look*
> *at me, and I look back and do not say anything.*[6]

Stafford won the National Book Award in 1963 for *Traveling Through the Dark*.

❧ POETRY

Absolution. Knotting, Bedford, England: Martin Booth, 1980. Wrappers. One of 50 signed copies in a total limitation of 125. Accompanied by one of 75 unsigned copies.

All About Light. Athens, Ohio: Croissant & Company, 1978. Wrappers. One of 176 signed copies in a total limitation of 426.

Allegiances. New York: Harper & Row, 1970. Dust jacket. Published at $4.95.

Annie-Over: Poems, by William Stafford and Marvin Bell. Drawings by Barbara Stafford. Rexburg, Idaho: Honeybrook Press, 1988. Wrappers. One of 26 lettered copies, signed by both authors and the illustrator on the centerfold, in a total limitation of 298.

"Anniversaries." Waldron Island, Washington: Brooding Heron Press, 1988. Broadside; one of a collection of 14

under the overall title "Transition." Limited to 55
copies for sale signed by the authors, plus an
unspecified number for authors and friends of the press.
Enclosed in a cloth box with Japanese-style closures.

Around You, Your House, and A Catechism. Knotting,
Bedfordshire, England: Sceptre Press, 1979. Wrappers.
One of 50 signed copies in a total limitation of 150.
Accompanied by a copy of the trade issue of 100
copies.

"Artist, Come Home." Illustrated by Patricia M. Petrosky.
Pittsburgh, Pennsylvania: Slow Loris Press, 1976.
Broadside. One of 65 signed copies.

"Assurance." Dallas, Texas: Toothpaste Press for
Bookslinger, 1983. Broadside. Limitation not stated.

Braided Apart: Poems, by Kim Robert and William Stafford.
Lewiston, Idaho: Confluence Press, 1976. Wrappers.
One of 50 copies signed by both authors.

"Bristlecone." Illustrated by Patricia Waters. Santa Rosa,
California: Calliopea Press, 198–. Broadside. One of
150 copies signed by the author and the artist.

Brother Wind. Rexburg, Idaho: Honeybrook Press, 1986.
Wrappers. One of 26 lettered copies, with a signed
holograph poem, in a total limitation of 250.
Accompanied by a copy of the trade edition, one of
188 copies.

"Cutting Loose." Winston-Salem, North Carolina:
Palaemon Press, 1983[?]. Broadside. One of 76 copies
signed by the author.

The Design on the Oriole. Mount Horeb, Wisconsin: Night
Heron Press, 1977. Boards. One of 200 copies signed by
the author and printed at Walter Hamady's Perishable
Press.

Eleven Untitled Poems. Mount Horeb, Wisconsin: Perishable Press, 1968. Wrappers. One of 250 copies.

Fin, Feather, Fur. Rexburg, Idaho: Honeybrook Press, 1989. Wrappers. One of 26 lettered copies signed by the author in a total limitation of 274.

A Glass Face in the Rain: New Poems. New York: Harper & Row, 1982. Dust jacket. Published at $12.95.

Going Places. Reno, Nevada: West Coast Poetry Review, 1974. Wrappers. Published at $2.50.

History is Loose Again: Poems. Rexburg, Idaho: Honeybrook Press, 1991. Wrappers. One of 26 signed copies in a total limitation of 278.

Holding onto the Grass: Poems. Rexburg, Idaho: Honeybrook Press, 1992. Wrappers. One of 26 signed copies in a total limitation of 268.

How to Hold Your Arms When it Rains: Poems. Linocuts by Christy Hale. Lewiston, Idaho: Confluence Press, 1990. Wrappers. One of 308 copies.

"I Would Also Like to Mention Aluminum: Poems and a Conversation," ed. William Heyen. N.p.: Slow Loris Press, 1976. Wrappers. Offprint from *Rapport 9,* vol. 3, no. 3 (Spring 1976). Signed by Stafford and Heyen.

In the Clock of Reason. Illustrated by Nancy S. Craig. Victoria, British Columbia: Soft Press, 1973. Wrappers. One of 300 copies signed by the author and the illustrator.

Kansas: Poems, ed. Denise Low. Topeka, Kansas: Washburn University, Woodley Memorial Press, 1990. Wrappers. Published at $7.00.

Listening Deep: Poems. Illustrated by Michael McCurdy. Great Barrington, Massachusetts: Penmaen Press, 1984. Wrappers. One of 50 copies signed by the author and the artist in a total limitation of 200.

The Long Sigh the Wind Makes: Poems. Introduction by Grey Elliot. Monmouth, Oregon: Adrienne Lee Press, 1991. Wrappers. Published at $15.00.

My Name is William Tell: Poems. Lewiston, Idaho: Confluence Press, 1992. Dust jacket. Winner of the 1992 Western States Book Award for Lifetime Achievement in Poetry.

"Notes for the Refrigerator Door." Binghamton, New York: Bellevue Press, 1976. Broadside. One of 65 copies signed by the author.

An Oregon Message. New York: Harper & Row, 1987. Dust jacket. Published at $17.95.

"Over the Miles." Austin, Texas: Cold Mountain Press, 1973. Poetry postcard. "Cold Mountain Press Series I, Number 2."

"Passing a Crèche." Seattle, Washington: Sea Pen Press & Paper Mill, 1978. Folded broadside. One of 200 copies signed by the author.

The Quiet of the Land. New York: Nadja, 1979. Wrappers. One of 200 copies signed by the author in a total limitation of 226.

The Rescued Year. New York: Harper & Row, 1966. Dust jacket. Published at $4.95.

Roving Across Fields: A Conversation and Uncollected Poems 1942–1982, ed. Thom Tammaro. Daleville, Indiana: Barnwood Press Cooperative, 1983. Paperback; not issued in cloth. This copy is signed by the author on the title page.

A Scripture of Leaves. Elgin, Illinois: Brethren Press, 1989. Wrappers. This copy is signed by the author on the title page.

Seeking the Way. Illuminations by Robert Johnson. Minneapolis: Melia Press, Minnesota Center for Book

Arts, 1991. Boards; glassine dust jacket. The total limitation consists of fifteen copies signed by Stafford. The images were developed as continuous-tone silver prints, after Liquid Light photographic emulsion was painted on the surface.

Segues: A Correspondence in Poetry, by William Stafford and Marvin Bell. Boston: David R. Godine, 1983. Boards, in slipcase as issued. One of 150 copies signed by both authors.

Smoke's Way: Poems from Limited Editions 1968–1981. Port Townsend, Washington: Graywolf Press, 1983. Boards. One of 26 copies signed by the author. Accompanied by a copy of the trade paperback published at $6.00.

Someday, Maybe. New York: Harper & Row, 1973. Dust jacket. Published at $5.95

Sometimes Like a Legend: Puget Sound Country Poems. Port Townsend, Washington: Copper Canyon Press, 1981. One of 26 lettered and signed copies, containing a holograph poem, in a total limitation of 290. Printed on beige paper.

Stories and Storms and Strangers. Rexburg, Idaho: Honeybrook Press, 1984. Wrappers. One of 400 copies.

Temporary Facts. Athens, Ohio: Duane Schneider, 1970. Boards; not issued in dust jacket. One of 200 copies signed by the author.

That Other Alone. Mount Horeb, Wisconsin: Perishable Press, 1973. Boards. One of 120 copies signed by the author.

Things That Happen Where There Aren't Any People: Poems. Brockport, New York: BOA Editions, 1980. One of 26 signed copies of 50 bound in boards in a total limitation of 1,200.

Traveling Through the Dark. New York: Harper & Row, 1962. Dust jacket. Published at $3.50. Signed by the author on the title page.

Tuft by Puff. Illustrated by Elizabeth Coberly. Mount Horeb, Wisconsin: Perishable Press, 1978. One of 240 copies printed on paper made "from the author's love-worn bathrobe . . . conjoined by the printer's similar garment."

Tuned in Late One Night. Illustrations by Timothy Engelland. Deerfield, Massachusetts: Deerfield Press, 1978. Dust jacket. One of 250 signed copies.

Two about Music. Knotting, Bedfordshire, England: Sceptre Press, 1978. Wrappers. One of 50 signed copies in a total limitation of 150.

"Waking at 3 A.M." Amherst, New York: Slow Loris Press, 1972. Broadside. One of 275 copies in a total limitation of 300.

Who Are You Really, Wanderer? Rexburg, Idaho: Honeybrook Press, 1993. Wrappers. One of 26 lettered copies signed by the author in a total limitation of 331.

"Why I Am Happy." Wood engraving by John De Pol. Roslyn, New York: Stone House Press, 1983. Broadside. One of 115 copies in a total limitation of 150, all signed by the author. "Portfolio One / 1983. Number 9."

Writing the World. Baltimore, Maryland: Alembic Press, 1988. Wrappers. Cover illustration by Rebecca Butcher.

Wyoming. Bristol, Rhode Island: Ampersand Press, Williams College, 1985. Wrappers. Published at $2.50. Second printing.

Wyoming Circuit. Tannersville, New York: Tideline Press, 1980. Glassine dust jacket. Accordion fold binding. One of 125 copies signed by the author.

You and Some Other Characters: Poems. Drawings by Barbara Stafford. Rexburg, Idaho: Honeybrook Press, 1987. Wrappers. One of 26 lettered and signed copies, containing a holograph poem, in a total limitation of 328. Accompanied by a copy of the trade edition.

✺ PROSE

The Animal That Drank Up Sound. New York: Harcourt Brace Jovanovich, 1992. Dust jacket. Published at $13.95. A juvenile.

Leftovers: A Care Package. Washington, D.C.: Library of Congress, 1973. Wrappers. A lecture by Stafford. Also contains Josephine Jacobsen's "From Anne to Marianne: Some Women in American Poetry."

You Must Revise Your Life. Ann Arbor: University of Michigan Press, 1986. Boards; not issued in dust jacket.

✺ TRANSLATION

Poems, by Ghalib. Translated by Aijaz Ahmad with William Stafford and Adrienne Rich. Forenote by Aijaz Ahmad. New York: Hudson Review, 1969. Wrappers. Published at 50 cents.

Mark Strand

Mark Strand (b. 1934) writes a stark, eerie poetry in which dreams and reality blend into each other, time is distorted, and the death or the alienation of the self is a constant possibility. Like Charles Simic, Strand draws on European and Latin American surrealism to create poems in which the rules of ordinary logic are transformed, made extraordinary and hermetic. The "poems become parables— brief tales which are fully lucid in their own terms and yet utterly beyond explanation in any other. . . . Each image in the sequence follows from and prepares for another. The poem thus has an Aristotelian logic. . . . This logical order rests, though, on an absolutely illogical premise."[1]

Strand explores traps of the self and of time. Efforts to give up or change the self fail. "I empty myself of my life and my life remains." Or if it does not remain, it will soon nightmarishly reappear. The poet gives up all the parts of his body, his clothes, and "the ghost that lives in them," for the sake of a lover, but in vain because "you will have none of it because already I am beginning again without anything."[2] Or he may lose himself by accident, as one might a pen, as in "Letter (for Richard Howard)," where pens fall out of the pockets of men running, and

> *People out walking will pick them up.*
> *It is one of the ways letters are written.*
>
> *How things fall to others!*
> *The self no longer belonging to me, but asleep*
> *in a stranger's shadow, now clothing*
> *the stranger, now leading him off.*

> *It is noon as I write to you.*
> *Someone's life has come into my hands.*
> *The sun whitens the buildings.*
> *It is all I have. I give it all to you. Yours,*[3]

The self, and what it writes, are not owned but in constant exchange. This sense of random circulation is both liberating and disquieting.

More recently, in a series of prose poems from *The Continuous Life*, Strand engages authors and fictional characters in a kind of debate about the nature of reality, extending fictions (a letter written by Franz Kafka's Gregor Samsa after his metamorphosis) and inventing lost authors. Strand is also an acclaimed translator of Latin American and Spanish poetry.

Strand was United States Poet Laureate in 1990–1991, and was awarded the Bollingen Prize in Poetry in 1993.

≈ POETRY

The Continuous Life: Eighteen Poems. Two Woodcuts by Neil Welliver. Iowa City, Iowa: Windhover Press, 1990. Wrappers. One of 225 copies in a total limitation of 251.

The Continuous Life: Poems. New York: Alfred A. Knopf, 1990. Dust jacket. Published at $18.95. First trade edition. A limited edition was published by the Windhover Press.

Dark Harbor: A Poem. New York: Alfred A. Knopf, 1993. Dust jacket. Published at $19.00.

The Famous Scene. Frontispiece portrait by Sidney Chafetz. Columbus, Ohio: Logan Elm Press & Papermill, 1988. Wrappers. One of 100 copies signed by the author and the artist.

"From Two Notebooks." Evanston, Illinois: No Mountains Poetry Project, 1975. Broadside. One of 150 copies signed by the author.

"The Garden for Robert Penn Warren." Winston-Salem, North Carolina: Stuart Wright, 1981. Broadside. "Fifteen copies have been privately printed for Stuart Wright and Mark Strand on the occasion of Robert Penn Warren's birthday, 24 April 1981."

The Late Hour. New York: Atheneum, 1978. Dust jacket. Published at $6.95.

The Monument. New York: Ecco Press, 1978. Dust jacket. Published at $7.95.

"My Mother on an Evening in Late Summer." Winston-Salem, North Carolina: Palaemon Press, 1984. Broadside, signed by the author. Limitation not stated.

"My Son." Hand silkscreen by Darcie Sanders. Evanston, Illinois: Whole Earth Center, 1976. Broadside. One of 150 copies signed by the author. "Based on Carlos Drummond de Andrade's poem, 'Ser.'"

The Planet of Lost Things. Illustrated by William Pène duBois. New York: Potter, 1982. Dust jacket. Published at $9.95. A juvenile.

Poems: Reasons for Moving, Darker & The Sargentville Notebook. New York: Alfred A. Knopf, 1992. Paperback, not issued in cloth. Published at $11.00. First combined edition.

Prose: Four Poems. Drawings by Josef Albers. Portland, Oregon: Charles Seluzicki, 1987. Wrappers. One of 187 copies signed by the author.

Reasons for Moving: Poems. New York: Atheneum, 1968. Dust jacket. Published at $4.50.

The Sargeantville Notebook. Providence, Rhode Island: Burning Deck, 1973. Wrappers. One of 400 copies.

Selected Poems. New York: Atheneum, 1980. Dust jacket. Published at $10.95.

The Story of Our Lives: Poems. New York: Atheneum, 1973. Paperback, not published in cloth. Published at $2.95.

Strand: A Profile. With an interview and with critical essays by Octavio Armand (translated by Carol Maier) and David Brooks. Iowa City, Iowa: Grilled Flowers Press, Profile Editions, 1979. Wrappers. One of 26 lettered copies signed by Mark Strand.

"Wisdom in a dull man . . . " Providence, Rhode Island: Burning Deck, n.d. Poetry postcard.

⚜ PROSE

Mr. and Mrs. Baby and Other Stories. New York: Alfred A. Knopf, 1985. Dust jacket. Published at $11.95.

Rembrandt Takes a Walk. Illustrations by Red Grooms. New York: Clarkson N. Potter, 1986. Dust jacket. Published at $14.95. A juvenile.

William Bailey. New York: Harry N. Abrams, 1987. Dust jacket. Plates. Published at $29.95.

⚜ TRANSLATIONS

18 Poems from the Quechua. Cambridge, Massachusetts: Halty Ferguson, 1971. Boards; not issued in dust jacket. One of 1,000 copies.

The Owl's Insomnia, by Rafael Alberti. Translated by Mark Strand. New York: Atheneum, 1973. Paperback; not issued in cloth. Published at $4.95.

Souvenir of the Ancient World, by Carlos Drummond de Andrade. Translated by Mark Strand. New York: Antaeus Editions, 1976. Wrappers. One of 50 copies signed by the author and translator in a total limitation of 500.

May Swenson

May Swenson (1913–1989), is a poetic shape-shifter whose studies or definitions of objects break things down into their most elemental, mysterious forms. She is much concerned with the visual aspect of poetry, the appearance of words on a page, as her title *Iconographs* suggests; her typographic innovations highlight the words themselves as magical objects. For Swenson, as for her friend and contemporary Elizabeth Bishop, poetic description is a means of discovery. As William Stafford says, "Her work often appears to be proceeding calmly, just descriptive and accurate; but then suddenly it opens into something that looms beyond the material, something that impends and implies. . . ."[1]

Swenson has a persistent urge to break herself down as well, to take on the forms of her objects and then lose form altogether, to "leave her own impinging selfhood in the paralyzed region where names are assigned, and assume instead the energies of natural process."[2] Sometimes a homely metaphor yields to a metaphysical vastness, as in "While Seated in a Plane" or "A City Garden in April," from her acclaimed *Half Sun Half Sleep*. In the former, she sees a cloudscape as a living room full of overstuffed chairs; but the

insubstantial, drifting quality of the clouds undoes the meta-
phor. One piece of furniture shifts into another; beds and
tables "ebbed to ebullient chairs, / then footstools that,
degraded, / flowed with the floor before I could get there."
Ultimately, instead of imposing shape upon the clouds, she
allows them to undo hers:

> One must be a cloud to occupy a house of cloud.
> I twirled in my dream, and was deformed
> and reformed, making many faces,
>
> refusing the fixture of a solid soul.[3]

In the "Daffodils" section of "A City Garden in April," set
in her beloved adopted city, New York, she compares daffodils
to telephones in a way that unsettles both.

> Yellow telephones
> in a row in the garden
> are ringing,
> shrill with light.[4]

This effect of synesthesia reduces the objects to pure color and
pure sound, to mystery:

> Look into the yolk-
> colored mouthpieces
> alert with echoes.
> Say hello to time.

Her use of alliteration, incantation, and riddle (she has
published two books of riddle-poems for children and adults)
goes hand in hand with her typographic innovation, which
includes shape poems; columns composed of the same word,
which cut concretely into the other sense of the poem; and
lines of widely spaced words intersected by squiggly dark lines
that divide the poem into sections, encouraging a variety of
possible readings in addition to the straightforward linear one.
As she says in "Teleology," we are accustomed to moving
forward; our eyes "look front," so that we cannot easily see the
world's multiplicity, as "the housefly sees in a whizzing
circle."[5] Swenson encourages a wider and less stable view.

In 1981, Swenson shared the Bollingen Prize in Poetry with Howard Nemerov.

❧ POETRY

"Evolution." Winston-Salem, North Carolina: Palaemon Press, 1984. Broadside, signed by the author. Limitation not stated.

Iconographs. New York: Charles Scribner's Sons, 1970. Boards; not issued in dust jacket.

In Other Words: New Poems. New York: Alfred A. Knopf, 1987. Dust jacket. Published at $16.95.

The Love Poems. Boston: Houghton Mifflin, 1991. Paperback; not issued in cloth. Published at $9.95.

More Poems to Solve. New York: Charles Scribner's Sons, 1971. Dust jacket. Poems for young readers.

Poems to Solve. New York: Charles Scribner's Sons, 1966. Dust jacket. Published at $3.50. Poems for young readers.

"Questions : Answers." Artwork by Karyl Klopp. Cambridge, Massachusetts: Pomegranate Press, 1973. Broadside. One of 250 copies.

❧ PROSE

New Voices: Selected University & College Prize-winning Poems, 1979–1983, ed. May Swenson. New York: Academy of American Poets, 1984. Wrappers. With a foreword by Swenson.

❧ TRANSLATIONS

"Sketch in October," by Tomas Tranströmer. Translated by May Swenson. N.p., 197–. Folded broadside. Swedish / English text. Limitation not stated.

Windows & Stones: Selected Poems, by Tomas Tranströmer
   Translated by May Swenson with Leif Sjöberg.
   University of Pittsburgh Press, 1972. Dust jacket.
   Published at $5.95.

Diane Wakoski 🌿

Diane Wakoski (b. 1937) says, "I think of myself as . . . a poet creating both a personal narrative and a personal mythology."[1] Poetry is the process by which she continually remakes herself. "The poems were a way of inventing myself into a new life."[2]

Wakoski's digressive and repetitive form is an extension of content, of the process of her transforming imagination at work. As Hayden Carruth says, "Wakoski has a way of beginning her poems with the most unpromising materials imaginable, then carrying them on, often on and on and on, talkily, until at the end they come into surprising focus, unified works. . . . [H]er poems are deeply, rather than verbally structured."[3] Digression and repetition are emotional and creative strategies to deal with her persistent sense of inadequacy and fear of betrayal. Wakoski explores the idea of repetition in "Filling the Boxes of Joseph Cornell," from her acclaimed, surrealist *Inside the Blood Factory*. Repetition is self-assertion, is obsession, is a structure for creation. There is the fear of repeating mistakes, but also the need to be heard, the need to understand: "The structure of anger is repetition"; and

The structure of repetition is one that makes songs
and dances and boxes
   I don't want to repeat myself.
   It seems to be the only way of getting a point across
   though[4]

Wakoski forges luminous poems and versions of self, combining images from popular American mythology, classical mythology, and daily life. Born in California, she often mythologizes the American West. In "The Silver Surfer on the Desert," she is "skimming past [the desert] in a blue silver car" with a cat ("downy as Teddy Bear Cholla"), or an owl, or the mythical silver surfer running beside her. This myth connects her Michigan life, where a grey cat looks in the window at her, to a mythic desert life that they share. She and the cat

               . . . *both recognize*
the invisible Silver Surfer
standing also behind us.
We both know that the cat ran
on his padded feet
next to the winter car
in the Sonoran desert. That someone
whispered in the ears
of both cat and woman,
and that the light which haloed
our silvery-haired bodies was not
indefinable. That anyone
who followed us
could never be lost
in total darkness.

We teach a new physics.
That there is nothing
which does not reflect
light.[5]

☙ POETRY

Abalone. Los Angeles: Black Sparrow Press, 1974.
Unprinted dust jacket. One of 126 copies in boards
signed by the author in a total limitation of 626. A
New Year's greeting for friends of the Press.

*Cap of Darkness: Including Looking for the King of Spain &
Pachelbel's Canon.* Santa Barbara, California: Black
Sparrow Press, 1980. Glassine dust jacket. One of 750
hardcover trade copies.

Celebration of the Rose: For Norman on Christmas Day.
Montclair, New Jersey: Caliban Press, 1987. Wrappers.
Signed by the author. Limitation not stated.

"Claws." Providence, Rhode Island: Burning Deck, ca.
1972. Poem postcard. One of an unspecified number of
signed copies.

Coins & Coffins. New York: Hawk's Well Press, 1962.
Wrappers. The author's first published book, preceded
by "Justice is Reason Enough," issued on
mimeographed sheets in 1959, and a poem in *Four Young
Lady Poets*, 1962.

The Collected Greed, Parts 1–13. Santa Barbara, California:
Black Sparrow Press, 1984. Glassine dust jacket. One of
50 hardbound copies signed by the author and with an
original holograph poem tipped in.

"Comparisons." Providence, Rhode Island: Burning Deck,
1973. Poem postcard. One of an unspecified number of
signed copies.

Dancing on the Grave of a Son of a Bitch. Los Angeles: Black
Sparrow Press, 1973. Glassine dust jacket. One of 300
copies in boards, numbered and signed by the author.

Discrepancies and Apparitions. Garden City, New York:
Doubleday, 1966. Dust jacket. Published at $2.95. With
the author's presentation inscription. Loosely inserted is

an invitation to the publication day party for *The Motorcycle Betrayal Poems*.

Emerald Ice: Selected Poems, 1962–1987. Santa Rosa, California: Black Sparrow Press, 1988. Glassine dust jacket. One of 200 hardcover copies signed by the author.

"The Empress No. 5." N.p., n.d. Broadside, signed by the author. Limitation not stated.

"Exorcism." Cambridge, Massachusetts: My Dukes, 1970. Broadside. Trade edition; there were also ten signed copies with a different final line.

The Fable of the Lion & the Scorpion. Milwaukee, Wisconsin: Pentagram Press, 1975. Wrappers. One of 100 signed copies in a total limitation of 1,000.

Four Young Lady Poets. New York: Totem Press, 1962. Wrappers. Published at $1.25. Correct first edition with the cover printed in yellow and black. The other contributors were Carol Berge, Barbara Moraff, and Rochelle Owens.

"The Frame." Illustrated by Richard Zauft. Cleveland Heights, Ohio: Leslietown Press, 1983. Broadside. One of 32 copies signed by the author.

The George Washington Poems. New York: Riverrun Press, 1967. Wrappers. Second issue, with the numeral 2 stamped to the left of the dollar bill on page one. This copy is signed by the author.

George Washington's Camp Cups. Madison, Wisconsin: Red Ozier Press, 1976. Wrappers. One of 100 copies signed by the author in a total limitation of 150.

Greed. See *The Collected Greed, Parts 1–13*.

Greed, Parts 5–7. Los Angeles: Black Sparrow Press, 1971. Glassine dust jacket. One of 200 hardbound copies numbered and signed by the author.

Greed, Parts 8, 9, 11. Los Angeles: Black Sparrow Press, 1973. Glassine dust jacket. One of 50 hardbound copies numbered and signed by the author and with a holograph poem. Accompanied by a copy of the broadside flyer for the book, reproducing a poem; one of 100 copies signed by the author.

"Having Replaced Love with Food and Drink: A Poem for Those Who've Reached 40." Huntington, New York: A Poem A Month Club, 1977. Broadside, signed by the author. Limitation not stated.

Husks of Wheat: Two Poems. Illustrated by Hans Burkhardt. Northridge, California: Santa Susana Press, 1987. Loose signatures in cloth slipcase as issued. One of 65 copies signed by the author and the artist.

Inside the Blood Factory. Garden City, New York: Doubleday, 1968. Dust jacket. Published at $4.50. First issue, with red endpapers. Signed by the author on the title page.

The Lady Who Drove Me to the Airport. Worcester, Massachusetts: Metacom Press, 1982. Wrappers. One of 150 copies signed by the author in a total limitation of 176.

The Laguna Contract. Madison, Wisconsin: Crepuscular Press, 1976. Wrappers. Illustrated. One of 125 copies signed by the author, this copy signed twice. Half of the edition was reportedly destroyed.

The Last Poem, by Diane Wakoski, & Tough Company, by Charles Bukowski. Santa Barbara, California: Black Sparrow Press, 1976. Wrappers. One of 740 copies. Published as a New Year's greeting for friends of the Press.

"The Liar." New York: L. Lutes, 1974. Broadside. One of 200 signed copies.

Looking for Beethoven in Las Vegas. New York: Red Ozier Press, 1981. Loose sheets in wrappers. One of 200 copies signed by the author.

Looking for the King of Spain. Los Angeles: Black Sparrow Press, 1974. Wrappers. Published at 50 cents. Twelve hundred twenty copies printed. "Sparrow 21."

"Love, the Lizard." Providence, Rhode Island: Burning Deck, 1975. Broadside. Limitation not stated.

"A Lover Disregards Names." Providence, Rhode Island: Burning Deck, ca. 1972. Poem postcard. One of an unspecified number of signed copies.

The Magellanic Clouds. Los Angeles: Black Sparrow Press, 1970. Glassine dust jacket. One of 250 hardbound copies signed by the author.

The Magician's Feastletters. Santa Barbara, California: Black Sparrow Press, 1982. Glassine dust jacket. One of 750 hardcover trade copies.

Making a Sacher Torte: Nine Poems. Illustrated by Ellen Lanyon. Mount Horeb, Wisconsin: Perishable Press / Minor Confluence, 1981. Boards. One of 225 copies. Accompanied by a copy of the broadside prospectus for the book.

The Man Who Shook Hands. Garden City, New York: Doubleday, 1978. Dust jacket. Published at $6.95.

The Managed World. New York: Red Ozier Press, 1980. Wrappers. One of 185 copies signed by the author in a total limitation of 200.

Medea the Sorceress. Santa Rosa, California: Black Sparrow Press, 1991. Glassine dust jacket. One of 110 hardbound copies signed by the author. Volume I of *The Archaeology of Movies and Books.*

The Moon Has a Complicated Geography. Palo Alto, California: Odda Tala, number three, 1969. Wrappers. Limitation not stated. This copy is signed by the author.

The Motorcycle Betrayal Poems. New York: Simon and Schuster, 1971. Dust jacket. Published at $5.95. Review slip loosely inserted.

On Barbara's Shore: A Poem. Los Angeles: Black Sparrow Press, 1971. Glassine dust jacket. One of 100 hardcover copies signed by the author in a total limitation of 513. The one-hundredth publication of the Press and published gratis.

Overnight Projects with Wood. Madison, Wisconsin: Red Ozier Press, 1977. Wrappers. One of 170 copies signed by the author. Title page collage by Steve Miller.

Pachelbel's Canon. Santa Barbara, California: Black Sparrow Press, 1978. Wrappers. Published at 75 cents. Twelve hundred twenty-eight copies printed. "Sparrow 71."

"Peaches." West Branch, Iowa: Toothpaste Press for Bookslinger, 1981. Broadside. One of 85 signed copies. Issued on the occasion of a reading by the author at the Walker Art Center, 26 February 1981.

"The Purple Finch Song." Mount Horeb, Wisconsin: Perishable Press, 1972. Broadside. One of 97 copies "for Walter & Mary's Purple Finch Paper."

The Ring. Santa Barbara, California: Black Sparrow Press, 1977. Glassine dust jacket. One of 140 hardcover copies signed by the author in a total limitation of 180.

"The Ring." N.p.: Walker Art Center, 1978. Broadside. One of 474 copies in a total limitation of 500.

The Rings of Saturn. Santa Rosa, California: Black Sparrow Press, 1986. Glassine dust jacket. One of 200 hardcover copies signed by the author. Accompanied by a copy of the hardcover trade edition limited to 300 copies.

Roses. Montclair, New Jersey: Caliban Press, 1987. Stiff wrappers silkscreened by Donna Moran. One of 100 copies signed by the author.

Saturn's Rings. New York: Targ Editions, 1982. Tissue dust jacket. One of 250 copies signed by the author.

Smudging. Los Angeles: Black Sparrow Press, 1972. Glassine dust jacket. One of 250 hardbound copies signed by the author. Accompanied by a copy of the broadside prospectus for the book.

"A Snowy Winter in East Lansing." Santa Barbara, California: Table-Talk Press, 1985. Broadside. One of 100 signed copies.

"Sometimes a Poet Will Hijack the Moon." Providence, Rhode Island: Burning Deck, 1972. Broadside. Limitation not stated.

Spending Christmas with the Man from Receiving at Sears. Santa Barbara, California: Black Sparrow Press, 1977. Unprinted dust jacket. One of 176 hardbound copies signed by the author. A Christmas greeting for friends of the Press.

"Stillife: Michael, Silver Flute and Violets." Storrs: University of Connecticut, 1973. Single sheet folded to make four pages. One of 250 copies issued on the occasion of a reading by the poet on 6 November 1973.

"Talking from Christmas Country." Los Angeles: Black Sparrow Press, 1968. Wrappers. One of 300 copies in a total limitation of 400. A Christmas greeting from the publisher under the overall title of *A Play and Two Poems.* Other contributors are Robert Kelly and Ron Loewinsohn.

Thanking My Mother for Piano Lessons. Mount Horeb, Wisconsin: Perishable Press, 1969. Wrappers. One of 190 copies signed by the author in a total limitation of 250.

"This Water Baby." Santa Barbara, California: Unicorn Press, 1971. Poetry postcard.

Trilogy. Garden City, New York: Doubleday, 1974. Dust jacket. Published at $6.95. Contains *Coins & Coffins*, *Discrepancies and Apparitions*, and *The George Washington Poems*.

Trophies. Santa Barbara, California: Black Sparrow Press, 1979. One of 200 hardcover copies signed by the author in a total limitation of 250.

Two Poems, by Galway Kinnell and Diane Wakoski. Wood engraving by Barry Moser. Madison, Wisconsin: Red Ozier Press, 1981. Wrappers. Publisher's New Year greeting, signed by Kinnell and Wakoski. Limitation not stated. Wakoski's poem is "Gardenias."

Virtuoso Literature for Two and Four Hands. Garden City, New York: Doubleday, 1974. Dust jacket. Published at $4.95.

"Vulture Weather." Illustrated by Elizabeth Quandt. N.p: Calliopea Press, n.d.. Broadside. One of 150 copies signed by the author and the illustrator. "Poetry / Art Broadside Series."

Waiting for the King of Spain. Santa Barbara, California: Black Sparrow Press, 1976. Glassine dust jacket. One of 250 hardcover copies signed by the author.

Why My Mother Likes Liberace: A Musical Selection. Illustrated by Rebecca Gaver. Tucson, Arizona: Sun-Gemini Press, 1985. Glassine dust jacket. One of 50 *hors commerce* copies signed by the author and the artist and with a holograph poem by Wakoski.

"Winter Sequences." Santa Barbara, California: Black Sparrow Press, 1973. Broadside folded twice and tipped into paper wrappers. One of 126 copies signed by the author in a total limitation of 626. A New Year's greeting from the press.

The Wise Men DRAWN *to Kneel in Wonder at the* FACT *So of* ITSELF. Los Angeles: Black Sparrow Press, 1971. Wrappers. Publisher's Christmas greeting. Five hundred twenty-five copies printed. Wakoski contributed "The Magi" to the booklet. Other contributors are Robert Kelly and David Bromige.

☙ PROSE

Creating a Personal Mythology. Los Angeles: Black Sparrow Press, 1975. Wrappers. "Sparrow 31." Published at 50 cents; 1,208 copies printed. This copy is signed by the author.

Form is an Extension of Content. Los Angeles: Black Sparrow Press, 1972. Wrappers. Published at 50 cents. Seven hundred twenty copies printed. "Sparrow 3."

Toward a New Poetry. Ann Arbor: University of Michigan Press, 1980. Paperback, not issued in cloth.

Variations on a Theme (An Essay on Revision). Santa Barbara, California: Black Sparrow Press, 1976. Wrappers. Published at 75 cents. Fourteen hundred seventy-six copies printed. "Sparrow 50."

Theodore Weiss

As poet, critic, professor of English at Princeton, and editor of *The Quarterly Review of Literature*, Theodore Weiss (b. 1916) has for more than fifty years been passionately engaged with the question of poetry's relevance—to its time, to his life, to everyone's life. In *A Controversy of Poets* he says, "I am concerned in a proudly snippety time with the sustained poem, one that is more than merely personal and lyrical and happily fragmented. It is easy to go with the time or to cry out against it; but to do something with it, to take it by surprise, to make more of it . . . than it can do itself— might that not still occupy poets?"[1]

Hayden Carruth describes Weiss's often complex, difficult syntax as winding "ever back on itself in the search for more precise discrimination of feeling, moral and aesthetic judgment and descriptive rightness."[2] Weiss takes change, aging, destruction, and doubt as occasions for making and remaking himself and his world, as in "The Last Letters," about the laws of a life's energy

consumed,
even as it consumes itself forever
in its own private flame, now breaking loose,

like some great moth
throwing itself into the fire
which is itself to enlarge it, but lost to it

in the very moment of having.³

This process by which we make and are made by our worlds is played out in very different ways by Weiss's two book-length poetic monologues, *Gunsight*, where a wounded soldier in surgery reaches down to recover layers of his past, and *Recoveries*, which explores, from the vantage point of a secondary figure in a Florentine fresco, the relation between painting and viewer, subject and creator. In the recent "Variations on a Favorite Theme," Weiss addresses his wife Renée, his co-editor and artistic collaborator, who is also a violinist:

Through
your strings the world, more spacious
as it turns upon itself, is passing,
our maple riding its dappled tide.⁴

☞ POETRY

The Catch. New York: Twayne Publishers, 1951. Dust jacket. Published at $2.25. Review slip loosely inserted. The author's first book, after an earlier edited volume of Gerard Manley Hopkins' poems.

Fireweeds. New York: Macmillan, 1976. Dust jacket. Published at $9.95.

From Princeton One Autumn Afternoon: Collected Poems 1950–1986. New York: Macmillan, 1987. Dust jacket. Published at $27.50.

Gunsight. New York: New York University Press, 1962. Dust jacket. One of 500 copies signed by the author. Publisher's flyer loosely inserted.

The Last Day and the First: Poems. New York: Macmillan, 1968. Dust jacket. Published at $4.95. Inscribed by the author.

The Medium: Poems. New York: Macmillan, 1965. Dust
jacket. Published at $3.95.

Recoveries: A Poem. New York: Macmillan, 1982. Dust
jacket. Published at $11.95. Review copy with
photograph and promotional material laid in.

A Slow Fuse: New Poems. New York: Macmillan, 1984. Dust
jacket. Published at $15.00.

The World Before Us: Poems 1950–1970. New York:
Macmillan, 1970. Dust jacket. Published at $6.95. With
the author's presentation inscription.

ᤂ PROSE

*The Breath of Clowns and Kings: Shakespeare's Early Comedies
and Histories.* London: Chatto & Windus, 1971. Dust
jacket. First English edition.

Selections from the Note-Books of Gerard Manley Hopkins, ed.
Theodore Weiss. Norfolk, Connecticut: New
Directions, 1945. Dust jacket. Published at $1.00. "The
Poets of the Year" series. Precedes Weiss' first published
book of poetry.

Reed Whittemore

Reed Whittemore (b. 1919), former editor of *Furioso* and *The New Republic* and now Poet Laureate of Maryland, has an engagingly unpretentious and humorous style. As James Dickey describes him, Whittemore is "as wittily cultural as they come, he has read more than any . . . man anybody knows, has been all kinds of places, yet shuffles along in an old pair of tennis shoes and khaki pants, with his hands in his pockets."[1] Whittemore has written a biography of William Carlos Williams, and has adapted Williams's loose and natural free verse form into his own style—colloquial, at times prosy, full of clever end and internal rhymes, almost like someone talking to himself. Also like Williams, Whittemore is concerned with the ordinary. "The properties of mind I most admire are the daytime properties—those that get us to the store or shop and back, and put us on the radio discussing poetry or arguing about communism and democracy."[2]

Whittemore frequently presents us with forms he confesses he has invented for fun or for the sake of argument, as in his comic treatment of the life-art dichotomy, "A Tale of a Poem and a Squash." He poses a poem against an acorn squash "grown in my garden," later admitting that his garden "as a matter of fact has no squashes"; squash and poem seem equally real or unreal.[3] In "Waves in Peoria," the poet critiques his own image immediately after writing it. The waves' beat

> Carries over the land like the longest freight train
> Ever to pass through Peoria.
> Possibly.
> I am not much on similes, and I think I have
> Never been to Peoria.[4]

But Whittemore legitimizes this activity of invention even as he humorously demystifies it. In "The Party" he demonstrates an absolute acceptance of children's make-believe:

> They served tea in the sandpile, together with
> Mudpies baked on the sidewalk.
> After tea
> The youngest said that he had had a good dinner,
> The oldest dressed for a dance,
> And they sallied forth together with watering pots
> To moisten a rusted fire truck on account of it
> Might rain.[5]

Whittemore's humor is often turned to serious subjects. The long title poem from *The Boy from Iowa* critiques both self-serving poets producing epics by the ton and, not unrelated, our consumer values:

> . . . he who has made me pen up pick,
> An earnest, honest, American epic hick.
> Born on a big old farm, he grew up with the notion
> That land was a good thing for man, even better than the
>   ocean.[6]

"Lines Composed upon Reading an Announcement by Civil Defense Authorities Recommending that I Build a Bomb Shelter in my Backyard," the first poem to take on the nuclear age, compares the bomb shelter to a child's game of self-sufficiency.[7] And poems like "The Feel of Rock," about his childhood, achieve an emotional depth with simplicity and wryness of tone and diction. Here is his portrait of his father:

The ground by the house was gravel like grandmother's
      heart.
He had his pride,
But God and he stood apart.
He slept with his radio by him as bride.[8]

❧ POETRY

The Boy from Iowa: Poems and Essays. New York: Macmillan, 1962. Dust jacket. Published at $4.00.

The Fascination of the Abomination: Poems, Stories, and Essays. New York: Macmillan, 1963. Dust jacket. Published at $5.00.

From Zero to the Absolute. New York: Crown, 1967. Dust jacket. Published at $4.95.

Heroes and Heroines: Poems. Drawings by Irwin Touster. New York: Reynal and Hitchcock, 1946. Dust jacket. Published at $2.50. Whittemore's first book.

New York Poems. Ausgewählt und herausgegeben von Ferdinand Schunck. Stuttgart: Philip Reclam jun., 1991. Paperback. An anthology containing Whittemore's "Ode to New York." English text with footnotes in German. A gift from the poet to the Milberg Collection.

The Past, the Future, the Present: Poems Selected and New. Fayetteville: University of Arkansas Press, 1990. Dust jacket. Published at $29.95. A gift from the poet to the Milberg Collection.

Poems New and Selected. Minneapolis: University of Minnesota Press, 1967. Dust jacket. Published at $4.00.

The Self-Made Man and Other Poems. New York: Macmillan, 1959. Paperback; not issued in cloth. "The Macmillan Poets" series.

☙ PROSE

Little Magazines. Minneapolis: University of Minnesota Press, 1963. Wrappers. Published at $1.25. "University of Minnesota Pamphlets on American Writers Number 32." A gift from the poet to the Milberg Collection.

Poets and Anthologists: A Look at the Current Poet-Packaging Process. Washington, D.C.: Library of Congress, 1986. Wrappers. A lecture delivered at the Library of Congress, 6 May 1985. A gift from the poet to the Milberg Collection.

Pure Lives: The Early Biographers. Baltimore, Maryland: Johns Hopkins University Press, 1988. Dust jacket. With the author's presentation inscription to Howard Woolmer. A gift from the compiler to the Milberg Collection.

Ways of Misunderstanding Poetry. Washington, D.C.: Library of Congress, 1965. Wrappers. A lecture delivered at the Library of Congress, 12 October 1964. A gift from the poet to the Milberg Collection.

Whole Lives: Shapers of Modern Biography. Baltimore, Maryland: Johns Hopkins University Press, 1989. Dust jacket. Published at $19.95. A gift from the poet to the Milberg Collection.

William Carlos Williams, Poet from Jersey. Boston: Houghton Mifflin, 1975. Dust jacket. Published at $10.95. Illustrated with photographs. With the author's presentation inscription to John Pauker.

William Carlos Williams: "The Happy Genius of the Household." Washington, D.C.: Library of Congress, 1984. Wrappers. A lecture delivered at the Library of Congress, 1 November 1983. A gift from the poet to the Milberg Collection.

Richard Wilbur

A prolific and career-long translator of Molière and Racine, Richard Wilbur (b. 1921) writes intricately brocaded, baroque poems that take so much pleasure in their status as artifacts that they maintain reference largely as foundation for his dazzling wit. In "Thyme Flowering among Rocks" he takes a close, even beautiful look at a stem of thyme in lines that could have been written by a plant taxonomist who loves his work:

> One branch, in ending,
> Lifts a little and begets
> A straight-ascending
>
> Spike, whorled with fine blue
> Or purple trumpets, banked in
> The leaf-axils . . .[1]

But even here Wilbur never forgets that his poem is a construction. He contrasts this simple, almost taxonomic view with the representational character the thyme would assume in Japanese art, and uses a 5 - 7 - 5 syllable count in his three-line stanzas to allude to haiku form.

More characteristic of Wilbur is the metaphysical mode

employed in "Black November Turkey," where a turkey and several chickens symbolize the dialectics of a complex system of metaphysical contraries.[2] Through his poetic attentiveness, Wilbur turns an ostensibly simple barnyard scene into a ritual occasion displaying death, timelessness, and a solemn obedience to fate in strict counterpoint to a vulgar, loud, and joyous absorption in the workings of time. Wilbur's diction and attention to sound, meter, and rhyme overwhelm the referential sense of the scene and make it permeable to a neo-Platonist complex of ideas.

In "A Voice from Under the Table" and the title poem from *Walking to Sleep* we see highly crafted meditations on the failed longing for transcendence which weave strands of mythological echo, literary allusion, and dream image in a learned rush that ends in the speaker's virtual annihilation, giving him the wisdom of distance.[3] This is in keeping with the Wilbur who says that "One perpetual task of the poet is to produce models of inclusive reaction and to let no word or thing be blackballed by sensibility."[4]

Wilbur's extraordinarily adroit translations of Molière and Racine capture the wit and grace of the French alexandrine in English couplets. In his version of Molière's *Tartuffe*, for example, Wilbur conveys the babbling sound quality of Madame Pernelle's indictment of parties—

> *C'est véritablement la tour de Babylone,*
> *Car chacun y babille, et tout du long de l'aune*

—with a pun that seems to reduce all language to redundancy—

> *Parties are Towers of Babylon, because*
> *The guests all babble on with never a pause . . .*[5]

Wilbur won the Pulitzer Prize and the National Book Award in 1957 for *Things of This World*. In 1971 he was awarded the Bollingen Prize in Poetry, and in 1989 the Pulitzer Prize for *New and Collected Poems*.

☙ POETRY

Advice from the Muse. Illustrations by Timothy Engelland. Old Deerfield, Massachusetts: Deerfield Press, 1981. Dust jacket. One of 300 copies signed by the author.

"Advice to a Prophet." N.p.: Privately printed, 1959. A greeting card. "From Richard and Charlee Wilbur."

"A Barred Owl." London: Turret Bookshop, 1992. Broadside. Published by Bernard Stone and Raymond Danowski. Reprinted from *Sewanee Theological Review* 35, no. 2 (1992). None for sale.

A Bestiary. Compiled by Richard Wilbur. Illustrated by Alexander Calder. New York: Pantheon Books, 1955. Boards, in slipcase as issued. One of 750 copies signed by Wilbur and Calder in a total limitation of 825.

"A Black Birch in Winter." N.p.: Privately printed, n.d. Greeting card. "The Season's Greetings from Charlee & Richard Wilbur." The photograph is by Larry Webster.

Candide, by Voltaire. Lyrics by Richard Wilbur. Music by Leonard Bernstein. New York: New York City Opera, 1956. Program for the world premiere, 1 December 1956, at the Martin Beck Theatre.

Candide. A Comic Opera Based on Voltaire's Satire. Book by Lillian Hellman. Score by Leonard Bernstein. Lyrics by Richard Wilbur. New York: Random House, 1957. Dust jacket. Published at $2.95. Illustrated with plates.

"A Christmas Hymn." N.p.: Privately printed for the author, n.d. Single sheet folded to make four pages. Christmas greeting. Inscribed, but not signed, by the author.

Complaint. New York: Phoenix Book Shop, 1968. Wrappers. One of 26 lettered copies in a total limitation of 126 signed copies.

"4/5/74." Illustrated by Dwight Little. Lenox, Massachusetts: Hawthorne Press, 1974. Broadside. One of 80 copies signed by the author and the artist. "An Arts Action Press broadside printed by Keith Thompson."

Hamlen Brook. New York: Albondocani Press, 1982. Wrappers. Holiday greeting, limited to 400 copies. Together with the original stiffener and unprinted envelope.

"A Late Aubade." N.p.: Privately printed for the author, n.d. Single sheet folded to make four pages. Christmas greeting. Previously printed in *The New Yorker.*

Lying and Other Poems. Omaha, Nebraska: Cummington Press, 1987. Wrappers. One of 160 copies.

The Mind-Reader: New Poems. New York: Harcourt Brace Jovanovich, 1976. Dust jacket. Published at $6.95.

"More Opposites." N.p.: Rowfant Club / Sea Cliff Press, 1988. Broadside. Limited to 80 copies for members of the Rowfant Club and 100 copies for distribution by Sea Cliff Press. Issued on the occasion of a Wilbur evening, 20 January 1988.

More Opposites. Illustrated by the author. New York: Harcourt Brace Jovanovich, 1991. Dust jacket. Published at $12.95.

New and Collected Poems. New York: Harcourt Brace Jovanovich, 1988. In publisher's slipcase as issued. One of 100 copies signed by the author. Accompanied by a copy of the trade edition in dust jacket, published at $27.95; a review copy with promotional material laid in.

Opposites. Illustrated by the author. New York: Harcourt Brace Jovanovich, 1973. Dust jacket. Published at $3.75.

Pedestrian Flight: Twenty-One Clerihews for the Telephone. Illustrated by the author. Winston-Salem, North

Carolina: Palaemon Press, 1981. Wrappers. Erratum slip. One of 110 copies signed by the author in a total limitation of 181.

Peter. Northampton, Massachusetts: Privately printed, 1972. Glassine dust jacket. Tributes to Peter Boynton by Richard Wilbur, James Merrill, William Meredith, and others. Printed at the Gehenna Press in an edition of 110 copies.

Poems 1943–1956. London: Faber and Faber, 1957. Dust jacket. Published at 15s. No comparable American edition.

"Prince Souvanna Phouma: An Exchange between Richard Wilbur & William Jay Smith." N.p., 1963. Single sheet folded to make four pages. One of 100 copies printed for private distribution on Wilbur's birthday, 1 March 1963. Signed by both Wilbur and Smith.

"The Proof." N.p.: Privately printed for the author, n.d. Single sheet folded to make four pages. Christmas greeting. Signed by the author.

"The Ride." New York: The Grolier Club, 1982. Broadside, signed by the author. Limitation not stated. "A keepsake for members & guests of The Grolier Club, November 10, 1982."

Seed Leaves: Homage to R.F. Prints by Charles Wadsworth. Calligraphy by Lance Hidy. Foreword by the author and afterword by the artist. Boston: David R. Godine, 1974. Wrappers, slipcase. One of 160 copies signed by the author and the artist. Printed on green paper.

Seven Poems. Omaha, Nebraska: Abattoir Editions, University of Nebraska, 1981. Wrappers. One of 200 copies.

Some Atrocities. Cleveland, Ohio: Bits Press, 1990. Wrappers. One of 300 copies.

Some Opposites: For Children and Others. New York: Nadja, 1990. Wrappers. One of 100 signed copies in a total limitation of 126.

"Transit." Winston-Salem, North Carolina: Palaemon Press, 1984. Broadside, signed by the author. Limitation not stated.

"Two Riddles from Aldhelm." Pittsburgh, Pennsylvania: Rook Press, 1975. Broadside, signed by the author. One of 100 illustrated copies in a total limitation of 300. "Rook Broadsides 3."

"Two Voices in a Meadow." N.p.: Privately printed for the author, n.d. Greeting card from Charlee and Richard Wilbur. Signed by the author.

"Under Cygnus." N.p.: Privately printed for the author, n.d. Single sheet folded to make four pages. A Christmas greeting.

"A Walk in the Woods." Cummington, New York: Privately printed, 1989. Single sheet folded to make four pages. One of 150 copies printed as a keepsake for a conference at Brown University; the conference never took place. Errata slip.

Walking to Sleep: New Poems and Translations. New York: Harcourt, Brace & World, 1969. Dust jacket. Published at $4.95.

⤳ PROSE

Conversations with Richard Wilbur. Edited with an introduction by William Butz. Jackson: University of Mississippi, 1990. Dust jacket. "Literary Conversation Series." Contains a chronology.

Edgar Allan Poe, 1809. Washington, D. C.: Library of Congress, 1959. Wrappers. Also contains Robert Hillyer's "Robert Burns, 1759" and Cleanth Brooks's

"Alfred Edward Housman, 1859." "The Gertrude
Whittall Lectures," published under the overall title
Anniversary Lectures.

Elizabeth Bishop: A Memorial Tribute. New York:
Albondocani Press, 1982. Wrappers. One of 174 signed
copies in a total limitation of 212. Published at $35.00.
The flyer advertising the book is loosely inserted.

Emily Dickinson: Three Views, by Archibald Macleish, Louise
Bogan, and Richard Wilbur. Amherst, Massachusetts:
Amherst College Press, 1960. Boards; issued without
dust jacket. "Papers delivered at Amherst College as
part of its observance of the bicentennial celebration of
the Town of Amherst . . . October 23, 1959." Signed by
Wilbur.

Responses: Prose Pieces 1953–1976. New York: Harcourt
Brace Jovanovich, 1976. Dust jacket. Published at
$10.00.

⮞ **TRANSLATIONS**

Andromache, by Jean Racine. Translated by Richard Wilbur.
Drawings by Igor Tulipanov. New York: Harcourt Brace
Jovanovich, 1982. Dust jacket. Published at $10.95.

"Andromache Speaks to Pyrrhus, from Jean Racine's
Andromaque, III, 6." Palo Alto, California: Matrix Press,
1982. Broadside. One of 50 copies signed by the author.
"Chimera Broadsides / Series 11."

"The Funeral of Bobo," by Joseph Brodsky. Translated by
Richard Wilbur. Ann Arbor, Michigan: Ardis, 1974.
Broadside. One of 100 copies signed by Brodsky.

The Learned Ladies, by Jean Baptiste Poquelin de Molière.
In a new English verse translation by Richard Wilbur.
New York: Dramatists Play Service, 1977. Wrappers, not
issued in cloth. Signed by Wilbur on the title page.

The Misanthrope, by Jean Baptiste Poquelin de Molière. Translated by Richard Wilbur. New York: Harcourt, Brace, 1955. Dust jacket. One of 1,450 copies in a total limitation of 1,500. This copy is signed by Wilbur. Published at $5.00.

The Pelican: From a Bestiary of 1120. N.p.: Stanbrook Abbey Press, 1963. Wrappers. One of 450 copies. A translation by Wilbur from Philippe de Thuan's Anglo-Norman bestiary of 1120. With the translator's presentation inscription.

Phaedra, by Jean Racine. Translated into English Verse by Richard Wilbur. Drawings by Igor Tulipanov. New York: Harcourt Brace Jovanovich, 1986. Dust jacket. Published at $15.95.

The School for Husbands, by Jean Baptiste Poquelin de Molière. Translated by Richard Wilbur. New York: Harcourt Brace Jovanovich, 1992. Dust jacket. Published at $18.95.

Tartuffe, by Jean Baptiste Poquelin de Molière. Translated by Richard Wilbur. New York: Harcourt, Brace & World, 1963. Dust jacket. Published at $3.95. With the author's presentation inscription.

The Whale and Other Uncollected Translations. Brockport, New York: BOA Editions, 1982. Boards, cloth spine. One of 10 copies signed by the author and with a holograph poem. Accompanied by a copy of the trade edition in dust jacket, one of 550 copies in a total limitation of 1,200, and with a copy of the poem-card prospectus.

C. K. Williams

For C. K. Williams (b. 1936), poetry is redemptive, a means by which to accept the ordinary for what it is, a way of using discursive language to reach beyond itself. He speaks urgently, in long lines and extended sentences that gather momentum and emotion, of the forces—whether our own ignorance or political oppression—that keep us from simply experiencing ourselves and our lives. Like William Carlos Williams writing in the 1950s, he believes that

> *It is difficult*
> *to get the news from poems*
> *yet men die miserably every day*
> *for lack*
> *of what is found there.*[1]

In "Yours," the poet's urgent work is to make poems as a way to awareness, as a way to make room for others to make poems:

> *listen! everyone! you have your own poem now*
> *it's yours as much as your heart as much as your own life is*
> *. . .*

I'm working as fast as I can I can't stop to use periods
sometimes I draw straight lines on the page because the
     words
are too slow . . .²

This sense of workmanship shows Williams's persistent affinity
with the working class. He is attuned both to the oppressive
relentlessness of a life that seems to offer no escape, and to the
joy that arises from working for its own sake. He explores the
warring forces of creation and destruction in poems like "To
Market,"³ where working on an assembly line provides both
a form for devotion and a means of self-destruction, and the
title poem from *Tar*, in which roofers live daily with the hot,
lethal substance, while the poet and his family adjust to the
presence of the deadly, invisible radiation emitted as a result
of the Three Mile Island nuclear accident. In "Sanctity" he
puzzles over the double life of a construction worker, who is
his friend and protector on the job, but at home is subject to
violent outbursts of inarticulate rage. The poem attempts no
facile resolution; instead it embraces its own inarticulateness
and allows the sounds of the construction site to speak for
themselves:

Listen: sometimes when you go to speak about life it's as
     though your mouth's full of nails
but other times it's so easy that it's ridiculous to even bother.
The eggs and the toast could fly out of the plates and it
     wouldn't matter
and the bubbles in the level could blow sky-high and it still
     wouldn't.
Listen to the back-hoes gearing up and the shouts and
     somebody cracking his sledge into the mortar pan.
Listen again. He'll do it all day if you want him to. . . .⁴

Here as elsewhere, Williams seeks to break through the
thinking mind into another dimension, simpler and more
basic. In the title poem from *With Ignorance*, written in his
discursive, interrogative mode, thoughts crowd each other in
their effort to get beyond thought:

What would release be? Being forgiven? No, never forgiven,
never only forgiven.
To be touched, somehow, with presence, so that the only
sign is a step, towards or away?

🖎 POETRY

A Day for Anne Frank. Philadelphia: Falcon Press, 1968.
Wrappers; limitation not stated. The author's first book,
this copy is signed and inscribed "The poem I learned
to write on . . . "

A Dream of Mind: Poems. New York: Farrar, Straus &
Giroux, 1992. Dust jacket. Published at $16.00.

Flesh and Blood. New York: Farrar, Straus & Giroux, 1987.
Dust jacket. Published at $12.95.

Lies. Boston: Houghton Mifflin, 1969. Dust jacket.

Poems 1963–1983. New York: Farrar, Straus & Giroux, 1988.
Dust jacket. Published at $19.95.

Tar: Poems. New York: Random House, 1983. Dust jacket.
Published at $10.00.

With Ignorance. Boston: Houghton Mifflin, 1977. Dust
jacket. Published at $7.95.

🖎 TRANSLATIONS

The Bacchae of Euripides: A New Version, by C. K. Williams.
Introduction by Martha Nussbaum. New York: Farrar,
Straus & Giroux, 1990. Dust jacket. Published at
$20.00.

Women of Trachis, by Sophocles. Translated by C. K.
Williams and Gregory W. Dickerson. Introduction by
the translators, and with an editor's foreword by
William Arrowsmith. New York: Oxford University
Press, 1978. Dust jacket. Published at $8.50.

Charles Wright

Charles Wright (b. 1935), a difficult poet to place in any particular American tradition, works at the interstices of the Tennessee language of his heritage, twentieth-century Italian surrealism (he has translated Dino Campana and Eugenio Montale), Catholic mysticism, and, especially in the earlier work, the American psychedelic culture of the 1960s and early 1970s. One might expect exaggeration, florid detail, and disjunctive, even heaped, orderings, as well as real spiritual yearning from bloodlines like these, but one hardly expects language torqued into the foreground of image with the beauty that is often his.

From "Dog Creek Mainline" we get a cluster of nouns moving on the rhythm of voice:

> *Odor of muscadine, the blue creep*
> *Of kingsnake and copperhead;*
> *Nightweed; frog spit and floating heart,*
> *Backwash and snag pool: Dog Creek.*[1]

It successfully repeats the sudden foregrounding of sense in its kaleidoscopic spin as images are grasped by consciousness so rapidly they become indistinguishable from the mind's order. The senses participate with each other and become so stimu-

lated, even aroused, that they break into hallucinatory constructs of their own: "floating heart" is the name of a plant that
Wright restores to its original strangeness.

In Wright, the visionary always threatens to overwhelm
logical order. He relinquishes individual identity and family
("The infinite rectitude / Of all that is past") in order to
encounter the archetypal, drowning small toe-holds of identity and sense in names of rivers or lines like "the stones
touched / All stall and worm to a dot"[2] as consciousness
becomes fluid and reference points dwindle to a far-off speck.

The poems of *China Trace* and *The Southern Cross* are
written out of a lush experience of a physical world more
quietly suffused with spirit and touched with a Christian air
that maintains deep and abiding faith in plants. This is a more
discursive voice, yet one that retains its beauty:

> *Like a bead of clear oil the Healer revolves through the*
> *   night wind*
>
> *Part eye, part tear, unwilling to recognize us*[3]

and

> *Time to gather the fire in its quartz bowl.*
>
> *I hope the one with the white wings will come.*
>
> *I hope the island of reeds is as far away as I think it is.*
>
> *When I get there, I hope they forgive me if the knot I tie is*
> *   the wrong knot.*[4]

In *Zone Journals* Wright composes in dated fragments,
shifting easily between Cherokee history, Renaissance Italian
art, the weather of the moment, or whatever is clear or
exciting and gets caught in the day's net of language.

Charles Wright's *Country Music: Selected Early Poems* was
co-winner of the National Book Award in 1983.

≈ **POETRY**

Bloodlines. Middletown, Connecticut: Wesleyan University Press, 1975. Dust jacket. Published at $6.00.

"California Spring." Washington, D.C.: Folger Library, 1979. Broadside. Limitation not stated. "Folger Evening Poetry Series 1979–80."

China Trace. Middletown, Connecticut: Wesleyan University Press, 1977. Dust jacket.

Colophons: Poems. Iowa City, Iowa: Windhover Press, 1977. Boards. One of 200 copies signed by the author.

Country Music: Selected Early Poems. Middletown, Connecticut: Wesleyan University Press, 1982. Dust jacket. Published at $15.00.

Dead Color. Illustrated by Leigh McLellan. San Francisco: Meadow Press for Charles Seluzicki, 1980. Wrappers. One of 285 copies signed by the author and the artist.

December Journal. Woodcut by William Hesterberg. N.p.: Geary Press, 1990. Wrappers. "Printed by Pam Beck to be distributed as gifts to friends of the poet, the artist and the printer." Limitation not stated. Signed by the poet and a gift from him to the Milberg Collection.

The Dream Animal. Illustrations by Charles Pachter. Toronto: Anansi, 1968. Boards; not issued in dust jacket. The author's first trade book.

"Equation." Illustrated by Karyl Klopp. Cambridge, Massachusetts: Pomegranate Press, 1975. Broadside. One of 26 artist's proofs signed by the artist; this copy is inscribed by Wright.

Five Journals. New York: Red Ozier Press, 1986. Tissue jacket. One of 25 copies bound in boards and signed by the author in a total limitation of 100. Printed on gray paper.

Four Poems of Departure. Portland, Oregon: Trace Editions, 1983. Wrappers. One of 425 copies in a total limitation of 500.

"Gate City Breakdown." Emory, Virginia: Iron Mountain Press, 1981. Broadside. One of 250 copies signed by the author.

The Grave of the Right Hand. Middletown, Connecticut: Wesleyan University Press, 1970. Dust jacket.

Hard Freight. Middletown, Connecticut: Wesleyan University Press, 1973. Dust jacket. Published at $6.00. This copy is signed by the author on the title page.

The Iron Mountain Review, Charles Wright Issue. Emory, Virginia: Emory & Henry College, 1992. Wrappers. Contains several poems by Wright and a bibliography. Signed by the poet and a gift from him to the Milberg Collection.

A Journal of the Year of the Ox. Iowa City: University of Iowa, 1988. Boards. One of 150 copies signed by the author.

"Nerval's Mirror." Illustrated by Karyl Klopp. North Cambridge, Massachusetts: Pomegranate Press, 1975. Broadside. One of 180 copies signed by the author and the artist.

The Other Side of the River: Poems. New York: Random House, 1984. Dust jacket. Published at $11.95.

Private Madrigals. Madison, Wisconsin: Abraxas Press, 1969. Wrappers. One of 200 copies signed by the author.

The Southern Cross. New York: Random House, 1981. Dust jacket. Published at $10.50.

The Venice Notebook. Boston: Barn Dream Press, 1971. Stiff wrappers. One of 100 signed copies in a total limitation of 500.

The World of the Ten Thousand Things: Poems 1980–1990. New York: Farrar, Straus, & Giroux, 1990. Dust jacket. Published at $25.00.

Wright, A Profile: New Poems. With an interview and a critical essay by David St. John. Iowa City, Iowa: Grilled Flowers Press, Profile Editions, 1979. Wrappers. One of 26 lettered copies signed by Wright.

Xionia: Poems. Iowa City: University of Iowa / Windhover Press, 1990. Boards. One of 250 copies signed by the author.

Zone Journals. New York: Farrar, Straus & Giroux, 1988. Dust jacket. Published at $14.95.

⤜ PROSE

Halflife: Improvisations and Interviews, 1977–87. Ann Arbor: University of Michigan Press, 1988. Cloth boards; not issued in dust jacket.

⤜ TRANSLATIONS

Mottetti = *Motets*, by Eugenio Montale. Translated by Charles Wright. Iowa City: Windhover Press at the University of Iowa, 1981. Glassine dust jacket. One of 220 copies.

Orphic Songs, by Dino Campana. Translated by Charles Wright. Introduction by Jonathan Galassi. Oberlin, Ohio: Oberlin College Press, 1984. Dust jacket. Published at $11.50. "Field Translation Series 9."

The Storm and Other Poems, by Eugenio Montale. Translated by Charles Wright. Introduction by Vinio Rossi. Oberlin, Ohio: Oberlin College, 1978. Dust jacket. Published at $8.95. "Field Translation Series 1."

James Wright

From his early formalist experiments all the way through his Deep Image work of the early and mid-1960s to his later quiet participations of voice in the loveliness of southern European light, James Wright (1927–1980) stood always in a deep vein of compassion running through himself and all things. He looked to art as an escape from the mills and the brutal indifference to beauty he found to be the southern Ohio of his youth, yet that heritage was not one he could ever allow himself to escape. This can be paralleled in the drama of "St. Judas," the title and final poem of the 1959 collection marking the end of his formal stage, where after betraying Christ, Judas, seeing a man being beaten, "held the man for nothing in my arms."

The rest of Wright's life as a poet can be seen as an exploration of the "nothing" one gets for embracing man and earth. *The Branch Will Not Break*, one of the greatest Deep Image works ever produced, shows remarkable range of feeling. It exhibits the Chinese mysticism of "Lying in a Hammock at William Duffy's Farm in Pine Island, Minnesota":

> *Down the ravine behind the empty house,*
> *The cowbells follow one another*
> *Into the distances of the afternoon . . .*

the comic and frustrated "Two Hangovers":

> *Drunk, mumbling Hungarian,*
> *The sun staggers in,*
> *And his big stupid face pitches*
> *Into the stove . . .*

the sorrow and wondering strangeness of "The sad bones of my hands descend into a valley / Of strange rocks," from "Rain"; and the sincere love and kindness for animals of "A Blessing," as in this evocation of a horse:

> *I would like to hold the slenderer one in my arms,*
> *For she has walked over to me*
> *And nuzzled my left hand.*

If *The Branch Will Not Break* is Wright's first acceptance of the mind's wildness and continuousness (notice how all passages selected show a dissolving and unifying of dissimilar substances), *Shall We Gather at the River* shows that wildness gone wrong in poems detailing human despair, bitterness, terror, and disgust, as when he writes

> *Soon I am sure to become so hungry*
> *I will have to leap barefoot through gas-fire veils of shame*[1]

or says that

> *A cop's palm*
> *Is a roach dangling down the scorched fangs*
> *Of a light bulb.*[2]

Toward the end of "The Minneapolis Poem," Wright does ask "What does my anguish / Matter?" and says,

> *something*
> *Is gone lonely*
> *Into the headwaters of the Minnesota.*[3]

His last collection, *This Journey*, published posthumously in 1982, evens his voice and brings it to his mature range. Despair and wonder are relinquished to a world lit from within, as in "Apollo," where the poet evokes

> *the young*
> *Fisherman's face:*
> *The only home where now, alone in the evening*
> *The god stays alive.*

Wright won the Pulitzer Prize in 1972 for *Collected Poems*.

≫ POETRY

"Autumn Begins in Martin's Ferry, Ohio." New York: Poetry Against the End of the World, 1982. Broadside. One of 150 copies.

Collected Poems. Frontispiece by Annie Wright. Middletown, Connecticut: Wesleyan University Press, 1971. Dust jacket. Published at $7.95.

"Entering the Kingdom of the Moray Eel & At Peace with the Ocean off Misquamicut." Huntington, New York: A Poem A Month Club, 1978. Broadside. One of 500 copies signed by the author.

"Fresh Wind in Venice." Pittsburgh, Pennsylvania: Slow Loris Press, 1976. Broadside. One of 65 copies, each signed by the author.

The Journey. Drawing by Marta Anderson. Concord, New Hampshire: William B. Ewert, 1981. Wrappers. One of 125 copies signed by the artist and by Christine Bertelson, the designer and printer.

"The Journey." Photographs by Robert Mahon. New York: Tideline Press, 1982. Folded broadside, with three mounted color photographs of Anghiari, Italy. One of 75 copies signed by Wright.

The Lion's Tail and Eyes; Poems Written out of Laziness and Silence, by James Wright, William Duffy, and Robert Bly. Madison, Minnesota: Sixties Press, 1962. Dust jacket. Published at $2.00.

Moments of the Italian Summer. Drawings by Joan Root. Washington, D.C.: Dryad Press, 1976. Wrappers. Published at $3.75. Trade edition; there were also 50 hardbound signed copies.

Remembering James Wright, by Robert Bly. Introduced by Thom Tamarro. St. Paul, Minnesota: Ally Press, 1991. Wrappers. Published at $6.00. Contains poems and translations by Wright and Bly.

A Reply to Matthew Arnold. Durango, Colorado: Logbridge-Rhodes, 1981. Wrappers. One of 22 numbered copies in a total limitation of 500.

Saint Judas. Middletown, Connecticut: Wesleyan University Press, 1959. Dust jacket. Published at $3.00. The author's second book, with his presentation inscription on the front endpaper.

Shall We Gather at the River. Middletown, Connecticut: Wesleyan University Press, 1968. Dust jacket. Published at $4.00.

Shall We Gather at the River. London: Rapp & Whiting, 1969. Dust jacket. Published at 25s. "Poetry USA Series 8." This edition drops one poem from the American edition and adds an introduction by Robert Bly.

The Snail's Road. Amherst, New York: Slow Loris Press, 1971. Broadside. One of 175 copies in a total limitation of 200.

The Summers of James and Annie Wright: Sketches and Mosaics, by James and Annie Wright. New York: Sheep Meadow Press, 1981. Wrappers. Published at $4.95.

The Temple in Nîmes. Worcester, Massachusetts: Metacom Press, 1982. One of 26 hardbound and lettered copies, not for sale, in a total limitation of 176. Accompanied by a copy of the trade edition, one of 150 copies in wrappers.

To a Blossoming Pear Tree. New York: Farrar, Straus & Giroux, 1977. Dust jacket. Published at $7.95.

Two Citizens. New York: Farrar, Straus & Giroux, 1973. Dust jacket. Published at $6.95.

"With the Gift of a Fresh New Notebook I Found in Florence." New York: Aeraiocht Press, n.d. Broadside. "Broadside Series, Special, No. One."

☙ PROSE

A Secret Field: Selections from the Final Journals, ed. Anne Wright. Durango, Colorado: Logbridge-Rhodes, 1985. Wrappers. Published at $3.25.

☙ TRANSLATION

Twenty Poems, by Pablo Neruda. Translated by James Wright and Robert Bly. Madison, Minnesota: Sixties Press, 1967. Dust jacket. Published at $2.00. With Pablo Neruda's presentation inscription.

Notes ⪘

⪘ AMMONS

1. The title poem from *Corsons Inlet: A Book of Poems* (Ithaca, New York: Cornell University Press, 1965).

2. Ammons, "Event: Corrective: Cure," *Acts of Mind: Conversations with Contemporary Poets*, ed. Richard Jackson (Tuscaloosa: University of Alabama Press, 1983), p. 33.

3. "Easter Morning," from *A Coast of Trees: Poems* (New York: W. W. Norton, 1981).

⪘ ASHBERY

1. The title poem from *Self-Portrait in a Convex Mirror* (New York: Viking Press, 1975); the poem originally appeared in *Poetry* magazine.

2. From *Three Poems* (New York: Viking Press, 1972), pp. 8–9.

3. "October at the Window," from *April Galleons: Poems* (New York: Viking Press, Elisabeth Sifton Books, 1987).

⪘ BERRY

1. "Introduction," *Wendell Berry*. American Authors Series, ed. Paul Merchant (Lewiston, Idaho: Confluence Press, 1991), p. 3.

2. "History," from *Clearing* (New York: Harcourt Brace Jovanovich, 1977).

3. Ibid.

4. "An Anniversary," from *The Country of Marriage* (New York: Harcourt Brace Jovanovich, 1973).

⪘ BERRYMAN

1. Daniel Hoffman, "John Berryman," *Contemporary Poets*, ed. James Vinson and D. L. Kirkpatrick. Third edition (London: Macmillan Press Ltd., 1980), p. 1736.

2. "A Professor's Song," from *His Thought Made Pockets & the Plane Buckt* (Pawlet, Vermont: C. Fredericks, 1958).

3. "Life, friends," from *The Dream Songs* (New York: Farrar, Straus & Giroux, 1969).

4. Berryman, "Note," *The Dream Songs*, p. vi.

✒ BISHOP

1. "Questions of Travel," from "Brazil," in *Questions of Travel* (New York: Farrar, Straus & Giroux, 1965); also in *The Complete Poems* (New York: Farrar, Straus & Giroux, 1969).

2. "The Sandpiper," one of the poems of "Elsewhere," in *The Complete Poems*.

3. "At the Fishhouses," from *Poems: North & South—A Cold Spring* (Boston: Houghton Mifflin, 1955); also in *The Complete Poems*.

4. "Squatter's Children," from "Brazil," in *Questions of Travel*; also in *The Complete Poems*.

5. *Anthology of Contemporary Brazilian Poetry* (Middletown, Connecticut: Wesleyan University Press, 1972).

✒ BOGAN

1. "Women," from *Body of This Death* (New York: Robert M. McBride, 1923).

2. Letter of 5 July 1969, quoted in Jaqueline Ridgeway, *Louise Bogan* (Boston: Twayne Publishers, 1984), p. 41.

3. Quoted in *Contemporary Authors*, New Revision, ed. James G. Lesniak (Detroit: Gale Research, 1991), vol. 33, p. 46.

4. "Medusa," from *Body of This Death*.

5. "The Meeting," from *The Blue Estuaries: Poems 1923–1968* (New York: Farrar, Straus & Giroux, 1968).

6. "Night," from *The Blue Estuaries*.

✒ BOOTH

1. "Forecast," from *Weathers and Edges* (New York: Viking Press, 1966).

2. Hayden Carruth, "Philip Booth," *Contemporary Poets*, ed. James Vinson (New York: St. Martin's Press, 1980), pp. 142–143.

3. "The Day the Tide," from *Weathers and Edges*.

4. "The Way Tide Comes," from *Available Light* (New York: Viking, 1976).

⌇ BRODSKY

1. Quoted in *Contemporary Authors*, New Revision, ed. James G. Lesniak (Detroit: Gale Research, 1992), vol. 37, p. 52.

2. "Nobel Lecture, 1987," *Brodsky's Poetics and Aesthetics*, ed. Loseff, Lev, and Valentina Polukhina (London: Macmillan Press, 1990), p. 9.

3. Stephen Spender in *The New Statesman* 88 (14 December 1973), p. 915.

4. Czeslaw Milosz in *New York Review of Books* 27, no. 13 (14 August 1980), p. 13.

5. "Nobel Lecture, 1987," pp. 2, 10.

6. "The Fifth Anniversary," from *To Urania* (New York: Farrar, Straus & Giroux, 1988).

⌇ CLAMPITT

1. This was her first commercially published book; an earlier collection, *Multitudes, Multitudes*, appeared in 1973.

2. "Beach Glass," from *The Kingfisher: Poems* (New York: Alfred A. Knopf, 1983).

3. Helen Vendler, "On the Thread of Language," *New York Review of Books* 30, no. 3 (3 March 1983), p. 19.

4. "Witness," from *What the Light Was Like* (New York: Alfred A. Knopf, 1985).

5. Mona Van Duyn on the back cover of *What the Light Was Like*.

6. "Gooseberry Fool," from *What the Light Was Like*.

7. Clampitt, on the back cover of *Archaic Figure: Poems* (New York: Alfred A. Knopf, 1987).

⌇ CORN

1. Quoted in *Contemporary Poets*, 3d ed., ed. James Vinson (New York: St. Martin's Press, 1980), p. 301.

2. "Songs for Five Companionable Singers," from *The Various Light* (New York: Viking Press, 1980).

3. "The Beholder," Section II of "Songs for Five Companionable Singers," from *The Various Light*.

4. "Passages," from *All Roads at Once* (New York: Viking Press, 1976).

✿ CREELEY

1. *The New American Poetry: 1945–1960*, ed. Donald M. Allen (New York: Grove Press, 1960), p. 410.

2. Charles Olson, "Projective Verse" and "Letter to Elaine Feinstein," in *Selected Writings of Charles Olson*, ed. Robert Creeley (New York: New Directions, 1966), p. 16. "Projective Verse" was first published in *Poetry New York*, No. 3 (1950).

3. "Preface," *For Love: Poems 1950–1960* (New York: Charles Scribner's Sons, 1962), p. 7.

4. "I Know a Man," from *For Love*.

5. Louis Martz, "Recent Poetry: The End of an Era," *Yale Review* 10, no. 2 (Winter 1970), p. 261.

6. "Echo Of," from *Pieces* (New York: Charles Scribner's Sons, 1969).

7. "Prospect," from *Mirrors* (New York: New Directions, 1983).

✿ DAVENPORT

1. George Steiner in *The New Yorker*, quoted on the back cover of *Thasos and Ohio: Poems and Translations 1950–1980* (Manchester, England: Carcanet, 1985).

2. "Ohio" and "For Lorine Niedecker" are from *Thasos and Ohio: Poems and Translations 1950–1980* (San Francisco: North Point Press, 1986); "The Resurrection in Cookham Churchyard," from *The Resurrection in Cookham Churchyard* (New York: Jordan Davies, 1982).

3. "Springtime and Autumn," from *Thasos and Ohio*.

4. The title poem from *The Medusa* (N.p.: Weng & Associates, 1984).

5. "Wo Es War, Soll Ich Werden," from *The Drummer of the Eleventh North Devonshire Fusiliers* (San Francisco: North Point Press, 1990).

6. "Badger," from *The Drummer of the Eleventh North Devonshire Fusiliers*.

✿ DI PRIMA

1. Robert Creeley, "Foreword," *Pieces of a Song: Selected Poems* (San Francisco: City Lights, 1973), p. vii.

2. *Rocky Ledge*, No. 7 (February–March 1981), p. 48.

3. "More or Less Love Poems," from *Dinners and Nightmares* (New York: Corinth Books, 1961).

4. "Poetics," from *Selected Poems 1956–1976* (Plainfield, Vermont: North Atlantic Books, 1977).

5. George Butterick, "Diane di Prima," *Dictionary of Literary Biography*, vol. 16: *The Beats: Literary Bohemians in Postwar America*, ed. Ann Charters (Detroit: Gale Research, 1983), p. 152.

6. "Poetics," from *Selected Poems 1956–1976*.

7. Untitled essay by Diane di Prima in *Beneath a Single Moon: Buddhism in Contemporary American Poetry*, ed. Kent Johnson and Craig Paulenich (Boston and London: Shambhala, 1991), p. 58.

8. "Tassajara, 1969," from *Selected Poems 1956–1976*.

≈ DICKEY

1. *The Longman Anthology of Contemporary American Poetry, 1950–1980*, ed. Stuart Friebert and David Young (New York and London: Longman, 1983), p. 174.

2. "The Flash," from *Poems 1957–1967* (Middletown, Connecticut: Wesleyan University Press, 1967).

3. "Pursuit from Under," from *Poems 1957–1967*.

4. "Cherrylog Road," from *Poems 1957–1967*.

5. *Falling, May Day Sermon, and Other Poems* (Middletown, Connecticut: Wesleyan University Press, 1981); *Puella* (Garden City, New York: Doubleday, 1982).

6. "Bread," from *Poems 1957–1967*.

≈ DORN

1. Books I–III, published between 1968 and 1972, were titled *Gunslinger*; the 1975 volume, which includes Books I–III and adds a fourth, is titled *Slinger*.

2. Preface to *Gunslinger*, ed. Marjorie Perloff (Durham, North Carolina: Duke University Press, 1989), p. xvii.

3. Quoted in *Contemporary Authors*, ed. Frances C. Locher (Detroit: Gale Research, 1980), vols. 93–96, p. 127.

4. From "Slinger I" in the 1989 edition of *Gunslinger*. In *Gunslinger, Book I* (Los Angeles: Black Sparrow Press, 1968), the first line of this quotation reads "And why do you have a female horse," as does an earlier version of the passage in "An Idle Visitation," from *The North Atlantic Turbine* (London: Fulcrum Press, 1967), pp. 60–61.

5. Edward Dorn, as quoted by Marjorie Perloff in *The New Republic*, 24 April 1976, p. 22.

6. Preface to *Gunslinger*, ed. Marjorie Perloff (1989), p. viii.

7. "Slinger, Book III," section ii, p. 198 in the Perloff edition.

8. Ibid., p. 155.

9. From *Yellow Lola* (Santa Barbara, California: Cadmus Editions, 1981).

❧   EBERHART

1. "Notes on Poetry," from *Twenty-five Dartmouth Poems*. Selected, with notes on poetry and a postscript by Richard Eberhart (Hanover, New Hampshire: Dartmouth Publications, 1966).

2. "A Commitment," from *Collected Poems 1930–1960* (London: Chatto & Windus, 1960).

3. Jean Garrigue, quoted in *Contemporary Authors*, New Revision, ed. Ann Evory (Detroit: Gale Research, 1981), vol. 2, p. 197.

4. "The Groundhog," from *Reading the Spirit* (London: Chatto & Windus, 1936).

5. "The Fury of Aerial Bombardment," from *Poems New and Selected* (Norfolk, Connecticut: New Directions, 1944).

❧   GINSBERG

1. "Howl," from *Howl and Other Poems* (San Francisco: City Lights Books, 1956).

2. Richard Eberhart, "West Coast Rhythms," *On the Poetry of Allen Ginsberg*, ed. Lewis Hyde (Ann Arbor: University of Michigan Press, 1984), p. 25.

3. From *Howl: Original Draft Facsimile, Transcript & Variant Versions* . . . , ed. Barry Miles (New York: Harper & Row, 1986), p. 152.

4. For the transcript of the court proceedings, see J. W. Erlich, *Howl of the Censor* (San Carlo, California: Nourse, 1961).

5. Ginsberg, "A Blake Experience," in Hyde, *On the Poetry of Allen Ginsberg*, pp. 120–130; see also Blake's "Ah! Sunflower," *The Complete Writings of William Blake*, ed. Geoffrey Keynes (London: Oxford University Press, 1966), p. 215.

6. The title poem from *Wichita Vortex Sutra* (N.p.: Coyote Books, 1966).

7. Quoted in *Collected Poems 1947–1980* (New York: Harper & Row, 1984).

8. "Going to the World of the Dead," from *White Shroud: Poems, 1980–1985* (New York: Harper & Row, 1986).

⤳ GLÜCK
1. *The Harvard Book of Contemporary American Poetry*, ed. Helen Vendler (Cambridge, Massachusetts: The Belknap Press of Harvard University Press, 1985), p. 416.
2. "Mythic Fragment," from *The Triumph of Achilles* (New York: Ecco Press, 1985).
3. "Lamentations," from *Descending Figure* (New York: Ecco Press, 1980).
4. "Pomegranate," from *The House on Marshland* (New York: Ecco Press, 1975).

⤳ GRAHAM
1. "Syntax," from *Hybrids of Plants and of Ghosts* (Princeton: Princeton University Press, 1980).
2. Thomas Gardner, "An Interview with Jorie Graham," *Denver Quarterly* 26, no. 4 (1992), pp. 79–104.
3. "For Mark Rothko," from *Hybrids of Plants and of Ghosts*; "Masaccio's Expulsion," from *Erosion* (Princeton: Princeton University Press, 1983); "Pollock and Canvas," from *The End of Beauty* (New York: Ecco Press, 1987).
4. "I Watched a Snake," from *Erosion*.
5. "From the New World," from *Region of Unlikeness* (New York: Ecco Press, 1991).

⤳ GROSHOLZ
1. "Nietzsche in the Box of Straws," from *Shores and Headlands* (Princeton: Princeton University Press, 1988).
2. "Dark Tents and Fires," from *Eden* (Baltimore, Maryland: Johns Hopkins University Press, 1992).
3. "Dream-Tree and Moon," from *Eden*.

⤳ GUEST
1. "The View from Kandinsky's Window," from *Fair Realism* (Los Angeles: Sun & Moon Press, 1989).
2. Quoted in *Contemporary Poets*, 5th ed., ed. Tracy Chevalier (Chicago and London: St. James Press, 1991), p. 360.
3. "The Advance of the Grizzly," *American Poetry Review* 21, no. 4 (July / August 1992), p. 21.
4. "The Altos," from *Defensive Rapture* (Los Angeles: Sun & Moon Press, 1993).

🗩 HALL

1. "An Airstrip in Essex, 1960" and "The Old Pilot" are from *The Alligator Bride* (New York: Harper & Row, 1950).

2. "Swan" and "Apples" are from *The Alligator Bride.*

3. "The Black-Faced Sheep," from *Kicking the Leaves* (Mount Horeb, Wisconsin: Perishable Press, 1975).

🗩 HALPERN

1. Derek Walcott's comment is on the dust jacket of Halpern's book, *Tango* (New York: Viking Press, 1987).

2. "The Ethnic Life," from *Traveling on Credit* (New York: Viking Press, 1972).

3. The title poem from *Foreign Neon* (New York: Alfred A. Knopf, 1991).

4. "Aubade," from *Life Among Others* (New York: Viking Press, 1978).

5. "Señor Excellent," from *Tango.*

🗩 HARPER

1. "Blue Ruth: America," from *History Is Your Own Heartbeat* (Urbana: University of Illinois Press, 1971).

2. Quoted in *Contemporary Poets*, 3d ed., ed. James Vinson (New York: St. Martin's Press, 1980), p. 644.

3. "Smoke," from *Images of Kin* (Urbana: University of Illinois Press, 1977).

4. "Don't They Speak Jazz?" from *Melus* 10, no. 1 (Spring 1983), pp. 3–6.

5. "Here Where Coltrane Is," from *History Is Your Own Heartbeat.*

🗩 HASS

1. "Misery and Splendor," a broadside (Berkeley, California: Black Oak Books, 1989).

2. Stanley Kunitz, *A Kind of Order, A Kind of Folly: Essays and Conversations* (Boston and Toronto: Atlantic, Little Brown, 1975), p. 282.

3. *Field Guide* (New Haven, Connecticut: Yale University Press, 1973).

4. Hass, quoted in *Young Contemporary Poets*, ed. Paul Carroll (New York: Follett Publishing Company, 1968), p. 189.

5. "On the Coast near Sausalito," from *Field Guide*.

6. Charles Molesworth, "Some Recent American Poetry," *Ontario Review* 11 (Fall–Winter 1979–1980), p. 100.

7. "Spring Drawing," from *Human Wishes* (New York: Ecco Press, 1989).

⇗ HECHT

1. "Peripeteia," from *Millions of Strange Shadows* (New York: Atheneum, 1977).

2. Peter Sacks, "Hecht's 'Rites and Ceremonies,'" in *The Burdens of Formality: Essays on the Poetry of Anthony Hecht*, ed. Sydney Lea (Athens: University of Georgia Press, 1989), p. 66.

3. Lea, *Burdens of Formality*, p. xii.

4. "The Gardens of the Villa d'Este," from *The Hard Hours* (New York: Atheneum, 1967).

5. Anthony Hecht, "On the Methods and Ambitions of Poetry," *Hudson Review* 18, no. 4 (Winter 1965–1966), pp. 489–505.

6. Laurence Lieberman, "Recent Poetry in Review: Risks and Faiths," *Yale Review* 57, no. 4 (Summer 1968), p. 601.

7. "More Light! More Light!," from *The Hard Hours*.

8. "Sestina d'Inverno," from *Millions of Strange Shadows*.

9. "The Ghost in the Martini," from *Millions of Strange Shadows*.

10. The title poem from *The Venetian Vespers* (New York: Atheneum, 1979); "See Naples and Die," from *The Transparent Man* (New York: Alfred A. Knopf, 1990).

⇗ HOLLANDER

1. Richard Poirier, quoted in *Contemporary Authors*, New Revision, ed. Ann Evory (Detroit: Gale Research, 1981), vol. 1, p. 276.

2. "The Great Bear," from his first volume, *A Crackling of Thorns* (New Haven, Connecticut: Yale University Press, 1958).

3. "Steady Work," from *In Time and Place* (Baltimore, Maryland: Johns Hopkins University Press, 1986).

4. "A Defense of Rhyme," from the "In Time" sequence, *In Time and Place*.

☙ HUDGINS

1. Robert Shaw, review of *Saints and Strangers*, in *Poetry* 148, no. 1 (April 1986), pp. 41–42.

2. Hudgins, as quoted in the *Dictionary of Literary Biography*, vol. 120, p. 144.

3. Henri Coulette, quoted in *Contemporary Authors*, ed. Susan M. Trosky (Detroit: Gale Research, 1991), vol. 132, p. 184.

4. "A Christian on the Marsh," from *After the Lost War* (Boston: Houghton Mifflin, 1988).

5. The title poem from *After the Lost War.*

6. "Praying Drunk," from *The Never-Ending* (Boston: Houghton Mifflin, 1991).

☙ IGNATOW

1. David Ignatow, untitled review of James Wright's *Shall We Gather at the River*, in *New York Times Book Review*, 9 March 1969, p. 31.

2. Marvin Bell, "Homage to the Runner," *American Poetry Review* 5, no. 2 (March–April 1976), p. 32.

3. Quoted in *Contemporary Authors*, First Revision, ed. Clare D. Kinsman and Mary Ann Tennenhouse (Detroit: Gale Research, 1974), vols. 9–12, p. 417.

4. "Business," from *Poems, 1934–1969* (Middletown, Connecticut: Wesleyan University Press, 1970).

5. "All Quiet," from *Rescue the Dead: Poems* (Middletown, Connecticut: Wesleyan University Press, 1968).

6. "Nice Guy," from *Rescue the Dead.*

7. "The Sky Makes No Sense to Me," from *Tread the Dark: New Poems* (Boston: Little, Brown, 1978).

☙ JARRELL

1. John Crowe Ransom, "The Rugged Way of Genius: A Tribute to Randall Jarrell," *Southern Review*, New Series 3, no. 2 (Spring 1967), p. 266.

2. *Little Friend, Little Friend* (New York: Dial Press, 1945); and *Losses* (New York: Harcourt, Brace, 1948).

3. Hayden Carruth, "Melancholy Monument," *The Nation* 209, no. 1 (7 July 1969), p. 20.

4. "Eighth Air Force," from *Losses* (New York: Harcourt, Brace, 1948).

5.   Helen Vendler, "Randall Jarrell, Child and Mother, Frightened and Consoling," *New York Times Book Review*, 2 February 1969, pp. 5, 42.

6.   Randall Jarrell, *Poetry and the Age* (New York: Alfred A. Knopf, 1953), p. 12.

7.   *The Bat Poet* (New York: Macmillan, 1964); and *The Animal Family* (New York: Pantheon, 1965).

8.   "Well Water," from *The Lost World* (New York: Macmillan, 1965).

⤳   JUSTICE

1.   "Bus Stop; Or, Fear and Loneliness on Potrero Hill," from *Platonic Scripts* (Ann Arbor: University of Michigan Press, 1984), p. 211.

2.   Ibid., p. 215.

3.   "Bus Stop," from *Night Light* (Middletown, Connecticut: Wesleyan University Press, 1967).

4.   "Elsewheres," from *Night Light*.

5.   "A Dancer's Life," from *Departures* (New York: Atheneum, 1973).

6.   "White Notes," from *Departures*.

7.   "Dreams of Water," from *Night Light*.

8.   "Sonatina in Yellow," from *Departures*.

⤳   KELLY

1.   "Going With the Poem," from *Beneath a Single Moon* (Boston: Shambhala, 1991).

2.   " (prefix:" from *Finding the Measure* (Los Angeles: Black Sparrow Press, 1968).

3.   "Sentence," from *Spiritual Exercises* (Santa Barbara, California: Black Sparrow Press, 1981).

4.   Jed Rasula, "Ten Different Fruits on One Different Tree: Reading Robert Kelly," *Credences: A Journal of Twentieth-Century Poetry and Poetics*, New Series 3, no. 1 (Spring 1984), p. 148.

5.   "The Devotees," from *Kill the Messenger Who Brings Bad News* (Santa Barbara, California: Black Sparrow Press, 1979).

6.   "Where is the root? / It lies beneath the tongue." The lines appear in "Towards the Day of Liberation," from *Not This Island Music* (Santa Barbara, California: Black Sparrow Press, 1987).

7.   "Foresong," Fourth Rune, in *Credences: A Journal of Twentieth-Century Poetry and Poetics*, New Series 3, no. 1 (Spring 1984), p. 54.

✺ KENNEDY

1. Quoted in *Contemporary Poets*, 5th ed., ed. Tracy Chevalier (Chicago and London: St. James Press, 1991) p. 502.

2. The title poem from *Emily Dickinson in Southern California* (Boston: David R. Godine, 1973).

3. The title poem from *Hangover Mass* (Cleveland, Ohio: Bits Press, 1984).

4. Quoted in *Contemporary Authors*, New Revision, ed. Ann Evory (Detroit: Gale Research, 1981), vol. 4, p. 342.

5. "Epiphany," from *Cross Ties: Selected Poems* (Athens: University of Georgia Press, 1985).

✺ KINNELL

1. "On the Oregon Coast," from *Flower Herding on Mount Monadnock* (Boston: Houghton Mifflin, 1964).

2. "Poem of Night," from *Flower Herding on Mount Monadnock*.

3. Charles Molesworth, "'The Rank Flavor of Blood': The Poetry of Galway Kinnell," *The Fierce Embrace: A Study of Contemporary American Poetry* (Columbia: University of Missouri Press, 1979), p. 99.

4. The title poem from *Flower Herding on Mount Monadnock*.

5. "The Bear," from *Body Rags* (Boston: Houghton Mifflin, 1968).

✺ KIZER

1. "A Muse of Water," from *The Ungrateful Garden* (Bloomington: Indiana University Press, 1961).

2. "Pro Femina," from *Knock Upon Silence* (Garden City, New York: Doubleday, 1965).

3. "Fanny," from *Yin: New Poems* (Brockport, New York: BOA Editions, 1984).

4. "A Widow in Wintertime," from *The Ungrateful Garden*.

5. "A Month in Summer," from *Knock Upon Silence*.

✺ KOCH

1. David Lehman, "When the Sun Tries to Go On," in *Poetry* 114, no. 6 (September 1969), pp. 401–409.

2. "On the Great Atlantic Rainway," from *Thank You and Other Poems* (New York: Grove Press, 1962).

3. "The Art of Poetry," from *The Art of Love: Poems* (New York: Random House, 1975).

4. "Variations on a Theme by William Carlos Williams," from *Thank You and Other Poems*.

ᵜᵄ KUNITZ

1. "King of the River," from *The Testing-Tree* (Boston: Atlantic Monthly Press, 1971).

2. James Whitehead, "Leaping Ghazals and Inside Jokes Concealed in Tropes," in *Saturday Review*, 18 December 1971, p. 40.

3. Quoted by Daniel Halpern in "Things That Make the World Worth Saving: An Introduction to a Poetry Reading," *A Celebration for Stanley Kunitz: On His Eightieth Birthday* (Riverdale-on-Hudson, New York: Sheep Meadow Press, 1986), p. 130.

4. "The Portrait," from *The Testing-Tree*.

5. "Father and Son," from *Passport to the War, A Selection of Poems* (New York: Henry Holt, 1944).

6. "The Science of the Night," from *Selected Poems 1928–1958* (Boston: Little, Brown, 1958).

7. "An Old Cracked Tune," from *The Testing-Tree*.

8. "The Mulch," from *The Testing-Tree*.

ᵜᵄ LATTIMORE

1. Quoted in *Contemporary Authors*, New Revision, ed. Ann Evory (Detroit: Gale Research, 1981), vol. 1, p. 365.

2. "Dry Light from Pylos," from *Poems* (Ann Arbor: University of Michigan Press, 1957).

3. "Notes from the Odyssey," from *Poems from Three Decades* (New York: Charles Scribner's Sons, 1972).

ᵜᵄ LEVERTOV

1. Kenneth Rexroth, "Poets Old and New," *Assays* (Norfolk, Connecticut: New Directions, 1961), p. 235.

2. Levertov, "A Testament and a Postscript, 1959–1973," *The Poet in the World* (New York: New Directions, 1973), p. 3.

3. "Caedmon," from *Breathing the Water* (New York: New Directions, 1987).

4. Levertov, "A Testament and a Postscript," p. 6.

❧ LEVINE

1. "Heaven," from *Not This Pig* (Middletown, Connecticut: Wesleyan University Press, 1968).

2. "Angel Butcher," from *They Feed They Lion* (New York: Atheneum, 1972).

3. Calvin Bedient, "An Interview with Philip Levine," *Parnassus*, Spring / Summer 1978, p. 46.

4. "Something Has Fallen," from *Ashes: Poems Old and New* (New York: Atheneum, 1979).

❧ McCLATCHY

1. Quoted in *Contemporary Authors*, ed. Frances C. Locher (Detroit: Gale Research, 1982), vol. 105, p. 320.

2. Quoted in "What One Wants to Get Near: A Conversation about Poetry," *Shenandoah* 34, no. 4 (1983), p. 38.

3. "Blue Horses," from *Scenes from Another Life* (New York: George Braziller, 1981).

4. "Little Elegy," from *Scenes from Another Life*; "The Lesson in Prepositions," from *Stars Principal* (New York: Macmillan, 1986).

5. "First Steps," from *Stars Principal*.

❧ MEREDITH

1. The title poem from *The Wreck of the Thresher* (New York: Alfred A. Knopf, 1964).

2. Dickey, "Falling," from *Falling, May Day Sermon, and Other Poems* (Middletown, Connecticut: Wesleyan University Press, 1981); Meredith, "Hazard's Optimism," from *Hazard, the Painter* (New York: Alfred A. Knopf, 1975).

3. "Roots," from *The Wreck of the Thresher*.

4. "Walter Jenks' Bath," from *Earth Walk: New and Selected Poems* (New York: Alfred A. Knopf, 1970).

❧ MERRILL

1. *The Changing Light at Sandover*, comprising "The Book of Ephraim," "Mirabell's Books of Number," and "Scripts for the Pageant" (New York: Alfred A. Knopf, 1992).

2. "The Book of Ephraim," from *The Changing Light at Sandover*. David Jackson is Merrill's lifelong companion.

3. Susan Howe, *Singularities* (Middletown, Connecticut: Wesleyan University Press; Hanover, New Hampshire: University Press of New England, 1990), p. 410.

4. James Merrill, "Condemned to Write About Real Things," *New York Times Book Review*, 21 February 1982, p. 33.

5. "F" from "The Book of Ephraim," *The Changing Light at Sandover*.

6. Ibid.

⇗   MERWIN

1. "Witnesses," from *The Moving Target*, (New York: Atheneum, 1963).

2. "Left Open," from *Travels* (New York: Alfred A. Knopf, 1993).

3. "Departure's Girl-friend," from *The Moving Target*.

4. "The Last One," from *The Lice* (New York: Atheneum, 1967).

5. "After Douglas," from *Travels*.

6. "Lives of the Artists," from *Travels*.

⇗   MORGAN

1. "When it rained and rained . . . ," from *Poems of the Two Worlds* (Urbana: University of Illinois Press, 1977).

2. Guy Davenport, quoted in *Contemporary Authors*, New Revision, ed. Deborah A. Straub (Detroit: Gale Research, 1987), vol. 21, p. 309.

3. "Saying," from *Poems of the Two Worlds*.

⇗   NEMEROV

1. "The Goose Fish," from *The Salt Garden* (Boston and Toronto: Little, Brown, 1955).

2. Willard Spiegelman, "Alphabetizing the Void: Poetic Diction and Poetic Classicism," *Salmagundi* 42 (Summer–Fall 1978), p. 134.

3. "A Spell before Winter," from *The Next Room of the Dream: Poems and Two Plays* (Chicago: University of Chicago Press, 1962).

4. "Life Cycle of the Common Man," from *New & Selected Poems* (Chicago: University of Chicago Press, 1960).

5. "Walking the Dog," from *Sentences* (Chicago: University of Chicago Press, 1980).

🦊 O'HARA

1. John Ashbery, "Introduction," *The Collected Poems of Frank O'Hara*, ed. Donald Allen (New York: Alfred A. Knopf, 1971), p. vii.

2. "Personism: A Manifesto," *The Collected Poems of Frank O'Hara*, p. 499.

3. "In Memory of My Feelings," from *The Collected Poems of Frank O'Hara*.

4. "Getting Up Ahead of Someone (Sun)," from *The Collected Poems of Frank O'Hara*.

5. "Music," from *The Collected Poems of Frank O'Hara*.

🦊 PINSKY

1. Barry Goldensohn in *Contemporary Poets*, 5th ed., ed. Tracy Chevalier (Chicago and London: St. James Press, 1991), p. 762.

2. "Essay on Psychiatrists," from *Sadness and Happiness* (Princeton: Princeton University Press, 1975).

3. From *An Explanation of America* (Princeton: Princeton University Press, 1979).

4. "The Figured Wheel," from *History of My Heart* (New York: Ecco Press, 1984).

5. The title poem from *The Want Bone* (New York: Ecco Press, 1990).

🦊 PLATH

1. Robert Lowell, quoted in *Contemporary Authors*, New Revision, ed. Ann Evory (Detroit: Gale Research, 1991), vol. 34, p. 356.

2. Anne Sexton, quoted in *Contemporary Authors*, New Revision, vol. 34, p. 356.

3. "Lady Lazarus," from *Ariel* (New York: Harper & Row, 1965).

4. "Sheep in Fog," from *Ariel*.

5. Marjorie Perloff, "The Two *Ariels*: The (Re)Making of the Sylvian Plath Canon," *Poems in Their Place: The Intertextuality and Order of Poetry Collections*, ed. Neil Fraistat (Chapel Hill: University of North Carolina Press, 1986), pp. 308–333.

6. "Wintering," from *Ariel*.

~ RICH

1. The title poem from *Diving into the Wreck: Poems 1971–1972* (New York: W. W. Norton, 1973).

2. "The Burning of Paper Instead of Children," from *The Fact of a Doorframe: Poems Selected and New, 1950–1984* (New York: W. W. Norton, 1984).

3. The title poem from *Diving into the Wreck.*

4. From *Twenty-One Love Poems* (Emeryville, California: Effie's Press, 1976).

~ RICHARDSON

1. "Post-Romantic," from *As If* (New York: Persea Books, 1992); Amy Clampitt, quoted on the back cover of *As If.*

2. "Post-Romantic," from *As If.*

3. "Anyway," from *As If.*

4. "Blue Heron, White Thunder," from *As If.*

5. "Cat among Stones," from *As If.*

6. "The Will," from *Reservations: Poems* (Princeton: Princeton University Press, 1977).

~ ROETHKE

1. Roethke, "On Identity," in *On the Poet and His Craft: Selected Prose of Theodore Roethke,* ed. with an introduction by Ralph J. Mills, Jr. (Seattle and London: University of Washington Press, 1965), p. 27.

2. Ibid.

3. Roethke, *Straw for the Fire: From the Notebooks of Theodore Roethke, 1943–63* (Garden City, New York: Doubleday, 1972), p. 229.

4. "Cuttings," and "Cuttings (*later*)," from *The Lost Son* (Garden City, New York: Doubleday, 1948).

5. Theodore Roethke, quoted in *Contemporary Authors,* ed. Frances C. Locher (Detroit: Gale Research, 1979), vols. 81–84, p. 478.

6. Quoted in *Contemporary Authors,* vols. 81–84, p. 476.

7. The title poem from *The Far Field* (Garden City, New York: Doubleday, 1964).

8. "Once More, the Round," from *The Far Field.*

≈ SCHUYLER

1. "Light from Canada," from *The Crystal Lithium* (New York: Random House, 1972).

2. Quoted in *Contemporary Authors*, ed. Frances C. Locher (Detroit: Gale Research, 1981), vol. 101, p. 445.

3. "Closed Gentian Distances," from *The Crystal Lithium*.

4. George Butterick in *Contemporary Poets*, 5th ed., ed. Tracy Chevalier (Chicago and London: St. James Press, 1991), p. 861.

5. "Blizzard," from *The Morning of the Poem* (New York: Farrar, Straus & Giroux, 1980).

≈ SCHWARTZ

1. Quoted in *Contemporary Authors*, New Revision, ed. James G. Lesniak (Detroit: Gale Research, 1992), vol. 35, p. 416.

2. "Dogs Are Shakespearean, Children Are Strangers" and "A Dog Named Ego, the Snowflakes as Kisses" are from *In Dreams Begin Responsibilities* (Norfolk, Connecticut: New Directions, 1938).

3. From *Genesis, Book One* (New York: New Directions, 1943).

4. "Dogs Are Shakespearean, Children Are Strangers," from *In Dreams Begin Responsibilities*.

5. "In the Naked Bed, in Plato's Cave," from *In Dreams Begin Responsibilities*.

6. "Seurat's Sunday Afternoon along the Seine," from *Summer Knowledge: New and Selected Poems, 1938–1958* (Garden City, New York: Doubleday, 1959).

≈ SEXTON

1. Patricia Marx, "Interview with Anne Sexton (1965)," *Anne Sexton: The Artist and Her Critics*, ed. J. D. McClatchy (Bloomington: Indiana University Press, 1978), p. 32.

2. Ibid., pp. 39–40.

3. Interview with Anne Sexton, in *Talks with Authors*, ed. Charles F. Madden (Carbondale and Edwardsville: Southern Illinois University Press; London and Amsterdam: Fefer & Simons, 1968), p. 161.

4. "Flee on Your Donkey," from *Live or Die* (Boston: Houghton Mifflin, 1966).

5. "The Fortress," from *All My Pretty Ones* (Boston: Houghton Mifflin, 1962).

⁊   SHAPIRO

1.   "The Leg," from *V-Letter and Other Poems* (New York: Reynal and Hitchcock, 1944).

2.   Shapiro, *Start with the Sun: Studies in the Whitman Tradition* (Omaha: University of Nebraska Press, 1960), p. 29.

3.   Shapiro, *In Defense of Ignorance* (New York: Random House, 1960), p. 275.

4.   "Lower the Standard: That's My Motto," from *The Bourgeois Poet* (New York: Random House, 1964).

5.   "Big Sonnet," from *Selected Poems* (New York: Random House, 1968).

⁊   SIMIC

1.   Charles Simic, *The Uncertain Certainty: Interviews, Essays, and Notes on Poetry* (Ann Arbor: University of Michigan Press, 1985), p. 36.

2.   "Spoon," from *Selected Poems, 1963–1983*, revised and expanded edition (New York: George Braziller, 1990).

3.   Simic, *The Uncertain Certainty*, p. 7.

4.   "Shirt," from *Classic Ballroom Dances* (New York: George Braziller, 1980).

5.   Simic, *The Uncertain Certainty*, p. 77.

6.   Ibid.

7.   *White: A New Version* (Durango, Colorado: Logbridge-Rhodes, 1980).

8.   "Invention of Nothing," from *Dismantling the Silence* (New York: George Braziller, 1971).

9.   "Windy Evening," from *The Book of Gods and Devils* (New York: Harcourt Brace Jovanovich, 1990).

⁊   SIMPSON

1.   "Why Do You Write about Russia?" from *Caviare at the Funeral: Poems* (New York: Franklin Watts, 1980).

2.   "My Father in the Night Commanding No," from *At the End of the Open Road: Poems* (Middletown, Connecticut: Wesleyan University Press, 1963).

3.   "Chocolates," from *Caviare at the Funeral*.

❧ SNODGRASS

1. Quoted in Robert Phillips, "W. D. Snodgrass and the Sad Hospital of the World," in *The Poetry of W. D. Snodgrass: Everything Human*, ed. Stephen Haven (Ann Arbor: University of Michigan Press, 1971), p. 88.

2. Quoted in Stanley Moss, "To the Dispossessed," in *The Poetry of W. D. Snodgrass*, p. 49.

3. The title poem from *Heart's Needle* (New York: Alfred A. Knopf, 1959).

4. Quoted in Paul L. Gaston, *W. D. Snodgrass* (Boston: Twayne, 1978), pp. 153–154.

5. "Magda Goebbels (19 April 1945)," from *The Führer Bunker: A Cycle of Poems in Progress* (Brockport, New York: BOA Editions, 1977).

6. Quoted in *Contemporary Poets*, 5th ed., ed. Tracy Chevalier (New York and London: St. James Press, 1991), p. 931.

❧ SNYDER

1. *Earth House Hold: Technical Notes & Queries to Fellow Dharma Revolutionaries* (New York: New Directions, 1969), p. 34.

2. David Kherdian, *Six Poets of the San Francisco Renaissance* (Fresno, California: Giligia Press, 1967), p. 52.

3. "Burning the Small Dead," from *The Back Country* (New York: New Directions, 1968).

4. Charles Olson, "Projective Verse," in *The New American Poetry: 1945–1960*, ed. Donald M. Allen (New York: Grove Press, 1960), p. 387.

5. Snyder, "Some Yips and Barks in the Dark," *Naked Poetry*, ed. Stephen Berg and Robert Mezey (Indianapolis, Indiana: Bobbs-Merrill, 1969), p. 358.

❧ STAFFORD

1. Quoted in *Contemporary Poets*, 5th ed., ed. Tracy Chevalier (Chicago and London: St. James Press, 1991), p. 952.

2. Stafford, "Vocation," from *Traveling Through the Dark* (New York: Harper & Row, 1962).

3. M. L. Rosenthal, quoted in *Contemporary Authors*, New Revision, ed. Deborah A. Straub (Detroit: Gale Research, 1988), vol. 22, p. 441.

4. Peter Ellsworth, "A Conversation with William Stafford," *The Chicago Review* 30, no. 1 (Summer 1978) p. 97.

5. Quoted in *Contemporary Authors*, New Revision, ed.
Deborah A. Straub (Detroit: Gale Research, 1988), vol. 22, p. 440.
6. "Visions," from *Poetry Northwest* 12, no. 1 (Spring 1971).

⇗ STRAND

1. Donald Sheehan, "Varieties of Technique: Seven Recent
Books of American Poetry," *Contemporary Literature* 10, no. 2 (Spring
1969), pp. 292–293. Sheehan's remarks concern Strand's *Reasons for
Moving* (New York: Atheneum, 1968).
2. "Giving Myself Up," from *Darker* (New York: Atheneum,
1970).
3. "Letter, " from *Darker.*

⇗ SWENSON

1. William Stafford, "A Five-Book Shelf," *Poetry* 111 (October
1967), p. 184.
2. Richard Howard, "May Swenson: Turned Back to the Wild
by Love," *Alone With America: Essays on the Art of Poetry in the United
States Since 1950* (New York: Atheneum, 1969), p. 519.
3. "While Seated in a Plane," from *Half Sun Half Sleep* (New
York: Charles Scribner's Sons, 1967).
4. "Daffodils," from "A City Garden in April," *Half Sun Half
Sleep.*
5. "Teleology," from *New & Selected Things Taking Place* (Bos-
ton: Little, Brown, 1978).

⇗ WAKOSKI

1. Quoted in *Contemporary Poets*, 5th ed., ed. Tracy Chevalier
(Chicago and London: St. James Press, 1991), p. 1021.
2. Quoted by Sandra M. Gilbert in "A Platoon of Poets,"
Poetry 128 (August, 1976), p. 294.
3. Hayden Carruth, "Poetry Chronicle," *Hudson Review* 27,
no. 2 (Summer 1974), pp. 311–312.
4. "Filling the Boxes of Joseph Cornell," from *Inside the Blood
Factory* (Garden City, New York: Doubleday, 1968).
5. "The Silver Surfer on the Desert," from *Medea the Sorceress*
(Santa Rosa, California: Black Sparrow Press, 1991).

❧ WEISS

1.   Quoted in *A Controversy of Poets*, ed. Paris Leary and Robert Kelly (Garden City, New York: Doubleday, 1965), p. 553.

2.   Hayden Carruth, "The Cycle of Sensibility," *The Nation*, 4 January 1971, p. 26.

3.   "The Last Letters," from *The World Before Us: Poems 1950–1970* (New York: Macmillan, 1970).

4.   "Variations on a Favorite Theme," from *A Slow Fuse: New Poems* (New York: Macmillan, 1984).

❧ WHITTEMORE

1.   James Dickey, quoted in *Contemporary Authors*, New Revision, ed. Ann Evory (Detroit: Gale Research, 1981), vol. 4, p. 596.

2.   Whittemore, quoted in *Contemporary Authors*, New Revision, vol. 4, p. 596.

3.   "A Tale of a Poem and a Squash," from *The Self-Made Man and Other Poems* (New York: Macmillan, 1959).

4.   "Waves in Peoria," from *The Self-Made Man*.

5.   "The Party," from *The Self-Made Man*.

6.   The title poem from *The Boy from Iowa: Poems and Essays* (New York: Macmillan, 1962).

7.   "Lines Composed upon Reading an Announcement by Civil Defense Authorities Recommending that I Build a Bomb Shelter in my Backyard," from *The Mother's Breast and the Father's House* (Boston: Houghton Mifflin, 1974).

8.   The title poem from *The Feel of Rock: Poems of Three Decades* (Washington, D.C.: Dryad Press, 1982).

❧ WILBUR

1.   "Thyme Flowering among Rocks," from *Walking to Sleep: New Poems and Translations* (New York: Harcourt, Brace & World, 1969).

2.   "Black November Turkey," from *Things of This World* (New York: Harcourt, Brace, 1956).

3.   "A Voice from Under the Table," from *Things of This World*.

4.   Wilbur, "Poetry and Happiness," in *Responses: Prose Pieces, 1953–1976* (New York and London: Harcourt Brace Jovanovich, 1976), p. 98.

5.   *Tartuffe*, by Jean Baptiste Poquelin de Molière. Translated by Richard Wilbur (New York: Harcourt, Brace & World, 1963).

～ WILLIAMS

1. William Carlos Williams, "Asphodel, That Greeny Flower, Book I," from *Journey to Love* (New York: Random House, 1955).

2. "Yours," from *Poems 1963–1983* (New York: Farrar, Straus & Giroux, 1988).

3. "To Market," from *Lies* (Boston: Houghton Mifflin, 1969).

4. "Sanctity," from *With Ignorance* (Boston: Houghton Mifflin, 1977).

～ C. WRIGHT

1. "Dog Creek Mainline," from *Hard Freight* (Middletown, Connecticut: Wesleyan University Press, 1973).

2. "Nightdream," from *Hard Freight*.

3. "Stone Canyon Nocturne," from *China Trace* (Middletown, Connecticut: Wesleyan University Press, 1977).

4. "Hawaii Dantesca," from *The Southern Cross* (New York: Random House, 1981).

～ J. WRIGHT

1. "In Terror of Hospital Bills," from *Shall We Gather at the River* (Middletown, Connecticut: Wesleyan University Press, 1968).

2. "The Minneapolis Poem," from *Shall We Gather at the River*.

3. Ibid.